RE\

"First of all, thank you Cecilia for allowing me the honor to review several chapters from your memoir. For years I would admire you from afar: a Latina woman, the mother of two young children with the guts, brains and savvy to take on law school. I started at ASU about the time you were beginning law school. As I started to meet more and more Chicano students on campus, your name would be mentioned as one of the few women and Chicanos at the law school. As an undergraduate, law school had that mystique of being one of the top degrees to reach in the university system. And you were setting the bar for many more to come. I remember my aunt, who was an elementary teacher in Flagstaff, speaking highly of your community activism on behalf of Chicanos/Mexicanos in the Guadalupe/Tempe schools. Word about your strong, community activism did get around.

"So as I read through several of your chapters, many of the events, causes and political scenes are familiar because I grew up reading the newspapers on what was happening in Phoenix and Arizona as a teenager. I eventually studied and became one of the few Latina journalists working in Arizona media during the late 70's, 80's and 90's.

"To hear you recount some of the political insider stories gave me a different picture than what I remember of some of the higher profile stories. That information may have been what I might have read in the papers or brief snippets we would show on the TV news. Too rarely did we show any Latinos with real working knowledge of what was going on talking about these very news events. Usually, it was the middle aged, white male politician or leader who was often quoted or who got the TV sound bite. The opportunity you take to share this in your memoir again points out the voice-less Latino, not because we didn't have Chicano/Latino leaders like you, but because the mainstream media did little to seek out and air diverse voices. Little by little that began to change during my broadcast career, and like you, while it appears we are making strides, the struggle never ends. It was almost a daily battle for the few minority journalists in our newsrooms to consciously call out the lack of diverse voices on the air or on news pages. (We were always challenging our news managers to make sure that diverse voices be heard in our daily news coverage. It takes voices inside media organizations as well as in the public to always be reminding colleagues to seek out diverse voices and perspectives.)

"When you would recount specific stories, naming the players, it is almost like having a front row seat watching you in action. While I never had that privilege, you make it come alive. I found myself chuckling several times on hearing your incredulousness at someone's behavior. Astonishment that someone did not realize the formidable opponent you could be. I enjoyed your ability to gently chide a person about the obvious, but with good humor. After having a few opportunities to interview you in person, your humor, self-deprecation and honesty jump off the pages. Your struggles as a young mom, who with the strong support of Elías, had to figure out how to strike a balance with your family, education, career and community activism. You call it miraculous; I call it strength of character. It seems to continue to tear at you as you try to reconcile if those struggles were worth the cost to your family. You do not get to your level of success without having some regrets, but what you have done to help others does balance out in the long run to reflect a life well-lived. Your personality and dedication will never let you pull away from your involvement and dedication, just slow it down... slightly.

"Cecilia you blazed a trail. Your challenges, pitfalls, causes and successes have broke ground many of us were able to follow and you helped make it just a little bit easier. Your example, mentorship and encouragement have helped and inspired so many others including me."

Anita Luera, Director
High School Programs
ASU Cronkite Journalism School

"To read Cecilia Esquer's personal memoir is to step back in time to the Phoenix and the Valley of the Sun of the 1960s and 1970s. It was a period of a far different metropolitan area, and it was also a period of considerable social injustice, as racial and ethnic minorities were just beginning in earnest the struggle for rights that are still not, today, fully won. It was a period of emerging organizations and voices, of a group of young people committed to social justice and determined to make their voices heard and their agenda respected. Of them, one of the most outstanding was Cecilia Esquer, a woman not to be daunted in the pursuit of her convictions, a woman who went on to become a major voice of her generation in Arizona. Told with wit and lucidity, Esquer is forthrightly honest, unstinting in both her praise for those who supported the Movement and unflinching in her criticism of those who sought to impede its progress. All in all, this is both a serious and a delightful book in its telling of an important segment of Arizona's social and political history."

David William Foster, Ph.D.
Regents' Professor of Spanish and Women and Gender Studies
Editor, Chasqui; revista de literatura latinoamericana

꒰꒱

"Cecilia Esquer fought to be heard during the early days of Chicano activism in Arizona, her political skills sharpening with each new challenge. This blunt reflection of her experiences follows the remarkable journey of a Chicana who opened doors and created positive change for women and minorities – especially Mexican-Americans. Her story details the struggles of the Arizona Chicano movement, and explores the toll her activism took on her family as she juggled their needs with her education and career."

Congressman Ed Pastor, J.D.

꒰꒱

THE LIE ABOUT MY INFERIORITY

Evolution of a Chicana Activist

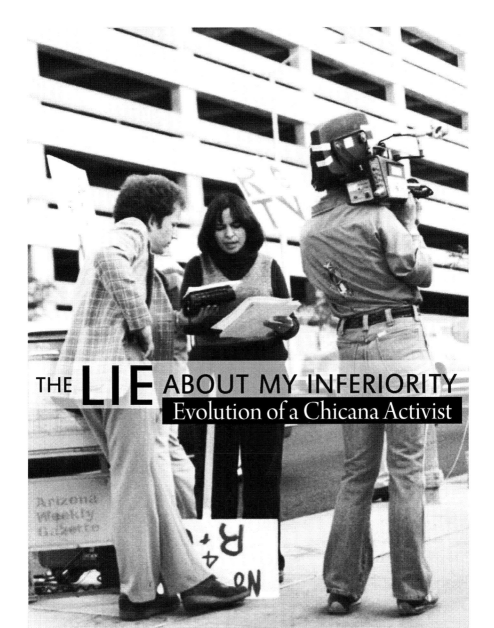

THE LIE ABOUT MY INFERIORITY
Evolution of a Chicana Activist

Cecilia D. Esquer, J.D.

Introduction by Christine Marin, Ph.D.

Mesa, Arizona 2010
Latino Book Publisher, an Imprint of HISI

FIRST EDITION

Cover and interior designed by Yolie Hernandez

Photographs by Elías Esquer unless otherwise specified

Published by Latino Book Publisher, an Imprint of HISI as part of the
"Our History, Our Words" Series

Copyright © 2010 by Cecilia Teyechea Denogeán Esquer

All rights reserved.

Latino Book Publisher | HISI
PO Box 50553
Mesa, Arizona 85208-0028
480-983-1445 | hisi.org

Library of Congress Cataloging-in-Publication Data
Esquer, Cecilia D.
The Lie About My Inferiority: Evolution of a Chicana Activist/
Cecilia D. Esquer —1st ed.

pp. 276

ISBN 13: 978-1-4507-1883-7

Printed in the United State of America.

To Elías, mi costilla,
Andrea and Marcos.
Thank you for your patience, love, and support.

Elías, your beautiful photos helped preserve so many precious
memories. Te quiero mucho.

SPECIAL THANKS to those who provided valuable feedback on the manuscript: Dr. David W. Foster, Jaime Herrera, Dr. Trino Sandoval, Marcos E. Esquer, Clara Urbano, Raquel Gutiérrez, Rose Simpson and Priscilla-Chomina Bottz. Thanks to Barbara Jordan, my Memoir Workshop professor at Mesa Community College, for her encouragement and support.
I was moved by the comments submitted by Congressman Ed Pastor, Dr. David W. Foster, and Anita Luera. Special thanks to Dr. Christine Marin for her powerful and heartfelt Introduction.

Eduardo Barraza and Yolie Hernández:
Thank you for your guidance, support, and good work.

The materials in the Chicano Research Collection were invaluable. I commend Dr. Christine Marin* for establishing this valuable resource. I found photos, documents, and articles I used in the book. Other materials refreshed my recollection of events long ago forgotten.

*Dr. Christine Marin, Ph.D, Archivist Department of Archives and Special Collections, Hayden Library. The Chicano Research Collection, Arizona State University Libraries.

TABLE OF CONTENTS

INTRODUCTION
By Dr. Christine Marin

I N her honest and brutally frank political and personal memoir, Cecilia Teyechea Denogeán Esquer describes herself as a brown-skinned Chicana who stood up for herself and fought against those who sought to convince her of her ethnic and cultural "inferiority". The "lie of [her] inferiority" is dispelled in this book. But just why Cecilia ever bought into this lie has plagued her throughout her lifetime—until she finally sat down and wrote her story. It's a compelling, detailed and uncompromising story that her son, Marcos, said she had to write because it was her "duty to tell the truth" about what happened "back then". What happened in her lifetime and throughout the course of her educational, legal, and political career was that Cecilia encountered the ugly heads of racism, discrimination and unfair mistreatment against Mexican Americans, women, and the Yaqui Indians, and whenever she sought to overturn them—as an educator, an attorney, a university professor, and as a recognized state-wide and national political leader, she was called a "radical", a "trouble-maker". The battles were not pretty. They were harsh. They were downright brutal. And they are outright shameful—and sexist. One must never forget the battles in Guadalupe, Arizona and Tempe, Arizona.

The "lie" about Cecilia's so-called "inferiority" began in her birthplace, Superior, Arizona, where she attended Harding Elementary School in the early to mid-1950s. The school was a segregated school, established in the copper mining town in 1922 for Mexican children. Teachers told her to say she was "Spanish", and not Mexican. They anglicized her surname, Denogeán, and told her to pronounce it as "Den-o-gene" because it sounded "more American." And they punished children like her for speaking Spanish on the playground. The humiliation and shame she encountered as a young child remained with her; but none of that would defeat her. Instead, Cecilia sought and gained an education that took her away from Superior and placed her in the urban worlds of Phoenix and Tempe and into the world of local and international politics.

New challenges were thrown her way and she refused to run away from them. Instead, she used her education to initiate and create socio-economic, educational and political changes for ordinary people just like her—those who deserved to be treated fairly and with respect and whose votes and voices should not be taken for granted: the poor, the under-represented, the disadvantaged, the children, and the women.

Cecilia Esquer wasn't afraid to take risks in her career. She attended law school in the early 1970s while married and with two small children. She was unafraid of speaking out and claiming her voice on political issues when it was unpopular for women like her to do so. She made achievements in a political world dominated by men. Along the way, she encountered important political leaders in Mexico, Arizona, and in Washington, D.C.—leaders who influenced her, became her friends, and remained those who helped Cecilia make a humanitarian difference: former Arizona governor and ambassador to Argentina, Raúl Castro; Ethel Kennedy, widow of former U.S. Attorney General, Robert Kennedy; President Bill Clinton and current Secretary of State, Hillary Clinton; Arizona's current Attorney General, Terry Goddard; Arizona's current Congressman, Ed Pastor, to name a few.

Throughout her book, Cecilia calls herself "ordinary". However, you will see that Cecilia's story is far from "ordinary". She was there to help shape the political history of Chicanos in Phoenix in the period of the 1960s. She was there to turn away injustice in the schools of Tempe in the 1970s. She was there in the 1980s to challenge the questionable decisions of important judicial representatives in Phoenix. She was there in the 1990s at Phoenix College to direct their Legal Assisting Program and to prepare students for paralegal work and become their mentor.

Cecilia Teyechea Denogeán Esquer is just as apt to take on a new challenge today as she was "back then". This book is that challenge. In her book, Cecilia used the word "fearless" to describe her work and commitment to equal justice under the law. However, she rarely used the word "fearless" to describe herself. But I'll use it. Cecilia is fearless.

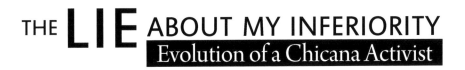

THE **LIE** ABOUT MY INFERIORITY
Evolution of a Chicana Activist

❦ 1 ❦

LAYING THE FOUNDATION

Separate but Equal?

FATE has offered me many unique opportunities, some of which I accepted, some I did not. Fate also has presented thorny challenges that affected my personal and political philosophy. The thorniest one was dealing with the reality that I grew up in a racist society. It took some time for me to realize that I was often treated differently because of the color of my skin, and the presumption by the dominant society that I was inferior, not their equal. To succeed, I had to learn how to react so that my spirit would not be broken or defeated. To this day I must say that I have suffered more due to the color of my skin than the fact that I am a woman.

So, what lessons have I learned? I first had to find my own identity. Then I had to develop a tough skin and "never let them see me cry." This made me overly cautious as I dealt with Anglo people through the years. Somehow, at some moment, like an albatross, the attitude that I was not equal would surface. Even some of my most liberal Anglo friends did not escape growing up with that presumption. As I grew, I learned to thrive on negative reinforcement. I took on some challenges, like law school, because someone told me I could not or should not do that. Always, I fought for respect and equal treatment.

Standing up for my beliefs was something that garnered respect and admiration from others. It also closed some opportunities because those in charge were afraid to have an individual who stood up for principle. Standing up for my beliefs led me to go to law school. Being a licensed attorney opened new horizons for me. Having three college degrees qualified me for a variety of positions; however, that albatross was always around, which sometimes made me question whether I could do it.

The most important factor in whatever success I may have achieved came from not being afraid to take risks: speaking out even though it closed some doors for me; going to law school while married with two children; accepting positions that were interesting though challenging.

None of this would have been possible without the constant support and encouragement from my husband, my children, my mother and the individuals who were there at critical moments that opened incredible doors to me. I did not do it alone.

Brief Bio

I was born in Superior, a small mining town in Arizona, located about 63 miles southeast of Phoenix. My father, Ramón Reel Denogeán, dropped out of school when he was in the fifth grade. My mother, Bertina Chávez Teyechea, dropped out during her junior year in high school to get married. Ramón and Bertina had nine children, four older and four younger than I. I attended Harding Elementary in Superior, a segregated elementary school, through seventh grade. Despite the fact that I developed excellent basic skills in the three Rs ('reading, 'riting, and 'rithmetic), I was made to feel that I was a second-class citizen. My teachers told us to say we were "Spanish," not "Mexican," and the pronunciation of our names was Anglicized because that sounded more "American." We would get punished for speaking Spanish at school.

My father worked as an underground miner for seventeen years for Magma Copper Company in Superior. He also worked as a self-employed mechanic on the side. In 1954 my mother packed up the family and moved us to Phoenix where she thought there would be more opportunities for her children. My father did not think he could support a family on a mechanic's salary. He commuted from Phoenix to his job at the mine in Superior until 1960, when a fire closed the mine for about a year. In 1968, at the age of fifty-five, he landed a job as a master mechanic for the City of Phoenix. He found the salary and benefits sufficient to support his family and worked there until 1983, when he turned seventy.

We moved to Phoenix in 1954, where I became an eighth grader at Lowell Elementary School. In 1959, I graduated from Phoenix Union High School. I was fortunate to receive a small scholarship to ASU and decided to live on campus. Even though I was only seventeen-years old, my mother supported my decision to move to a dorm. I was fortunate I did not have to ask my father for money to attend ASU, since I was able to pay my own way with the scholarship and a part-time job on campus. My father was furious when I moved to the dorm. He did not speak to me for about three months. In his family tradition, a daughter did not move out of the house until married or buried. When my grandmother would visit, she would ask my father: "¿Dónde está Cecilia? Falta Cecilia." (Where is Cecilia? She should be home).

During my undergraduate years at Arizona State University, in Tempe, I worked summers as a relief secretary at the Phoenix law firm of Lewis and Roca. If anyone had told me then that I would become a lawyer, I would have told them they were nuts. My highest priority in 1961 was to get my B.A. degree because I knew I did not want to be a legal secretary the rest of my life. I graduated from ASU in 1963 with a degree in Business Education and became a teacher.

Despite the fact that I received the Business Education Outstanding Student award and that I was the President of the Business Education Honorary, I was unable to find a teaching job in Maricopa County, the largest county located in the central part of Arizona. There were jobs in Maricopa County in 1963, but they were not hiring many minorities in those years. I was fortunate to be hired to teach at Ray High School in Kearny, Arizona, a small mining town about two hours southeast from Tempe. In addition to teaching business classes, I taught a general history class even though I did not have many credits in history. Teaching the history class opened new horizons for me and made me decide to pursue a master's degree in a liberal arts discipline. Working as a teacher in a small town is special. You get to know the students and their families very well. The entire town comes out for athletic events at home and away. My colleagues were supportive and helpful. While it was a great teaching experience in a wonderful community, I was still single and felt isolated from my friends and family. So, after one year, I returned to ASU for the fall 1964 semester and completed my course work in December 1965. In 1966 I graduated with a Master's degree in Spanish from the College of Liberal Arts.

I also got married during this time. I met my future husband when I was a student teacher during the 1963 spring semester at Tempe High School in Tempe, Arizona, home of Arizona State University. One day, as I drove into the parking lot at Tempe High, I almost ran into the campus cop. I had borrowed someone's car because my friend Becky Portillo's car broke down, so she could no longer give me a ride to Tempe High. The car I was driving was an old Dodge whose front seat was rusted in place, so I could not adjust it and had to stand to hit the clutch and the brake. The campus cop turned out to be Elías Esquer, a freshman student at ASU. It turned out he had the same time schedule I did, so he agreed to give me a ride. Who could know I would wind up marrying this guy who scolded me for almost killing him:

Elías: "Do you always drive that way?"

Cecilia: "Do you always get in people's way?"

Elías and I became good friends, but did not really start dating until I returned to Tempe to go to graduate school. Although he was a freshman, he was older than me.

Elías graduated from Tempe High in 1956. The economy was pretty flat in those years, so he could not find a job. He and his high school friend, Frank López, volunteered to join the U.S. Air Force. Elías returned to Tempe after completing his term and found a job as a tire recapper. This got old, so he took a State test which qualified him to be a State agricultural quarantine inspector. He worked at an inspection station located in Cameron, Arizona, which was part of the Navajo Indian Reservation. There, Elías met a young couple, Martín and Emily Téllez. Martín was a teacher at the Tuba City elementary school, and Emily worked for Social Services in the Bureau of Indian Affairs. Martin strongly encouraged Elías to go to college, which he did. Elías was also a Spanish major, so we had common interests and some of the same friends. We started dating during the 1964-65 school year and were married at St. Agnes Church in Phoenix in June 1965. Since Elías was still in undergraduate school at ASU, we lived in Tempe.

I was hired to teach Spanish at McClintock High School in Tempe in 1965. I taught there from 1965 to 1966, and again from 1968 to 1970. This experience turned me into a Chicana activist. I prefer to use the term Chicana because it is a political term which describes a Mexican American woman who believes in "La Causa." La Causa is a political movement seeking to achieve equality for Mexican Americans. César Chávez, a Mexican American farm worker, labor organizer, and civil rights activist, and the farm workers' movement were an integral part of La Causa.

As a young Chicana teacher at McClintock High School in 1969-70, I was faced with a difficult dilemma: speak out about the high school's discriminatory practices toward minority students, especially the students from the town of Guadalupe, or remain silent to avoid losing a job I thoroughly enjoyed. I was lucky to have a colleague and mentor, Sue Chemnick Chilton, who raised these difficult issues with me – issues about busing schedules, student discipline and student placement. The response from the administration was one of denials and subtle threats to my contract. [More in Chapter 2]

During this time my husband and I became volunteers for the United Farm Workers Organizing Committee, an experience that turned out to be life-changing. We became deputy registrars and spent many weekends going door to door with a team of party activists to register voters – often as many as 300 in one weekend. We also attended the weekly rallies —our two kids in tow— at the Santa Rita Center, in Central Phoenix, where we were given updates on the various boycotts and the efforts towards forming a union. César Chávez would attend from time to time.

At one of the rallies, César cited the great need for more Mexican American lawyers, a prospect that sounded interesting to me. It appeared that most of the positive social changes were taking place through court challenges. In addition, I was getting discouraged by the lack of interest in addressing the discriminatory practices at the high school, and also by the frequency with which I was summoned to the Principal's office to be questioned about his concerns over my activism, which consisted mostly of asking him questions about what I perceived were discriminatory practices. I was often asked to be a guest speaker in ASU classes and Valley high schools. I often mentioned the discriminatory practices at McClintock. Mr. Boyle told me that "radicals did not belong in [his] school." Finally after an incident in which I inadvertently became a whistleblower, my contract was threatened directly. I left McClintock High School in 1970 for the birth of our son, Marcos.

My husband and I were fortunate to become politically active during the late 1960s and early 1970s; I can't recall a more exciting time for young people to become involved, those "wild and crazy" years. In 1970, Elías was the first Hispanic ever elected to the Tempe Union High School District board. In 1973, as a result of our involvement in Chicano political issues and in the Democratic Party, I was elected to be a member-at-large of the Democratic National Committee (DNC)[1]. In 1972 I had been elected as a precinct committeeperson. In a period of

1   One of the outcomes of the 1972 McGovern for President Campaign was the adoption by the DNC of the "McGovern-Fraser Reform Rules." These reforms were adopted by the Democratic National Committee in response to the turmoil during the 1968 Democratic National Convention in Chicago. The rules called for proportional representation in the state delegations seeking to be sat at the Democratic National Presidential Nomination Convention. If they did not meet the requirement, the delegation could be challenged. The rules also created 25 at-large positions. These positions were intended to balance the make-up of the DNC, which was dominated by White males over 50. The hunt was on for women and minorities under 50 who were active in the Democratic Party.

one year, I was catapulted from being a precinct committeeperson to a member-at-large of the DNC – go figure! That fall of 1973 I also became a first-year law student at the ASU College of Law. Imagine the stress on a family with two young children, ages seven and three, and having to adjust from a two-income family to one income and no student loans!

The story presented in this book is focused on our efforts to help change the unfair and inequitable treatment of minorities, and on the educational and political experiences that depict the life of a Chicana activist who tried to make a difference. While there has been much progress in regard to the plight of women and minorities, we still have some work to do. To this day, I still come across individuals who see me as inferior. However, these days, I find that I am accepted fairly readily in most places.

I am tremendously encouraged by the historic victory of our 44th President, Barack Obama. I have to confess that I did not think he had a chance when he first announced he was running for president. I still get choked up when I recall his incredible victory speech on November 4, 2008. Because of him, I am more optimistic about the possibility for some positive changes in our society. I have faith in the younger generation; they have become more active politically, have incredible talent and seem unafraid and confident in their ability to move things forward. Young people were a key factor in President Obama's historical victory, and a sign that many young people do not share their parents' prejudices toward minorities.

OPPOSITE PAGE PHOTO CAPTIONS:
Top: 1st Grade – Mrs. Foraker, 1947-48 Harding Elementary School in Superior, Arizona, Cecilia is in the front row 4th from left

Middle: Main Street, Superior, Arizona, c1984

Bottom: 4th Grade – Mrs. Ryder, 1950-51 Harding Elementary School in Superior, Arizona, Cecilia is in the front row 2nd from left; and her sister Connie is in the second row 1st from left

Top: Arizona State University Commencement, June 5, 1963
Ramón and Bertina Denogeán, Connie Rojas (Bachelor of Arts), Cecilia Denogeán (Bachelor of Arts)

Middle: Arizona State University Commencement, Spring 1966
Cecilia (Master of Arts), Andrea, and Elías Esquer (Bachelor of Arts)

Bottom: Family picture, c1974

OPPOSITE PAGE PHOTO CAPTIONS:
Top: Award - Outstanding Business Education Student
Arizona State University - Spring 1963. Dr. Donald Tate, Cecilia Denogeán, Dr. Lohnnie Boggs

Bottom: Ramón and Bertina Denogean family: Front Row – Carmen Cook, Ramón Denogeán, Richard Denogeán, Irene Childress
Second Row – Rudy Denogeán, Connie Rojas, Cecilia D. Esquer, Ray Denogeán

2

POLITICAL AWAKENINGS

McClintock High School

AS mentioned earlier, I was hired to teach Spanish at McClintock High School beginning the 1965 fall semester. McClintock was a new high school, the second high school in the Tempe Union High School District. Mr. William Boyle was the Principal. I was the third Hispanic ever hired to teach in the Tempe Union High School District. The hiring was a direct result of the League of United Latin American Citizens' (LULAC) efforts, to pressure the school board to hire Hispanics. My first year at McClintock was exciting. I had great students. They thought they had a great teacher, so Mr. Boyle was happy he hired me. I left McClintock in March 1966 for the birth of our daughter Andrea.

My husband Elías worked as the first campus cop at Tempe High School from 1962 to 1965 while he attended ASU. He was hired by Mr. Boyle, the school Principal at Tempe High at the time. Mr. Boyle had been the Registrar and a coach when Elías was a student at Tempe High. They had a good relationship. If Mr. Boyle had not hired Elías that year, we probably would not have met. Elías had served in the U. S. Air Force and had worked at various jobs. He decided to attend ASU at the age of twenty-six. He completed his B.A. in Spanish in June of 1966 and then began looking for a teaching position.

We were interested in traveling, but could not afford it, so Elías began to look at out-of-state teaching positions. He came home from a recruiting fair at ASU and told me that we had an offer to teach Spanish from the Tacoma Public Schools in the state of Washington. I could not believe they would hire me without an interview. Besides, I was pregnant and did not know whether I could even teach that fall. In addition, I did not want to teach full time. That summer we moved to Tacoma, Washington. Elías was hired full-time at Jason Lee Junior High; I was hired part-time at Baker Junior High.

Tacoma Public Schools

We did not know anyone in Tacoma when we arrived, but the faculty there was very welcoming. We found an apartment overlooking Puget Sound, a complex of inland marine waterways in the northwestern part of Washington. Our landlady's daughter took care of our daughter Andrea while I was teaching. Foreign languages were taught beginning in the third grade and had a high priority in the courses offered. Because we were "native speakers," we received many dinner invitations. Through some teachers in the District we met a "colonia" of Cuban exiles living in the Northwest. Most Cubans initially fled to Miami, Florida, but there were not enough jobs for all the exiles. The U.S. Government offered a teacher-training program to help the Cuban exiles re-tool. Some of them had held positions in the Cuban government. Some were lawyers, others architects, all were from the professional class. Now many of them were foreign language teachers in the Tacoma Public schools. They treated us like family.

About once a month there was a party. Cubans came from as far away as Vancouver, Washington and Portland, Oregon. They were very homesick. There were excellent musicians in the group, so we were treated to fine Cuban music. More than anything, their pride in being Cuban helped me to understand the importance of knowing one's culture and language. When someone mentioned to our friend and colleague, Kiki Remos, that she was losing her Cuban accent, she was horrified: "I never want to lose that accent; I always want people to know that I am Cuban." This Cuban community reinforced my struggle to find my own identity.

Back to Tempe, Arizona

In 1968 we returned to Tempe so Elías could pursue graduate work. I was rehired to teach Spanish at McClintock. My teaching load included one class of bilingual Spanish. Most of the students in that class were from the town of Guadalupe, a community contiguous to Tempe and composed of Mexican American and Yaqui residents. Many of the other students at McClintock were from the Shalimar Country Club area, which had a population of high and middle income families. About 80 per cent of Guadalupe's population fell in the lower income level, so the student body reflected the extremes in social and economic status. If I had not been assigned to teach this one class, I probably would have remained in the District until retirement.

McClintock High School – Challenges

I soon discovered that many of the students from Guadalupe were not proficient in reading and writing. My colleague, Sue Chilton, had been teaching bilingual Spanish classes since McClintock first opened. She enjoyed a great rapport with the students from Guadalupe. They loved her and looked to her for guidance. My students from Guadalupe kept their distance from me and only spoke to me when I asked them a direct question. Sue advised that I had to become involved in their community to gain their confidence. I started making house calls to meet the parents and families and attended events in the community. The students responded immediately, and I soon became familiar with their plight.

These students were not well received at McClintock and were subjected to racist remarks by faculty, staff and fellow students. Many were placed in remedial classes without being tested. Their student files were replete with negative comments by their elementary school teachers comments like: "his brother was lazy, so he is lazy." In the faculty lounge, some of the teachers called the students from Guadalupe "losers."

A Million Moon Shots

Not only did teachers make comments in the faculty lounge, but they also expressed their opinions about "Mexicans" in the classroom. One of my student's sister came to my classroom in tears. She was in an advanced science class. It was the day a missile was launched by NASA, when her teacher told the class he would rather see a million moon shots than all the lazy Mexicans on welfare. This student was from Guadalupe and her mother was receiving welfare benefits. She was the only minority in the class and felt as if everyone was staring at her.

When I asked Mr. Boyle to speak with the teacher about this incident he told me he did not believe the teacher made the statement and, even if he did, there was nothing he could do about it. I continued to ask Mr. Boyle to address other students' complaints about the negative treatment they received, but he failed to address their concerns. This began my special relationship with Mr. Boyle and, ultimately, ended in my decision to go to law school.

"This Is Not Their School"

Sue Chilton and I sponsored the Spanish Club, which held its meetings at 7:30 a.m. before classes began at 8:10 a.m. The students from Guadalupe were not able to attend the meetings because their bus arrived on campus ten minutes before classes began. It would make no difference if we held the meetings right after school because the bus to Guadalupe left ten minutes after the last class period. Most students from Guadalupe did not have cars to drive to school. Guadalupe was about five to six miles from the high school, so the students had to ride the bus.

Sue and I went to see Mr. Boyle to see if something could be done about the bus schedules. He said they intentionally set the bus schedules that way because they did not want the students from Guadalupe on campus except during class times. We asked him why he felt this way. He said that there would be more problems if the students from Guadalupe were on campus any longer. He reminded us about the fights that developed during the lunch hour between some students from Guadalupe and some students from Tempe, and they did not need that. "Besides," he said, "this isn't their school and we just don't want them here." As difficult as it was, Sue and I decided against taking it any further at this time. Mr. Boyle did not appreciate our raising these thorny issues with him.

How Mr. Boyle Inspired Me to go to Law School

Here I was in Mr. Boyle's office again. He looked at me sternly, his 6'3" figure filling his principal's chair. I became pretty apprehensive when he told me he heard I was saying he was prejudiced. He asked me if I knew why I was hired by the District. I responded I was not sure, but thought to myself that I was hired because I was qualified to teach high-school Spanish. After all, I had a Master's degree in Spanish, I was totally bilingual, and had experience teaching Spanish. His next comments helped me to understand why the Tempe Union High School District routinely would hire their White alumni, but not their minority alumni. "You were hired because you are from a mining town, and mining town Mexicans do not have the same gripes against society as the Mexicans from the Valley. But it seems you have forgotten your place."

I asked him, "What is my place?" That took him aback a little. He shifted his big frame in the chair, a sure sign he was upset with me again. He said they expected me to behave like one of the other teachers who was from a mining town. He told me he had lived and taught in Superior, my hometown, and knew how people behaved. In fact, he married Eleanor Mahoney, a lovely woman from a prominent family in Superior.

I told him I knew who the Mahoneys were, but that I did not attend Roosevelt School, where the Mahoneys would have attended, because the elementary schools were segregated. I had to attend Harding Elementary School. "It was necessary to segregate students," he said. I asked him why the high school was not segregated. "By that time the students have set opinions and know what is expected of them."

Before he dismissed me, he cautioned me against associating with people from the League of United Latin American Citizens (LULAC) and the American Civil Liberties Union (ACLU) because they were radical, and radicals did not belong in "his" school. Members of LULAC had pushed for the hiring of Hispanics and other minorities in the District. The newspaper carried accounts of the exchanges with the School Board. That is the main reason I was hired in 1965. I was only the third Hispanic ever hired in the school district, which was established in 1908. The ACLU was very active in advocating for student rights and had filed at least one action against the District.

I left the meeting wondering how I could say the things I did to my principal and worrying how that would affect my contract. Perhaps it was that I had a lot of experience standing up to an authoritarian figure: my father. He was the oldest of eleven children and had to help with his younger siblings when his father died in 1940. My father was used to being in charge and not contradicted, until I came along. For example, even though he objected to my living in a dorm at ASU, I went ahead and did so. To begin with, he wanted me to attend Phoenix College with my sister Connie. He said if I stayed he would buy me a car. I rudely responded: "Yuh, you will buy me a car that will barely get me to school. It will often break down and you won't have the time to repair it. Besides, I cannot afford the gas and insurance." My father was not used to women going to college and thought his mother expected him to keep us at home until we were married. My mother always encouraged us to "do the right thing" and served as a role model when she would visit a teacher to discuss some action taken against one of her children that she thought needed some explanation. She strongly encouraged us to get an education and was very supportive.

Until I was hired at McClintock High School, I thought the world of teachers and looked up to them. One day, in the teacher's lounge, a few teachers were talking about the "losers" in their classes and how they were not going to make it. I realized they were talking about students from Guadalupe, students who were predominantly Mexican American or Yaqui Indian. I told them I was like these students and did not appreciate their comments. "You are different, you are not lazy and ignorant like them," they assured me. I told them I came from a similar background and they should not be lumping all these students into one category. This is one of the reasons I became known as a "troublemaker" and was ostracized by some of my colleagues. This made me more determined to work to eliminate the racist barriers facing minority students.

My Classroom is Searched

The students in my bilingual Spanish class had become very protective of me. The class met during the first period, so most mornings there were a few students waiting for me outside the classroom. One morning they could not contain themselves. When we went into the classroom, they told me that one of the math teachers had searched my classroom – the cabinets and my desk. How could this be? The first break I had, I went and confronted the math teacher. He was surprised I knew, and said he was just doing his job because Mr. Boyle was concerned I might be handing out political propaganda to the students. I told him he was not very professional. If Mr. Boyle wanted to know, all he had to do was to come to my classroom himself.

Some of my fellow teachers had told me that Mr. Boyle would listen to my class through the intercom. I went to see Mr. Boyle. "I didn't know you were interested in learning Spanish. You are welcome to sit in on the class anytime." He said some of the parents complained that I was putting ideas into their children's minds by discussing political issues. I assured him there was no time to do other than to teach Spanish during the class period. Mrs. Chilton and I sponsored the Spanish Club. The members of the club were interested in hearing about César Chávez and the farm worker's movement. Apparently some of the parents thought that was too radical.

Title I Dilemma – What next?

At the start of the fall 1969 semester, Carolyn Guerra, an English teacher, came to see me because Mr. Boyle told her that "Mrs. Esquer" knew about the changes to the placement of students in English classes. Apparently she taught a regular level English class, but found that most of her students this semester did not have the skills to be successful in the class. I told her I knew nothing about this, but that I would check it out. I went to see Barbara Shepard, the Department Chair for the Counseling Department.

And did she have a story! She said that over the summer, the Administration and its Title I reading consultant, ASU professor Dr. John Edwards, became concerned that McClintock might lose its Title I funding because they had not made sufficient progress with the students. Many of the students in the Title I reading program were from Guadalupe. Dr. Edwards and Mr. Boyle decided that one way to protect the funding was to place students in the Title I classes who were just below their reading level. Most of the students from Guadalupe were reading below the sixth-grade level.

When Barbara Shepard refused to change the student placements, Mr. Boyle and Dr. Edwards took over the student files and made the changes themselves. Barbara said the "Mrs. Esquer" Mr. Boyle was referring to was probably Lupe Esquer, my husband's sister-in-law, who was a member of the Title I Advisory Committee. I called her immediately. Dr. Edwards had called Lupe in the middle of the summer to get her approval to change student placements. Lupe recalled he told her they wanted to make some changes to the Title I program so that "those students who could really benefit from the program were placed in the classes." Then he asked if she could approve this change over the phone or whether they needed to call an emergency meeting. She thought it was a logical change and said there was no need for a meeting. Dr. William Podlich, a Professor in the ASU College of Education, and the Chair of the committee, was out of town for the summer.

When I described the situation, Lupe was furious. She called Dr. Podlich, who called an emergency meeting of the Title I Advisory Committee. Mr. Boyle was not very happy with me when he came to my classroom to tell me I had to attend the meeting, but that he would be out of town. That Friday, when I opened the door to the meeting room, I was stunned, scared out of my wits! Mr. Benedict, the Tempe Union High School District Superintendent was there, together with every Assistant Superintendent, the Business Manager and even the Athletic Director. The members of the Title I Committee were also present. Dr. Edwards called the meeting to order and announced the meeting was being taped because Mr. Boyle was unable to attend.

Dr. Edwards then stated the purpose of the meeting was "to catch the culprit who had tipped off the Advisory Committee." Dr. Podlich immediately interrupted him, declaring that the purpose of the meeting was to determine whether the District was in violation of Federal law. If it was, then the District needed to act immediately to come into compliance. Otherwise, he would have to alert the Federal Title I officials. The room was electrifying. Dr. Edwards stated his reasoning for advising Mr. Boyle to make the placement changes. Lupe Esquer said that had Dr. Edwards explained the changes they were making, she would not have approved of the changes without a meeting of the Title I Committee. Other members expressed their concern.

I was asked to explain how I became involved in this. So, I told them how Mrs. Guerra had come to see me and what happened after that. Superintendent Benedict assured Dr. Podlich they would immediately do what was necessary to ensure the District was in compliance. This abruptly ended the meeting. Mr. Benedict came up to me after the meeting. He had always appeared a kind, gentle and caring person. However, that day his eyes were steely and his jaw was tight. He told me that next time I thought something was wrong that I should go to him before calling someone outside the school. His tone was very threatening.

The following Monday, Carolyn Guerra came to tell me about the mass confusion, as students were transferred to the appropriate English class and thanked me for whatever I did to get this straight. I was summoned to Mr. Boyle's office when he returned from his trip. He assured me he was trying to do the right thing to protect the Title I funds. He asked if I knew I could lose my job for what I did. I responded that it seemed that he would be the one to lose his job if he violated Federal law. To this day I do not know where I found the courage to stand up to him in this way.

I am grateful to Dr. Podlich for his strong stance in forcing the

District to comply with the law. He empowered the parent members of the Committee to state their disapproval of what had happened. I use this experience as a model in advocating for justice and institutional change.

Elías runs for the High School Board

My husband and I were very concerned about the negative treatment of students and the failures of the high-school district to diversify its faculty. In 1968, he attended a meeting with a small group of community activists. They met to convince someone in their group to run for the high school board. When no one agreed, they drew straws and Elías pulled the short straw. We had never considered the idea of running for office. When he came home and told me he would be the candidate, I could not stop laughing. He ran against the incumbent, Howell Hood, a veterinarian who had served on the board for many years. Elías lost by 200 votes, which was quite an accomplishment. There were no incumbents running in the next election so we all thought Elías had a good chance of winning.

There were four candidates: Jim Phillips, a native Tempean, Helen Branch, a registered nurse, Larry Woodford, a dentist, and Elías, a community college professor. There were several forums. The discussions were cordial and fairly well attended. This time, Elías had more volunteers. Eliza Carney, a community activist, was one of the hardest working volunteers.

On election night, the paper ballots from the different voting precincts were being delivered to the Administration Building at Tempe High School, where the totals from each precinct were tallied. We were fairly paranoid during those years, knowing that Arizona had a history of voting violations, including the stuffing of ballot boxes and disappearance of ballots. We had volunteers monitoring the tallying of the votes at key precincts; some even followed the ballot box all the way to Tempe High.

There were no cell phones then, so our volunteers would call in the numbers to us at a phone at Tempe High. Ed Pastor, another Chicano activist, joined us that evening at Tempe High. When we passed by the Administration Building conference room, we noticed that the District Administrators and Principals looked pretty worried; they could hear us cheering each time we took a precinct. We were waiting for the final precinct, Mitchell School, where Jim Phillips' father was the principal. Hank Arredondo, who Elías knew since high school, was monitoring that precinct. He called to say the tally was being held up because of one questioned ballot and gave us the numbers they had at the time. As we expected, we lost Mitchell precinct. Elías and I concluded we had lost the election, but Ed Pastor quickly added up the totals and told Elías he had won – by seven votes! Hank called to tell us the questioned ballot was finally resolved in Elías's favor. Elías was elected with a margin of eight votes!

We then went to the conference room for the final tallying of the votes. The atmosphere was gloomy. They had heard us cheering again. They also had their volunteers calling in the numbers. When we walked in, they would not look at us. There was Mr. Benedict, the Superintendent, who knew Elías since he attended Tempe High. Then there was Mr. Boyle, one of Elías's high school coaches and my former Principal from McClintock High School. Dudley Stringer, the Business Manager, was there. He knew Elías because Dudley had been a teacher in the Business Department when Elías worked at Tempe High. I had met Dudley when I was a student teacher in the same department. Finally, there was Sam Fees, the elementary school Superintendent who had been an eighth grade teacher and track coach at Tempe Grammar school when Elías was a student. Mr. Fees coordinated sports during recess, so he knew Elías since then.

We walked in; no one acknowledged us. When the final tally was taken and it was clear Elías had won, not one of them congratulated Elías or shook his hand, a fine example of the All American good sportsmanship tradition! In walked Jim and Mr. Phillips, his father. They came right over, congratulated Elías, shook his hand and told him they were sure he would do a good job. What a contrast.

School Board Issues

It took a long time to understand that the school administrators were more cognizant of the potential power Elías could have as a Board member. We did not understand why they were so upset when Elías just had one vote out of five. Elías pretty much fulfilled their expectations and pushed for some badly needed changes in hiring practices and treatment of all students. He served for six years. My husband had some heated discussions with Mr. Boyle and some of the other board members. It was difficult for him because Mr. Boyle had been his high school coach and his principal and had hired him when he returned to attend ASU.

In a meeting in which Elías raised the need to hire more minority faculty, he was asked if he wanted to lower the hiring standards. Elías pointed out that the candidates he was thinking about had the same degrees and the same certification as the non-minority candidates, publicly exposing the administration and school board's attitude that minorities were inferior and not equal[1]. This began the move to diversify the faculty. He also led the efforts calling for the education of faculty and staff on cultural differences. Many of the administrators and faculty resented this.

When Elías served as Board President he would meet with Mr. Benedict, the Superintendent, to go over the Agenda. Elías described one of these meetings where they were discussing the hiring of minority faculty, when suddenly Mr. Benedict told Elías that he "could not take this; it's just too much pressure." Mr. Benedict stood up and walked out of the room. He retired before Elías's term was up.

Elías was the second board member who was not connected to agriculture. Jim Yount, a dentist, was the first; he supported Elías in some of these discussions. When Pat Fullinwider, another Party activist, was elected in 1974, the board became more representative of the community it served. Pat was also the first woman elected to the Board.

Arizona as a state was changing also; the State was entering a terrific growth spurt in the urban areas so its economy was no longer "Cattle, Climate, Cotton, Copper, and Citrus"; it was time for an attitude change. We can thank Elías Yescas Esquer for being instrumental in bringing to light the discriminatory practices and for his courage in standing up to his old coach and teachers. Although many urged Elías to run for re-election, he concluded that he had done all he was going to do in this arena.

Mr. Boyle Retires and runs for the School Board

The School Board held a yearly dinner in which they included the spouses and school administrators. Mr. Boyle made sure I was seated next to him at these dinners. At one of the yearly dinners in 1973 he

---

1   "Discrimination Charges Heard at TUHS Meeting," Tempe Daily News, October 3, 1972, p. 1.

said: "I hear you are going to law school."

"You heard right."

"Well, too bad you won't get to sue me because I am going to retire in four years."

I poked him in the ribs and said: "Law school only takes three years, so you better get ready!" At a subsequent meeting he told me he planned to run for the school board after he retired.

"Why would you run for the board," I asked.

"To get back my good reputation that you ruined," was his response. He was referring to the fact that I was often a guest speaker in university classes and community organizations where I spoke of the inequities in the Tempe Union High School District. Mr. Boyle ran and was elected in 1978.

To the end Mr. Boyle and I enjoyed a special relationship; we battled fiercely on the issues, but we admired each other somewhat. He was impressed by my courage and especially by my efforts to become a lawyer. He also cared for Elías and our children. He was a dedicated, hard-working principal. He cared about "his" teachers and "his" school dearly. He had intimate knowledge of what was going on inside and outside of the classroom. He knew every employee's name and the name of most of the students. He was loved, feared, and respected by most. However, he never saw minorities as equal and separated students and teachers into "good" and "bad" categories. Unfortunately most Chicanos and Yaquis fit into his "bad" category. I came to appreciate his frankness in dealing with me and with the minority students at McClintock. Principals who succeeded him were more subtle about their prejudices, so it became more difficult to expose their discriminatory attitudes against minorities.

In 2010, there are a fair number of minority teachers and administrators. The district has grown from two high schools to seven. The demographics of the City of Tempe and the school district have changed tremendously. There is no question about diversity now. The District has improved tremendously in the hiring of minorities at every level. However, the students from Guadalupe continue to experience the lowest reading scores and the highest dropout rates in the District.

Top: Elías and Cecilia
Esquer and Sue Chilton,
McClintock High School,
c1969-1970

Bottom: Hascall Hensaw
and Bill Boyle, Tempe
Union High School
District, 1975

WELCOME TO THE BOARD! — Elias Esquer, (left) is administered the oath of office to the Tempe Union High School District Board of Education by clerk of the board Dr. Howell Hood during Monday night's meeting of the board. Esquer narrowly defeated Jim Phillips in the October 6 balloting Mr. Esquer will take his place on the board at the end of this year.   Jan Young photo

Top: Elías Y. Esquer and Dr. Howell Hood, Swearing in ceremony – Tempe Union High School Board – Tempe Daily News, January 1971. Photo courtesy of Jan Young

Bottom: Spanish Club, McClintock High School, 1969 Historian, Tempe, Arizona

SPANISH CLUB—Front Row: John Bella, Fred Pastrano, Roy Lopez, Pete Bella, Manuel Ortiz, Bill Salazar, Joe Solarez, Ignacio Mori. Second Row: Armida Holquin, Josie Nunez, Angie Sanchez, Yolanda Cons, Lupe Terrazas, Frances Ojeda, Chris Coronado, Herlinda Abeyta. Back Row: Advisor Susan Chilton, Isabel Vasquez, Linda Ortega, Trini Ojeda, Frances Flores, Patsy Mendoza, Bertha Canez, Octaviana Trujillo, Rosie Garcia, Frances Garcia, Sue Gonzales, Monica Ortiz, Josie Mendoza, Carmen Canez, Mary Lou Alvarez, Rosa Mazon, Mary Figueroa, Alice Mazon, Advisor Cecilia Esquer.

SUPERINTENDENT FRANK
LIN BENEDICT consults James
G. Yount, president of the
Board of Education, about the
agenda for the next meeting.

Top left: Cecilia D.
Esquer, Classroom,
McClintock High School,
1968-69

Top right: Mr. Franklin
Benedict, Tempe
Union High School
Superintendent,
McClintock High School,
1969 Historian, Tempe,
Arizona

Bottom: Juni and
Kiki Remos, Tacoma,
Washington, October
1966

Top: Educators for Roy Elson, U.S. Senate, Tempe, Arizona, Fall 1968

Bottom l to r: Georgia Álvarez, Nellie Soto, Cecilia D. Esquer, Guadalupe Soza, Christine Marín, and Yolanda C. Kizer – Honoring 50 Women of the UFW César Chávez Foundation, Phoenix, Arizona, March 22, 2007

Top: Cecilia and Elías Esquer, Baker Junior High, Tacoma, Washington, 1991

Bottom: Elías Esquer, Jason Lee Jr. High, Tacoma, Washington, 1991

⌘ 3 ⌘

GRASSROOTS AT ITS BEST

The Guadalupe Organization, Inc. (GO)

A KEY factor in my growing political awareness was my involvement with the Guadalupe Organization, Inc. (GO) in 1968 when I was teaching at McClintock High School. GO was a non-profit established to provide services to the unincorporated community of Guadalupe. Lauro García, Jr. was the Executive Director; Esther Apodaca was the Deputy Director. A critical element of GO's mission was to train and empower individuals to improve their community and to secure the resources necessary to provide for the community. GO's history is very special.

I met Lauro García when I was teaching at McClintock High School. He was a source of information for me, and then became a source of inspiration. He and his wife Margie were members of a group of young Catholic activists who were trained organizers. He and a few other individuals were assigned to work in Guadalupe to organize its residents to bring about needed changes. They formed the Guadalupe Health Council, that later became GO.

As I began to make house calls in Guadalupe, I realized GO was a focal point in the community since Guadalupe was an unincorporated community prior to 1975. It fell under the auspices of the Maricopa County Board of Supervisors. The supervisors were not attentive to the needs of the residents from Guadalupe. GO lobbied the Board of Supervisors to provide better services to this community. GO helped parents deal with problems with the elementary and high school. They advocated for fair and just treatment of the students from Guadalupe. GO organized parents, who filed lawsuits when the district would refuse to respect the rights of their children. Their actions brought about a major change in the law concerning the placement of students in special education classes.

Mr. García invited me to attend elementary school board meetings from time to time. It was obvious that the board became uneasy and unhappy when Mr. García and residents from Guadalupe appeared at a board meeting. Despite the fact that about one-half of the students from Guadalupe attended Tempe Elementary Schools, they made it clear they preferred for them not to come to the board meetings. The negative reception by the Board was surprising to me.

Overflowing Septic Tanks

Mr. García often told me how, in 1964, the Guadalupe Health Council appeared before the Tempe Elementary School Board to ask the Board to remedy an unsanitary condition at Frank Elementary School in Guadalupe. Apparently the restrooms were located outside the school buildings and were placed over septic tanks. The septic tanks were full and overflowing, so the administration had them locked. The students had no access to restrooms during the school day. When a student asked where to go to the restroom, a teacher responded: "in the bushes, just like you do at home." Mr. García decried the treatment of the students and again asked the Board to order an immediate correction of the situation. On the Board was Dr. William Payne, a medical doctor. Mr. García expected Dr. Payne to push for the administration to take care of this horrendous problem; however, Dr. Payne had nothing to say. Instead the Board President thanked Mr. García for his statements, and then simply moved on to the next agenda item. None of the other board members had any comments.

Mr. García would remind the Board about this event from time to time. GO's requests to provide a better education for the students from Guadalupe were ignored. Mr. García was usually accompanied by ten or more GO members, which created friction with the Board. Many of these meetings were covered by the press. This brought to light the hostile attitude exhibited by the Board toward Guadalupe, and especially toward Lauro García and the Guadalupe Organization. The Board would meet in a small meeting room. Many present had to stand. Many years later, as a third-year law student, I led an effort to block the Governor's nomination of Dr. Payne to the Arizona Board of Regents. I did not feel he was worthy of such a prestigious position.

The Special Education Law Suit

One lawsuit in particular illustrates how the Board treated this group. Parents and one school counselor asked the administration to look at the placement of students in special education classes. They felt the practices discriminated against Spanish and Yaqui speaking children. A lawsuit was filed in Federal District Court when the District refused to take affirmative steps on its own. In 1971, GO and nine parents filed an action on behalf of thirteen children, claiming the District was improperly placing Spanish and Yaqui speaking children in classes for the mentally retarded.

The Board was so incensed over the filing of the lawsuit that they changed the rent-free status of the Guadalupe Organization asking GO to pay $9,600 yearly rent. For five years GO had rented classroom space for adult education classes at a nominal fee. This brought about the filing of another legal action by GO challenging the exorbitant fee. The court granted a preliminary injunction; the District settled out of court for a one-dollar-a year fee.

The special education lawsuit resulted in what is called "The Guadalupe Decision" due to its impact on all school districts[1]. The court found the Tempe Elementary School District was improperly placing children in classes for the mentally retarded. The court ordered the District to test the children in their dominant language. When properly tested, the finding was that all but one of the plaintiff children had been misplaced.

As a result of the "Guadalupe Decision," the Arizona Department of Education drew up regulations that in effect forced school districts throughout the state to review their practices in placing children in special education classes. Many of the provisions were incorporated into state statutes by the 1973 legislature. All Arizona children now must be tested in their dominant language, and the District must have written approval from the parents before they are placed in special education classes.

But, this was not the end for the District. Mrs. Socorro Bernasconi, a resident of Guadalupe and a counselor at Frank School, was responsible for bringing the discriminatory practices to light. As a result, she was summarily transferred to Rural Elementary School, a predominantly (95%) Anglo school. In 1971, Mrs. Bernasconi filed a lawsuit in Federal District Court challenging the transfer. A Federal District judge found that "the district retaliated against the plaintiff for her exercise of the constitutional right of free speech." The District filed an appeal in the 9th Circuit Court of Appeals. The Court finally issued its opinion on

1 Guadalupe Organization v. Tempe Elementary School District No. 3, U.S. District Court for the District of Arizona, No. CIV71-435, Phoenix, May 9, 1972.

February 22, 1977 in favor of Mrs. Bernasconi[2].

TD3 – Desegregation – Not an Alka Seltzer Tablet

In May 1971 two Health, Education, and Welfare (HEW) officials visited the school district and spoke to school and community people about the educational program in the Tempe Elementary School District. There were subsequent visits. As a result, the District was found to be in non-compliance with Title VI of the Civil Rights Act of 1964 for maintaining a segregated school district.

The Board formed a Mexican American Educational Advisory Committee to provide input concerning minority students. Al Jauregui, the principal from Frank School in Guadalupe, was the liaison to the committee. The initial meetings were "getting to know you" sessions. Mr. Jauregui and others made presentations concerning the various programs in the District. We wanted to provide input on possible solutions for improving minority achievement. One of the recommendations we made was to ask the District to establish a Bilingual Program. The Board did not seem interested. After a heated meeting, Tony Chávez, the Committee Chair, announced to the media that the school board refused to cooperate in the formation of a bilingual program. Immediately after this, the Board voted to "dissolve" the committee. They needed a committee that the Board "would have more control over."[3]

Mr. Chávez called a press conference. The committee had not been notified of the Board's decision. It became obvious the Board formed the committee to look good in the eyes of HEW. The District did not seriously want the committee's input. Finally, Mr. Chávez commented on the Board's decision to "dissolve" the committee: "We are not Alka Seltzer tablets; you cannot 'dissolve' this committee."

TD3 - Rules for Radicals – Bluffs Can Work

In 1972, the results of state-mandated reading tests showed that Frank School in Guadalupe had the lowest reading scores in Maricopa County. This, despite the fact that the school district had received almost $1 million in Federal Title I funds since 1965 to help the children

2 Bernasconi v. Tempe Elementary School District No. 3, 548 F.2d 857 (1977).

3 TD3 Drops Support for Advisory Group, Tempe Daily News, June 7, 1973 and "Advisory Unit Not Finished," Tempe Daily News, June 8, 1973. "Mexican American Panel Dissolved by Tempe District," Phoenix Gazette, p.8, n.d.

in Frank and Thew schools improve their reading scores. Thew school is located near the barrio of Victory Acres, which had a predominant Mexican American population. Some of the parents in the town of Guadalupe did not think TD3 was using Title I funds appropriately. The students were not making progress in reading, and the teachers were basically blaming the parents. In the spring of 1975, a group of parents presented petitions bearing more than 700 signatures asking the board to re-evaluate their reading programs. As usual, the Board president accepted the petitions and then moved on to the next item on the agenda.

Lauro García asked me and Max Valencia, a GO employee, to gather information at the District offices. I was now a first year-law student. We made a public records request to review the Title I documents. They were voluminous! Max and I went through the grant proposals.

Then we began to request the financial records, a couple of years at a time. Max and I would go to the District Offices on Fridays at 3:00 p.m. We generally stayed until 5:00 p.m.

Although we did not understand the documents we were reviewing, we made it a point to occasionally point out something in a rather loud voice "Did you see this?" We knew we were being monitored. We would also take extensive notes, not knowing what we were writing. About two months had passed. I was walking down the hallway to the assigned room. As I passed by the office of Sam Fees, the Superintendent of the Tempe Elementary School District, he came out and loudly yelled "Why don't you just go to hell!" I turned around, greeted him and asked if he was alright. Apparently the pressure was getting to him. They could not figure out what we kept exclaiming about, or why we took so many notes! This proved to be an effective bluff. Shortly after, we stopped going. Eventually, the Guadalupe Organization and some of the parents of Title I students filed a law suit.

I was impressed with the activism displayed by the parents and by GO's commitment and effective training to help the parents become advocates for their community. I was also affected by the changes an attorney could bring about by filing legal actions demanding compliance with the law. Jerry Levine, an attorney from Scottsdale, was the attorney for the Guadalupe Organization. He was an outstanding advocate for GO. He and Ted Jarvi founded Levine & Jarvi, a clinic type law firm. To this day Jerry is loved and respected by many Guadalupe residents.

I volunteered time with GO and participated as a trainer in

parent-training workshops, and I did some legal research. In the end, I learned more from the parents who were receptive to what I brought. I appreciated their willingness to offer constructive criticism.

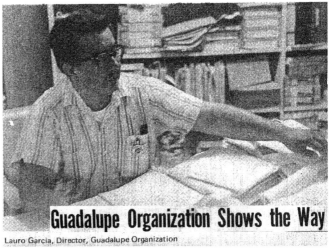

Guadalupe Organization Shows the Way

Lauro Garcia, Director, Guadalupe Organization

4

ARIZONA POLITICS
WE GET INVOLVED!

Democratic Party Delegate Selection – 1972

AS the 1972 Presidential Campaign approached, the farm worker movement changed its focus to support a candidate who would understand and work for changes in the farm workers' plight. Chicano Democratic activists wanted a voice in the delegate selection process. We formed a political organization called "Unidos" (United). Ed Pastor was the Chair. Unidos included members from throughout Maricopa County. We held regular meetings to discuss upcoming events and developed strategies to ensure our voices were heard.

We discovered that to participate in the delegate selection process, a person needed to be a precinct committee man. Of course most of us didn't know what that was, nor were we familiar with the local, state, and national Democratic Party structure. The deadline for filing petitions to become a precinct committee man had passed, but we found out we could run a write-in campaign. Across Maricopa County, Chicanos went door-to-door to collect the six to fifteen signatures needed to qualify to be a write-in candidate. Many of us collected the required signatures and asked voters to write in our names. About thirty of us were elected! Now what?

First, each legislative District met to elect its officers. That was followed by the meeting of each County Party to elect its officers. A day or two before the County meeting, Alfredo Gutiérrez asked me to meet with him and Joe Eddie López. They were members of Unidos and were known for their activism at Arizona State University. They were among the founders of the Mexican American Student Organization (MASO), which became Movimiento Estudiantil Chicano de Aztlán (MEChA). They were active at ASU and in the community. In 1968, they organized a sit-in of students in ASU President G. Homer Durham's office, demanding that the University sever its contract with Phoenix Linen and Towel Supply because of the company's mistreatment of its employees[1]. In the community, they held voter registration drives and worked to raise the community's political awareness.

Chicanos Open the Doors to the Democratic Party

Alfredo and Joe Eddie convinced me to run for Vice Chair of the County Party. They also convinced other Chicanos to run for other County offices. Alfredo instructed us to arrive early at the county party meeting. He introduced me to Matt Wheeler, a candidate for Chair of the Maricopa County Democrats. Matt pledged his support for me, and then took me around to get others to vote for me.

He made it a point to introduce me to union and party leaders. John Ahearn, the Arizona Chair for the Campaign of Senator George McGovern, and a long time party leader, pledged his support. When his good friend Sandy Massetto walked in, she asked John for his support. He apologized to Sandy telling her he had committed to vote for me. She checked with a couple of other party activists; they told her the same thing. The day or two before the convention, the Arizona Republic had published an article about Sandy stating she was running unopposed for the position. Apparently she did not call individuals to ask for their vote. She was shocked at the responses she received, turned around and left the meeting.

The thirty or so Chicano precinct committee men had a terrific impact on the outcome of this election. Party activists were eager to show their support for diversity. Matt Wheeler was elected County Chair. Several Chicanos were elected to County offices, including Carolyn Rosales as Sergeant-at-Arms and me as First Vice-Chair. Of course, none of us had any idea of the work before us. Being the first Vice-Chair, I automatically became a member of the State Executive Committee. It took me a while to figure out the role of that Committee. To this day, I feel some degree of guilt for Sandy Massetto's grief. She was not the culprit painted by Alfredo and Joe Eddie. I also learned an important lesson from Sandy: don't take anything for granted in politics.

The election of many Chicanos as precinct committee persons, then, gave Chicanos power when it came to electing delegates to the national presidential nominating convention. Alfredo Gutiérrez and Joe Eddie López established themselves as powerbrokers for Chicanos.

---

1   Albert Sitter, Sit-in at Durham's Office – Laundry Policy Protested, Arizona Republic, November 21, 1968, A1. (MSS150 Chicano). Chicano Research Collection. Department of Archives and Special Collections, Hayden Library. Arizona State University. Tempe, Arizona.

The Delegate Selection Process, 1971-72

I was asked by Ed Pastor, the Chair of Unidos, to attend and observe the meeting of the State Democratic Party Rules Committee. This Committee was assigned to draft the rules for selecting delegates to the 1972 Presidential Nominating Convention. I was selected because, according to Ed, I had "nothing else to do" since I was home caring for my son Marcos. When I asked the members of the committee if I could attend their meetings, I was told it was a public meeting. But, did I know they met at night [me being a married woman]? I simply asked for the time and address of the meeting.

The meeting was at the home of one of the members. When I showed up I was asked to sit at the corner of the table to observe the proceedings. They were discussing the possible options for delegate selection. I could stand it no more, so I asked if I could ask questions. Of course I could. When I asked my first question, there was an expression of surprise that I understood the discussion. All the members of the committee were lawyers. After this meeting I began to think seriously about going to law school.

The goal of the Committee was to ensure the representation of minorities and women in the Arizona delegation. The Democratic National Committee (DNC) had adopted the recommendations of the McGovern-Fraser Reform Commission, which provided for proportional representation of women and minorities in each State's delegation. The DNC had the right to refuse to seat any delegation that did not meet the proportional representation requirement.

The Arizona Rules Committee adopted the recommendation by Dick Wilks, an attorney and party activist, to provide for cumulative voting in the delegate selection process. Cumulative voting is the option used to protect the rights of minority shareholders in elections for boards of directors of large corporations. For example, assume there were five vacancies. This system allowed voters to allocate all of their five votes to one candidate, to allocate their votes to one-to-two candidates, or to vote for one candidate for each position. When minority shareholders gave all their votes to one candidate, they were often able to have representation on the corporation board.

Members of Unidos were supporting various Democratic candidates for the Party's nomination. The candidates included: Senator George McGovern from South Dakota, New York Mayor John Lindsay, former

Vice-President Hubert Humphrey, Eugene J. McCarthy, former Senator from Minnesota, and Senator Edmund Muskie, from Maine , among others. Unidos was committed to electing Chicano/a delegates, regardless of their candidate preference. Therefore, I offered to train representatives of the various candidates on the delegate selection rules, especially on how cumulative voting worked.

County Caucuses

After the election of precinct committee persons, the next step in selecting the delegates to the Democratic National Convention are the county caucuses. At the county caucuses, the delegates to the State caucus are elected. At the state caucus, the delegates to the national convention are selected.

The night before the county caucus, I received a call from John Ahearn, the State Chair for the George McGovern campaign. After the primary, McGovern was allocated two delegates and three alternates from Maricopa County. John wanted to let us know that he and a couple of other McGovern people thought it would be good for the McGovern delegates to include a Chicana (a "two-fer") and told me the name of their Chicana candidate.

John then proceeded to tell me he would be running for the other delegate seat from Maricopa County. These were heady days in the Chicano movement. I felt free to tell one of the most respected war veterans and party leaders that we would not support this effort. I reminded him the McGovern-Fraser Reform Rules were all about openness and no more "smoke-filled back room deals." As the McGovern State Chair he should go for the at-large delegate position. He responded they had agreed for that seat to go to George Miller, the Mayor of Tucson. That did it. I told him the Chicano McGovern delegates would withhold their votes, ensuring that none of them would be elected.

When we showed up at the Maricopa County party caucus, Chicanos seemed to be the only ones who understood the complexities of cumulative voting. Separate sessions were held for each candidate. To everyone's amazement, Chicanos won an unprecedented number of delegates. The county delegates then went to the State convention, where the twenty-two delegates and twenty-two alternates would be selected.

State Convention – Chicanos go to the National Convention

Elías and I did not attend the State convention because we had received a fellowship to attend a six-week Bilingual Teacher Training Program in Guadalajara, Mexico. The State convention proved historical. Following is a compilation of various accounts.

There was some uneasiness because of the large number of Chicano delegates. When the final tallies were completed, the names of the delegates were announced and they were asked to come forward. Of the 44 delegates and alternates, six Chicanos were elected as delegates and eight Chicanos were elected as alternates! Prior to this time, there had never been more than one Chicano delegate or alternate. The Anglo women were committed to electing minority delegates. Many of these women gave up their bids to support a minority candidate. Someone in the audience yelled "Where are our women?" objecting to the high number of Chicano delegates. Pandemonium broke loose. Individuals had to be physically restrained.

Elías and I laughed so hard when we heard about this, but we also realized that we had some challenges ahead of us in our own Democratic Party. The 1972 delegate selection process marked the beginning of increased Chicano participation in the Democratic Party structure.

Establishment of the Guadalupe Polling Precinct

People from Guadalupe were eager to participate in the delegate selection process; however, there was no polling place in or near their community. Socorro Bernasconi convinced us to push for the establishment of a polling place in Guadalupe. Since the Democratic Party had to pay for the election, our request was initially refused. Then I called one of the Democratic Party officials. If they were truly interested in minority representation, how could they refuse the request? After all, about ninety-five percent of registered voters in Guadalupe were Democrats. Finally, I threatened to go to the press, so we reached an agreement.

If we could find a polling place and volunteers to run the election, they would approve our request. And, Elías had to be the precinct captain. In reality, the Party did not think people in Guadalupe would turn out to vote and did not want to waste valuable resources. In addition, I don't think they thought we could get it together in such a short time. The elementary school district let us use Frank School in

Guadalupe at no cost, so we went to get the materials to set up the polling place.

Election Day was exciting! Candidates put up colorful campaign signs. Max Valencia drove up and down the streets with a megaphone reminding people to come out to vote. The Party had to follow the same rules used for all elections. We set up all the required signs just in time for the first group of voters. Even we were surprised by the turnout. At about 7:30 a.m., someone came to get Elías. John Simonds, one of the candidates, was raising a ruckus because he was told he could not post his sign on the school yard fence. Elías explained to Mr. Simonds that he could not post campaign signs within seventy-five feet of the polling place. Mr. Simonds yelled: "Then why did you let that guy 'Hoy' put up his sign on the fence?" The sign read: "VOTE HOY." Anybody would think the Director of the Bilingual Programs for the Tempe Elementary School District would know that this meant "VOTE TODAY!"

About four hundred people voted at that precinct. This gave Guadalupe enough votes to have one of its residents, Jesse Bravo, elected as an alternate Delegate to the National Convention. The same community made a difference in 1970 when Elías ran for the Tempe Union High School Board and was elected by eight votes. It was the first time a substantial number of Guadalupanos voted in a school board election.

Arizona Women's Political Caucus (AWPC)

Sometime in the 1970s I was asked to speak at a meeting of the Arizona Women's Political Caucus (AWPC). They were interested in the fact that I was a married Chicana, with children, and I was politically active. They also wanted me to join their organization. I was not particularly excited when I accepted this invitation. What did I have to offer Anglo women?

I gave a brief overview about myself and about my political involvement and then called for questions. I could not believe the questions asked!

"How do you do it? Being married with children and being so active? Does your husband approve?" a woman from the audience asked.

"Both my husband and I are active. We became political because we wanted to address issues facing Chicanos," was my response. "We try to schedule our time so we can spend time with our children. One of my husband's sisters helps tremendously. We often drop by and leave Andrea and Marcos to play with their many cousins."

"Our husbands would never be that supportive," said another woman.

I was a little stunned after this exchange. Somehow I had the impression that Anglo women were pretty liberated. Now I began to understand why the Rules Committee was all Anglo males. Next they asked for some advice on a couple of compelling issues:

"We are not allowed to wear pantsuits at work."

"We are required to wear nylons to work."

"How can we change that?"

"We are not paid the same wages as male employees doing the same work."

My response was rather insensitive and rude:

I was hesitant to come here today because my time is very limited. I need to concentrate my volunteer activities to promoting Chicano causes. For instance, while you are fighting to wear pantsuits, not to wear nylons and for equal pay, we are fighting for sanitary facilities for farm workers. Today farm workers in the fields do not have toilets. We are fighting to keep children from working in the fields – they need to be in school. And, we are fighting for the passage of laws that prohibit spraying the fields with pesticides while the workers are in the fields. We are fighting for decent wages, housing and health care for farm workers.

All of these things you take for granted. We need for your organization to support these efforts. I somehow feel I am wasting my time coming here. You are highly educated women and will figure out how to get the changes you are looking for. What you need to understand is that my time is too valuable to address your issues. Don't get me wrong: any rights you secure will surely benefit Chicanas.

After the meeting several women came up to me and said "Thank you! If you can do it, so can I!" Go figure.

Chicanos discuss MASO

Gus Chavez   Dian Sailas   Reyes Jimenez   Jerrie Trujillo   Robert Pastor

Mexican-Americans form first campus organızation

The first organization to be established on campus solely for the Mexican-American student will meet Tuesday at 3 p.m. in the Senate Chamber, MU 227.

Tentatively called the Mexican-American Student Association, it will choose an official name at the organizational meeting.

The group will extend community-directed efforts to teenagers, elementary school children, offering tutoring with educational problems.

Eventually, the student group hopes to publish a Spanish newspaper.

Representatives of the organization will be at a table on the Mall Monday.

Laundry Policy Protested

Sit-in at Durham's Office

Top: Gus Chávez, Diane Salas, Reyes Jiménez, Jerrie Trujillo, Robert Pastor, Arizona State University, MASO/MEChA Collection (MSS-110 Chicano). Chicano Research Collection. Department of Archives and Special Collections, Hayden Library, Arizona State University, Tempe, Arizona

Middle: State Press, ASU, October 18, 1968 [Chicano Research Collection]

Bottom: Headline, Arizona Republic, Phoenix, Arizona, Nov. 21, 1968 [Chicano Research Collection]

Top: Ed Pastor, Verma Méndez Pastor, Ed Young

Bottom: Elías, Marcos Esquer, Doña Luz Corral de Villa, widow of Pancho Villa, Andrea and Cecilia D. Esquer, Chihuahua, Chihuahua, México, July 1972. Photo by Pancho Villa Museum

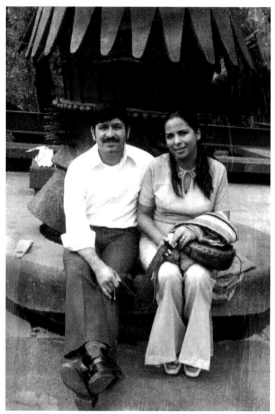

Top: Elías and Cecilia Esquer
México City, 1972

Bottom: Esquer Political Button
Collection, early years

5

TEMPE POLITICS
WATER IS THE ISSUE

Tempe Politics – The 1972 Tempe City Election

IN the spring of 1972, Richard Neuheisel and Dale Shumway ran for the Tempe mayoral slot. All signs pointed to a tight race, but Neuheisel seemed to have the edge. He sought Elías' support one day over coffee at Coco's. Elías told him he could not support him because of the disrespectful manner in which residents of the community of Guadalupe had been treated by former Mayor Elmer Bradley during a Tempe City Council meeting in November 1969. Elmer Bradley was defeated by Dale Shumway in the 1970 mayoral race. Richard Neuheisel was a Council member at that time and did not speak out or object. He told Elías he was not paying a lot of attention at that meeting and didn't remember exactly what had happened. We did not endorse or work for his opponent, Dale Shumway. In the end, Dale Shumway won the 1972 race by about twenty votes, twenty votes we could easily have garnered for Neuheisel. Many of the Tempe residents who were present at the November 1969 meeting worked to defeat Neuheisel despite the fact they were not enthusiastic about Shumway's candidacy.

So what happened at that Council meeting?

On November 6, 1969, about seventy residents from the then unincorporated Town of Guadalupe attended the regular Tempe City Council meeting. They were there to complain about problems with the water bills from the City of Tempe. In 1964, the City of Tempe purchased the Guadalupe Water Co. and became the water provider for the town of Guadalupe. The water system was inadequate. The City of Tempe made some improvements, but the problems with the system were not resolved.

Then City Manager Ken McDonald told the Council that the "water mains were too small and corroded, producing inadequate water pressure."[1] In addition to the inadequate water system, the residents of

---

1 Gene Luptak, "Guadalupe's anger at Tempe unsoothed by new pipeline," The Arizona Republic, No-

Guadalupe complained "about high water rates, lack of water pressure, contamination, and misreading of meters."[2]

About fifty Guadalupe residents attended the October 29, 1969 Tempe City Council meeting to present their complaints. Instead of hearing their complaints, the Council members slipped out a rear door.[3] They did so because the Guadalupe residents would not agree to let Mayor Bradley place a limit on the number of Guadalupe residents who would be admitted to the meeting. The Council was willing to meet with only five representatives. Lauro García, the Executive Director of the Guadalupe Organization, asked for the hearing to be held in the larger Council chambers, but the Mayor and Council refused. Mr. García offered to limit their number to seventeen. That was about the same number of City Council members and City staff attending the meeting.[4]

The water issue was not on the November 6, 1969 Council agenda, so the Guadalupe residents waited to present their requests under "Unscheduled Public Appearances," which are scheduled at the end of the Council meeting. The meeting included presentations by Tempe residents. They had no time limits. One person spoke for forty minutes even though he was asked to be brief. The chambers were small. There was not enough sitting room, so many of the seventy people were standing in the back and the aisles. There was a lot of shuffling in the audience.[5] The following editorial describes some details of that meeting:

> During a period between two speakers, some of the fifty people forced to stand . . . shifted from one foot to the other, cleared their throats, and a few went to the drinking fountains.
>
> At this point, Mayor Bradley, with his great jaw bone firmly set, announced that, "any further disturbances would result in the guilty persons being evicted from the room.

vember 28, 1969. (MSS132-Chicano. Chicano Research Collection. Department of Archives and Special Collections. Hayden Library. Arizona State University. Tempe, Arizona.

2 Luptak, Nov 28, 1969

3 The Arizona Republic, Friday, "Guadalupe sit-inners go home," October 31, 1969(MSS132-Chicano. Chicano Research Collection. Department of Archives and Special Collections. Hayden Library. Arizona State University. Tempe, Arizona.

4 Luptak, Nov 28, 1969

5 Editorial, David Leuser, "Citizens Tell Tempe Councilmen They Are Ashamed to Live There, The Voice of the city, November 13, 1969. (MSS132-Chicano. Chicano Research Collection. Department of Archives and Special Collections. Hayden Library. Arizona State University. Tempe, Arizona.

. . . .

When item 12 (Unscheduled Public Appearances) came up, Mayor Bradley generously allowed one person from Guadalupe to speak for a whole five minutes. Lauro Garcia . . . had only time to read a brief statement telling that Guadalupe wants to meet with the Tempe City Council and expressing concern over last week's treatment. During his time allotment, Garcia was interrupted twice. . . No time was added to his time allotment. Mayor Bradley then, at great length remonstrated Garcia, the people of Guadalupe, and anyone else who wouldn't listen to his reasons why only a couple of people from Guadalupe could meet to resolve problems.

. . . .

The Father Robert Coriell asked to speak [priest from Our Lady of Guadalupe church]. He was refused. The Father stated, "I have a right to be heard." Mayor Bradley, without hesitating, shot back, "You do not have that right!" Whereupon, a student in the audience called out (without being recognized) "What happened to freedom of speech?" At this point, Mayor Bradley had him forcibly ejected from the meeting.[6]

No one from the Council spoke up. Eliza Carney, a Tempe resident and community activist, stood up and chided the Mayor, telling him she was ashamed to be a Tempe resident when the Mayor mistreated visitors to the Council. Other individuals then stood up and objected. Even after this, no Council member or the Mayor apologized.[7]

Elías was at this meeting and was outraged by the disrespectful manner the Council treated the residents from Guadalupe. He agreed with Eliza that Neuheisel should have spoken up, so we decided not to support him. Elías liked Dick Neuheisel and felt badly when he lost.

In late November 1969, Tempe city officials announced that more than $40,000 would be spent to install new water mains in Guadalupe. However, Lauro García said, this did not resolve the issues around high water rates, lack of water pressure, contamination, and misreading of meters. Guadalupe residents were charged thirty percent higher rates than Tempe residents. Guadalupe residents without water meters were charged a $4 monthly flat fee; those with meters were charged up to

6   Ibid., Leuser Editorial
7   Ibid.

four times that amount.[8]

To this day, I marvel at the tenacity of the residents of Guadalupe. They are willing to stand up for their rights, and they are willing to stay with it, no matter how long it takes, and no matter how many times they are insulted and rejected. I learned a lot about human nature during this time. Once more, my feeling that Anglo people saw me as a second-class citizen was reinforced. But I was reminded once again that there are decent human beings, like Eliza Carney, who are Anglo who will publicly oppose racist and disrespectful behavior. I also learned that speaking out at public meetings is essential. Finally, my respect for my husband grew tremendously. It took a lot of courage for Elías to tell Dick Neuheisel that he could not back him for Mayor.

---

8 Luptak, Nov 29, 1969.

6

NATIONAL POLITICS THE DEMOCRATIC NATIONAL COMMITTEE (DNC)

O NE of the outcomes of the 1972 McGovern for President Campaign was the adoption by the Democratic National Committee (DNC) of the "McGovern-Fraser Reform Rules." In addition to providing for proportional representation in the state delegations to the DNC National Convention, the rules created twenty-five at-large positions. These positions were intended to balance the make-up of the DNC that was dominated by White males over fifty. The hunt was on for women and minorities under fifty who were active in the Democratic Party.

Unidos had met and recommended that Joe Eddie López be nominated by Charlie Pine, our State Chair. Bob Strauss from Texas was the Chair of the DNC. His son lived in Tucson, Arizona, so Strauss was open to supporting a candidate from Arizona. But, they needed a minority woman. Charlie Pine checked with Ed Pastor, the Unidos Chair, to make sure it was alright for him to nominate me. Charlie Pine called me. He sounded very excited and asked if he could submit my name for election. I didn't think anything would come of this, just a lot of hot air; but, I told him to go ahead. Charlie told me to stay by the phone because he would be calling back in a couple of hours. I failed to tell him that our family was just about to leave for Disneyland for the weekend.

When we returned on Sunday evening, we found our front door covered with newspaper articles and congratulatory notes. I had been elected![1] When Charlie returned, he chided me for not waiting for the phone call. Eliza Carney held a party to celebrate my election.

I was a first year-law student at the time. We had little money, and not enough for me to travel to the two to three meetings per year in

---

1 Arizona Republic, "Tempe woman is named to Dems' national panel," Arizona Republic, date missing

Washington, D.C. Rick DeGraw, a fellow Democrat, formed an ad hoc group called "Roots." Before each of my trips, he would write a letter to a circle of friends asking for contributions to help defray my expenses. Of course our friends had little money; however, they sent in checks, as small as $2.50 and as large as $25.00. Round-trip tickets at the time were around $600.00. Rick generally raised enough money for a one-way trip. I charged the rest of the ticket to our credit card.

I never had enough funds to pay for a hotel room. Joe Aragón, an attorney from California, was the head of the Latino Desk for the DNC. There were thirteen Latinos on the DNC. We relied on Joe to help us get through these meetings. Mary Ledesma, from California, was a member of the Executive Committee of the DNC. Her hotel room was paid for by the DNC. She graciously invited the Latinas who could not afford a hotel room to stay with her in her hotel room. Generally, it was Polly Baca from Colorado, Alicia Chacón from Texas, and me. We would share a king-size bed, taking turns sleeping on the floor. My husband did not have contact information for me until I called to let him know where I was staying. This created tension in the family, because sometimes I generally could not make contact with Mary Ledesma until late in the evening. Marcos would get very anxious not knowing where I was. Elías felt pretty helpless.

At one meeting, I went to register and was told I would have to pay a forty-five dollar registration fee. We had not been notified of this change in policy. I did not have the forty-five dollars and was told I could not go into the meeting. They refused to waive the fee. I became upset and raised my voice asking why I had to pay for the right to vote. A distinguished looking gentleman was in line behind me. Hearing the commotion he apparently indicated that he would pay my registration fee. I later found out he was Dale Bumpers, a Senator from Arkansas. If I recall correctly, we were not denied admission to future meetings if we did not have the registration fee.

There were 330 members on the DNC. I found it difficult to see how I could have an impact on its work. The agendas were generally around party rules and internal DNC issues. Joe Aragón convened a meeting of the thirteen Latinos on the DNC. We formed the Latino Caucus. Collectively we were able to address issues affecting Latinos. It was difficult to get support from the other Democratic Party National Committeemen. Joe would set up meetings with DNC Chair, Bob Strauss. Some of the meetings were fairly confrontational. Joe Bernal, a state senator from Texas, and Alicia Chacón, a probate judge from Texas, had a history of dealing with Bob Strauss. Senator Bernal did not hesitate to accuse the Chairman of ignoring Latino interests, and would call him a racist from time to time. Chairman Strauss responded in kind.

An issue surrounding the Watergate break-in surfaced concerning access to DNC files, files that Chairman Strauss refused to release. Alan Baron, a DNC employee, requested the files to use in a lawsuit he had filed against the Republican National Committee. His desk was one of the desks searched by the Watergate burglars. Alan felt the files would be useful in his case. He asked to meet with the Latino Caucus to get support for his request.

When I returned to Arizona, I wrote an article in the State Democratic Party newsletter criticizing Chairman Strauss for his refusal to release the files. Shortly after that, he came to a Democratic Party dinner in Arizona. Bob made sure I sat next to him at the head table. Besides the issues around the release of the files, he also wanted to discuss the status of Joe Aragón. I got the impression that he wanted to get a new person to head the Latino Desk. That discussion got a little heated. I told him Joe was very effective, especially in the support he provided the Latino Caucus. In the end, Joe Aragón remained on the job.

The DNC had several classes of members. One class was established to provide representation for the Democratic Governors. The DNC was a focal point for individuals interested in running for President. They were able to establish a nationwide network that was helpful when they launched their campaigns. Jimmy Carter served as the Governor from Georgia while I was on the Committee. Bill Clinton served as the Governor from Arkansas before his decision to run for President. They were each elected President in large part due to the support they gained from the Democratic Party members of the DNC. My term was up at the end of 1976.

I did not seek re-election in 1977 to the DNC because by that time I worked as an Assistant Attorney General in Arizona. At that time state law did not allow state employees to serve in partisan positions. I did not see Bob Strauss until sometime in June 1982. I was elected as an At-Large Delegate to the 1982 Democratic National Party Conference in Philadelphia, Pennsylvania. I ran into Bob Strauss as we entered the hotel. He grabbed my arm and pulled me over to introduce me to his wife. Then he said, "I want you to meet my new partner." I turned around, looked up, way up. In front of me was Vernon Jordan, a Black man who had served in the Carter administration and later in the Clinton administration. The unspoken message was: "Now call me racist!" Bob Strauss could not contain his laughter as I shook hands with Mr. Jordan. Of course, by the time I had served four years on the DNC, I came to realize that Bob Strauss was an incredibly talented politician. His quick gavel kept the left and the right factions in check. When he felt things were getting hot, his gavel worked extra fast. His work was instrumental in Democratic Party efforts to win elections. Bob later served as the Trade Envoy for President Clinton.

Looking back I wonder how I could sacrifice valuable time I could have spent with my family or studying for my law school classes. At any rate, it was an incredible experience. I felt guilty about placing the needs of my family below my political interests, but the feeling that I had to accept certain positions allowed me to set my guilt aside. I also did not consider the fact that ignoring my studies would contribute to my failure to pass the bar exam on the first try.

L to r: Linda Álvarez, n/a, Rick Hernández, Joe Eddie López, Earl Wilcox, Cecilia D. Esquer, Ed Pastor, White House, Washington, D. C., 1976

Top: Cecilia and Elías Esquer, Tempe, Arizona, Spring 1973

Middle l to r: Pat Fullinwider, Cecilia D. Esquer, Joe Eddie López, Tempe, Arizona, Spring 1973

Bottom l to r: Eliza Carney, Cecilia D. Esquer, Pat Fullinwider Tempe, Arizona, Spring 1973

⋘ 7 ⋙

LAW SCHOOL

ASU College of Law

AS I mentioned in a previous chapter, I became interested in going to law school after all the problems I experienced teaching at McClintock High School. I noticed that positive changes in education were taking place as a result of court decisions. At one of the farm worker rallies, César Chávez mentioned the need for more Mexican American attorneys, something which started me thinking about going to law school. In 1972, Ed Pastor was a second-year law student. At one of the farm worker rallies I asked Ed if law school was very difficult. He said it was not and asked if I was interested in going. I told him I was thinking about it. He said I was crazy to go, but that I could make it. He advised me to speak with my husband. If we decided that I should go to law school, he would help me get in.

After some discussion, Elías and I decided I should try it. I took the Law School Admissions Test (LSAT). When the results came in, I called Ed. He came by the house with an application for admission for me to complete and told me he would be back the following week. He called in the middle of the week to tell me he had made some appointments for me and would drop by to pick me up.

Our first meeting was with Willard Pedrick, the Dean of the ASU College of Law. Ed introduced me and told him I was going to be in the first-year class the following fall. I was caught off guard by this approach. Dean Pedrick asked me a few questions. We had a pleasant visit. Then Ed took me to meet with members of "El Grupo," the Chicano law students' association. At that time, student organizations had representatives on the Admissions Committee, so Ed asked the group to support my application for admission.

I was fortunate to be admitted to ASU because it would have been impossible for me to attend any other law school. My husband loved his teaching position at Mesa Community College and wanted to stay. Besides, we were going from two incomes to one, and had good support for child care in Tempe. As the beginning of the school year approached, I became very apprehensive about my prospects for success in law school. I vowed to try my best the first semester and promised myself I would not be too surprised if I didn't make it. The reception from a couple of the professors did not help at all.

Negative Reinforcement Works!

During law school orientation week, August 1973, I met Professor Jonathan Rose on the stairway by the rotunda in the law building. Professor Rose joined the faculty at the ASU College of Law in the college's second year. I had met him through the farm workers' organizing movement and through the Arizona Democratic Party in the late 1960s early 1970s. He often played the guitar at the rallies – his favorite song: "Solidaridad Pa' Todos" (Solidarity for All).

"Hi Cecilia. I was so surprised when I learned you were coming to law school. By the way, I looked up your index. Did you know you are in that percentage of students who generally do not make it through law school?"

Without waiting for an answer, he continued:

"Besides, you are a Chicana, married with children. You should be home taking care of your family. Also, you should not call me John at school."

Poking him in the chest:

"I wasn't even going to admit I knew you, much less call you John. I didn't even know whether I could make it through even one year, much less three. But, thanks to your encouragement, I know I am going to finish!" I don't think Professor Rose would speak this way to a male student, even a Chicano.

I was in Professor Rose's Contracts class that year. I entered with great trepidation. However, it turned out he was a very good teacher. I did well in his class. I served on the Community Legal Services Board of Directors with him. When the program came under fire by a very conservative board member, I was moved by Professor Rose's ardent defense of the program and of the mission of legal aid programs in general.

Another day during Orientation Week, we were divided into small groups of fifteen students. Professor Hal Bruff was the discussion leader for our group. I was the only minority in the group. The purpose of the group was to address student fears and concerns and to answer any questions. Toward the end of the discussion, one of the students asked if it was true that if we looked to our left, then to our right, that one of us would not make it to third year. Professor Bruff quickly discounted that. He said ASU only admitted students they thought would be successful in law school, so they expected all of us to make it, "except for those minority students we admitted." Miraculously, I did not say anything. But, I was very upset.

Having come to law school after having picketed and marched for the UFW, I went to Dean Pedrick's office. He told me Professor Bruff had already told him what had happened and that Bruff felt badly about it. Professor Bruff said if I wanted an apology, I could go to his office. I told Dean Pedrick I would do no such thing, and he could tell Professor Bruff to go to hell.

Sensitizing the Faculty

Nationally, the demographics of law school students were beginning to change. The Women's Movement and the Civil Rights Movement created a greater awareness about legal rights, but the majority of law students were still white males. Women and minorities sought admission to law schools in unprecedented numbers. The 1972 class included eight women. My first-year class of 150 students, the 1973 class, included thirty women, the largest number enrolled to date. Even though the ASU law school was relatively new, founded in 1967, it was clear the facilities planners did not anticipate many women students. Professors complained because women were often late to class. This was due mainly to the fact that there were not enough restroom stalls for the number of women, so the lines were long. Dean Pedrick helped resolve this by agreeing to convert one of the men's bathrooms to a woman's bathroom. He even attended the ceremony where the nameplate was changed from "Men" to "Women" and helped place a bouquet of flowers in one of the eight urinals.

Another dilemma was the insensitive comments made by some of the professors in class. They were not used to having women and minority students. The women had no problem challenging the vocabulary in class. Minorities were more reluctant because we did not feel totally accepted by some of the faculty and students.

I remember a situation in the first-year Criminal Law class with Professor Cohen during a discussion of the death penalty. He made a couple of remarks about the individuals who received the death penalty, then concluded with making a joke about what it must be like to "fry" on the electric chair. There was some laughter in the class.

A classmate sitting next to me did not find the professor's comments funny at all. In fact he was very upset by the comments: his father had been the last person in Arizona executed by lethal gas before the 1963 U.S. Supreme Court moratorium on the death penalty. After class I suggested he speak with Professor Cohen. He could not and would not.

I went upstairs to Professor Cohen's office and asked him if he knew anyone whose friend or relative had suffered the death penalty. He did not. I told him this year's first-year class was the most diverse class to date and brought a wider group of experiences, including friends or family who had encounters with the criminal justice system. I mentioned that I came from a large family and had close relatives who had done some jail time, some simply because they were Mexican American. Then I asked if he knew that the father of one of the students in the Criminal Law class had been executed in the Florence prison gas chamber. Professor Cohen turned pale. He could not believe this. I told him this student was very upset and offended by his comments. I refused to tell him the name of the student, but expected him to make some type of apology in class. He did not. I again was disappointed by the insensitivity and ignorance about the minority communities. This increased my commitment to work for change.

Democratic National Party Conference 1974
Internal Party Affairs

During first year, second semester of law school, I became involved with another delegate selection process. In even-numbered years between Presidential nominating conventions, the national Democratic Party holds a mid-term conference, the "Democratic National Party Conference." The 1974 Conference gave women and minorities an opportunity to make sure the 1972 successes were not a one-time thing, especially when it came to the "no more smoke-filled room" delegate selections.

We waited as long as we could to see if the "men" would call any of us for support of their candidates. There are not as many delegate positions for this conference as there are for the Presidential nomination convention. Karen Scates, a Party activist, and I decided we would like to see a woman candidate. Karen was an aide to Senator Alfredo Gutiérrez. Karen and I convinced Joyce Geyser to run. Joyce was the District 27 Democratic Party Chair and had become a very successful fundraiser for the Party and for individual candidates. We felt she would be the ideal candidate and were thrilled when she agreed to run. So, three weeks before the State Caucus, Joyce launched her campaign.

Karen and I worked hard to get statewide support for Joyce. We were pleased with the positive response. The night before the statewide convention to select the delegates, I received a call from John Ahearn. John was a long-time Democratic Party activist, a highly decorated war veteran, including the medals for Distinguished Service Cross and the Purple Heart. John was appointed to the Arizona Corporation Commission in 1979 and served until 1981. He was the Chair for the 1972 McGovern Campaign, which is where Elías and I met him. John was a strong advocate for public service and serving the poor. He became one of my heroes.

However, he and his circle of friends were having a hard time understanding what Democratic Party women expected in regard to our involvement in Democratic Party politics. Since this was not a Presidential nominating convention, we thought this was a good time for us to make our point. So, when John called asking us to support Sam Goddard for the at-large position, I told him we already had a candidate: "John, since you did not call us when you went to make your selection, we went ahead and found our own candidate." He did not seem too concerned. I understood why. Sam Goddard was a former Arizona Governor and a National Committee man from Arizona on the Democratic National Committee. At this time, I was a Member-at-Large of the Democratic National Committee.

The State Caucus took place on a Saturday at the old Adams Hotel (now the Wyndham) in Downtown Phoenix. I ran into John Ahearn as we headed for the meeting room. He seemed intrigued by the fact we had chosen our own candidate and asked: "When Sam gets elected, would you be willing to move to make the election unanimous by acclamation?" I responded: "I would be honored to do that; however, if somehow Joyce gets elected, would you be willing to do the same for Joyce?" His reaction was one of surprise. Until that moment, he did not see how anyone could defeat Sam Goddard. John did not respond and seemed relieved when someone came to greet him.

Jim Walsh, an attorney and Democratic Party activist, chaired the elections that day. The ballroom at the Adams Hotel was packed with at least 300 people. Jim called for nominations for the at-large position. Sam Goddard and Joyce Geyser were the only two nominated. The voting was open so individuals stood for the vote count. There were about four vote counters. After several attempts, they could not come up with the same totals. Finally, someone moved that the voting be by secret ballot. The Chair called for a secret ballot. I was still a little naïve about these issues, but I could tell the Goddard supporters felt very threatened by this move. And, they were right. Joyce Geyser won.

We did not know that Democrats in Tucson had strong feelings against anyone from Maricopa County. There has always been a "them (Maricopa County) v. us (Pima County)" attitude. It didn't take much for the Pima County individuals to seek ways of "getting even." They took this opportunity to let Sam know how they felt. I imagine the Goddard supporters knew this might happen when the voting turned to a secret ballot. Initially I don't think they considered Joyce was a threat because they did not campaign much before the State caucus. Apparently, as they went around asking for votes at the State caucus, many individuals told them they were committed to Joyce. We really worked hard to get Joyce elected.

The Arizona Republic and Phoenix Gazette, who thought Sam Goddard had been too liberal when he was Governor, turned this into a big story. They claimed the party faithful had rejected Governor Goddard.[1] I wrote a letter to the Editor of The Arizona Republic to let them know it was not a personal attack on Governor Goddard.[2]

Third Year Law School 1974-75
Arizona Politics & Governor Castro

The year 1974 turned out to be an historic year. Raul Castro, a Hispanic lawyer, former County Attorney, and Superior Court Judge from Tucson, was elected Governor of Arizona. He was the first Hispanic ever elected to this position in Arizona. No Hispanic has been elected since. Elías and I worked as volunteers on his campaign. We were ecstatic when he was elected.

Political issues seemed to find me wherever I was. One evening

1   John Kolbe, "Demos Reject Goddard; Tempe Woman Elected, Phoenix Gazette, October 1, 1974; Editorial, "Pragmatic Democrats," Arizona Republic, October 4, 1974
2   Cecilia D. Esquer, "Best lobbyist won," Letters to the Editor, Arizona Republic, October 14, 1974.

someone called Elías to ask if we knew the Governor was going to announce his nomination of Dr. William Payne to the Arizona Board of Regents at a press conference the next morning. Elías called Ed Pastor, who worked for Governor Castro. Ed did not know about the potential nomination, but said he would check it out. Ed had worked as the Director of Development for the Guadalupe Organization in the community of Guadalupe. Dr. Payne had served on the Tempe Elementary School District Board, whose District boundaries included parts of Guadalupe. Ed called back a few minutes later to confirm that indeed Dr. Payne was going to be nominated. When I told him the nomination was a big mistake, he suggested I call Manny Domínguez who also worked for Governor Castro.

I called Manny that same evening to ask for an appointment with the Governor so I could ask him to withdraw the nomination. On election night, the Governor had gone to our Tempe District election night party to thank us for the outstanding get-out-the-vote effort. It was the first time a Democratic gubernatorial candidate won this highly Republican district. I reminded Manny the Governor promised to ask our District Chair for feedback on any potential appointees from Tempe. Eliza Carney, the District Chair, told me no one had called her. She would have expressed our opposition. Manny mentioned the Governor had a policy of not speaking with anyone about a nomination on the morning of the announcement. However, he would check to see if either the Governor or Dino DeConcini, the Governor's Chief of Staff, would be willing to meet with us.

Manny called me early the next day to confirm that neither the Governor nor DeConcini could meet with us before the press conference. But, the Governor could meet with us that evening. The County Democratic Party was holding a victory celebration that evening, so Manny reserved a room in the hotel for our meeting with the Governor.

That evening a group of Democratic Party activists came to the meeting with the Governor. They included Matt Wheeler, the newly elected Chair for Maricopa County, Eliza Carney, our District Chair, Bill Canby, one of my law professors, Bruce Mason, a political science professor at ASU, John McCulloch, a Democratic Party activist, Elías and me. The Governor came in with Manny and his bodyguard. He sat across the table, directly in front of me. We exchanged greetings and introductions. I congratulated him on his historic victory.

The Guadalupe Factor

I reminded him of his promise to seek our input on any potential nominees from our District. I told him Dr. Payne did not represent a positive figure in higher education because of his negative attitude toward the children of Guadalupe during his fifteen-plus years on the Tempe Elementary School District Governing Board. He said he did not know Dr. Payne, and that he probably was an "S.O.B." Governor Castro told us we should understand that the day after he was elected, he had to start raising funds for his re-election and needed as broad support as possible. Everyone around the table expressed their concerns about Dr. Payne.

We asked him to reconsider his decision, but he said he could not; it was too late to withdraw the name. After he left, Manny asked if we were fine with this. I told him we were not. He asked us not to pursue this any further and I responded: "The Governor did what he did; now we will do what we have to do." He left pretty dejected. The nomination was subject to Senate confirmation.

Next morning, I called Alfredo Gutiérrez, the Senate Majority Leader. He told me Dr. Payne had to be confirmed unless we could provide strong documentation of the concerns I expressed. Then, there was only a possibility that he could be turned down. Senator Gutiérrez asked me to meet with him the next morning. At this meeting he brought in Senator Lela Alston, the majority whip. After I briefed them on the reasons for our opposition to Dr. Payne's appointment, they asked if I could document what I said about Dr. Payne. I told them I could. Then, both pledged their support. Senator Gutiérrez set up a desk for me in the basement of the Capitol building where some of their staffers worked.

I was a third-year law student, so I was able to devote some time during Spring Break to gathering the documentation: newspaper articles, tapes of the school board meetings, etc. It was easy to gather articles from the Arizona Republic. The paper had a "morgue" where they kept individual separate files on persons mentioned in the news. At that time it was open to the public and the public could request copies of the articles. There were quite a few articles with Dr. Payne's name.[3]

When the Governor told Senator Gutiérrez he would not

---

3   The easy access to these materials led to the closing to the public of the Arizona Republic "morgue." The paper did not want to provide resources for this type of effort.

withdraw the nomination, the Senator announced he would oppose the confirmation of Dr. Payne.[4] This became a front page story for several weeks. I then started calling people to see if they were willing to oppose the nomination. Lauro García, the Executive Director of the Guadalupe Organization, and Santo Bernasconi, a community activist from Guadalupe, agreed to help gather the documentation. Annetta McCulloch, another Party activist, offered to get copies of the school board minutes. Others indicated they would help too. The following Tuesday I took the documents I had collected to Senator Gutiérrez. Alfredo called a meeting to discuss the Payne appointment. The meeting included State Senators Marcia Weeks, Frank Félix, Lito Peña, Sue Dye, Tony Gabaldón, and Lucy Davidson. Only Senator Dye expressed some reservations; she wanted more specific documentation. I could not believe it! We actually had a chance to challenge the Governor's nomination.

With this, I called a meeting of interested individuals. They included: John McCulloch, Eliza Carney, Joyce Geyser, Dora Quesada (a teacher from Frank Elementary School in Guadalupe), Santo Bernasconi, Rose Martínez, a member of the Tempe Elementary School Board, and her husband Dick Martínez. We decided to proceed. Things were moving at a rapid pace, but I felt we were doing the right thing. It did bother me that here I was, challenging the actions of our first Latino Governor, one we had worked very hard to elect. But I did not feel I had a choice, and, there were others who agreed with me.

When Senator Gutiérrez sent a letter requesting the school board meeting tapes, the Board decided not to accept a letter signed by the Senator. They insisted the regulations required the request for tapes of the school board meetings be signed by the Senate President, Bob Stump, or the Education Committee Chair, Senator Tony Gabaldón. They did not think either would be willing to sign, but Senator Stump signed the letter, so the tapes had to be produced.

I spent most of Spring Break, March 15 – 19, 1976, listening to the tapes and selecting the portions to be transcribed. So much for quality time with my family. Then the political games began. Lauro García was contacted by ASU Dean of Students George Hamm. He commented that it was great that GO was doing better in regard to funding, but that

4   Mike Tulumello, "Senate Leader Says Governor's Nominee Not Suitable Regent," State Press, Vol. 58 No. 94, April 7, 1976. (MSS132-Chicano. Chicano Research Collection. Department of Archives and Special Collections. Hayden Library. Arizona State University. Tempe, Arizona.

it would be unfortunate if GO encountered funding problems again only because Lauro chose to testify against Dr. Payne. Joyce Geyser was asked by Al Rogers, who was in charge of appointments for the Governor, to testify on behalf of Dr. Payne. Another prominent Tempe doctor, Dick Flynn, asked Mike Geyser how he thought the votes for confirmation were going. Mike felt pressured by these individuals who could affect his company's contract with the hospitals.

I called Manny Domínguez to complain about the attempts to pressure people not to testify. If this continued, I would start calling State Committee people. He called back to tell me Al Rogers would not have others approached, and Al wanted to know if I was willing to call a truce. Dino DeConcini also reassured Eliza Carney there would be no more "strong arming." Our group met on April 4 to finalize our plans to testify before the Senate Education Committee on April 7. There was scuttlebutt that Bruce Babbitt, the Arizona Attorney General, was about to release an opinion requested by Governor Castro. The Governor asked the Attorney General whether Senate confirmation was required in light of the fact that the Arizona Constitution did not require Senate confirmation for members of the Board of Regents. The Constitution did list other positions that required Senate confirmation.

Wednesday, April 7, 1976 – "The Eleventh Hour." Around Noon on the eve of the confirmation hearing, I was in Senator Gabaldon's office to be briefed on how the hearing would be run and to give him an idea of the number of witnesses we planned to present. The phone rang. Senator Gabaldón told me Governor Castro was on the phone. The Governor called to find out how Senator Gabaldón thought the Committee would vote. Senator Gabaldón told him there were not enough votes to confirm; in fact there was only one vote in favor. This was followed by a heated exchange. The Governor told Senator Gabaldón that a page was on his way to deliver a letter withdrawing Dr. Payne's nomination. He had received an opinion from Attorney General Babbitt stating the nomination did not require Senate confirmation because the Arizona Constitution took precedent over the state statute that required senate confirmation.

Senator Gabaldón pleaded with the Governor not to do this. But at 4:00 p.m., the page delivered the letter withdrawing Dr. Payne's name. Until this moment, the battle over the nomination had been an internal one within the Democratic Party. Now the Republicans jumped in. They called a press conference and told the Governor that once he had submitted to the process, he should not "pull his marbles because he was losing the game." The next day the Senate filed a mandamus action against the Governor asking the Court to order Dr. Payne to appear for the confirmation hearing. The Court dismissed the action. Thus, we were unable to present our testimonies before the committee. The Senate then proceeded to pass a referendum that would amend the Arizona Constitution to require Senate confirmation of future nominees to the Board of Regents. The measure passed at the next General Election, diminishing the power of the Governor to make appointments to the Board of Regents.

Governor Castro resigned in 1977, before his first term was up, to accept an appointment by President Jimmy Carter to serve as Ambassador to Argentina. He had extensive experience as a diplomat, having served under President Johnson as Ambassador to El Salvador and to Bolivia. I think he preferred diplomatic circles.

In 1976, I was in Washington, D.C. to attend a function for Latinos at the White House. I was the only Chicana in the 11-member Arizona delegation. Governor Castro was part of our group. He was personally recognized at every function because he and Jerry Apodaca, the Governor of New Mexico, were the only Latino Governors in the country.

Governor Castro invited me to a function at the Organization of American States (OAS) in Washington, D.C. The OAS was hosting a reception in his honor because he had been elected Governor of Arizona. It was an elaborate affair. I was moved by the love and respect with which Governor Castro was received. I was also surprised that he would invite me to accompany him to the reception in light of the Payne nomination controversy.

To this day, I have mixed feelings about my actions. We worked so hard to get Governor Castro elected – the first Arizona Latino Governor. And here I was, a Chicana, challenging a person I admired greatly. I wonder whether I should have listened to Dino DeConcini, who personally asked me to consider the effect of my actions. In the end, though, I concluded that not challenging Dr. Payne's appointment would indicate a support of outrageous discriminatory policies and practices. I also look back and marvel that I was able to put this whole effort together and still have a successful last semester in law school. Always, I feel pangs of guilt about the little time I spent with my family.

Reflections

Law school was very challenging for me. I had not been in a classroom for about ten years, so I had to re-establish study habits and drop my outside activities. Because I was driven to law school by a desire to "change the system," I found it difficult to stay out of some of the political frays. I could not have made it without the help of my study group. Because I was so worried about me, I did not stop to think about the commitment my husband had made.

He was a full-time professor at Mesa Community College. In addition, he served on the high school board and also chaired a national committee for the National Education Association. He taught two evening classes to help make up for the loss of my income. Finally, he took over all the household duties during the first two years - from cleaning the house, doing the grocery shopping, preparing meals, handling babysitter problems - to taking care of any dilemmas with our two children. After my second year of law school, Elías told me I should be able to make it successfully through the third year, and suggested I start sharing duties at home.

It was difficult at first because Elías, Andrea, and Marcos had established a routine that did not include me. I had to elbow my way back in. During the first dinner I had prepared in a while, my son Marcos asked if it was alright if his Dad continued cooking! I am thankful for their love and support during these difficult years.

After graduation, came the bar exam. Imagine my disappointment when I did not pass the first time. However, I was successful the second time. I ran into Marcos's first-grade teacher at the grocery store one day. She told me she just had to tell me something that happened in "Show and Tell," even though she usually did not disclose the children's contributions. When I passed the bar exam, Marcos proudly announced in class, "My mother finally met a bar she could pass up." Some of the students came to hug him because they thought I had a drinking problem! When the teacher explained why Marcos was so proud, they cheered. I looked forward to new challenges.

Top: Cecilia and
Elías Esquer, Tempe,
Arizona, 1973

Middle: Ramón
Denogeán, Andrea
and Cecilia Esquer,
Bertina T. Denogeán,
Elías and Marcos
Esquer, Arizona State
University College of
Law Commencement,
Tempe, Arizona,
Spring 1976

Bottom: Socorro
Morales, Aaron
Kizer, Cecilia D.
Esquer, Manuel
Silvas, Arizona State
University College of
Law Commencement,
Spring 1976

Top: James P. Walsh, Cecilia D. Esquer, Phoenix, Arizona, 1974

Bottom: Teatro Familia, Marcos and Andrea Esquer, and audience, Hispanic Law Students National Conference, Guadalupe, Arizona, 1975

Pause
between
classes

Six first year members of "El Grupo," Chicano law student organization at the Arizona State University College of Law, relax in the school's lounge between classes. They are (seated) Manuel Silvas, Superior; Cecelia Esquer, Phoenix; Joe Rivera, Flagstaff; and Jose de la Vara, Yuma. Standing are Socorro Morales, Tempe; and Ronnie Martinez, Superior.

Top: Arizona State University, Tempe, Arizona, 1973-74

Bottom: Cecilia D. Esquer and Hon. Raúl Castro, Phoenix College, Phoenix, Arizona, November 29, 2009

8

MEXICO CITY 1976
"NI FU NI FA"

American Council of Young Political Leaders (ACYPL)

EARLY November 1976, I received a call from E. B. Bob Allen (Bob Allen), a leader in the Democratic Party and an advisor to Attorney General Bruce Babbitt. He asked if I would be willing to go on a goodwill trip to Mexico City through the U. S. State Department. The trip would involve a six-member delegation from the United States – three Democrats and three Republicans. We would be meeting with high-ranking officials in the Partido Revolucionario Institucional (PRI), at that time the ruling party in Mexico. We would return to Washington, D.C. for a debriefing with State Department officials. The State Department would arrange the ten-day visit. I was flabbergasted. How did my name come up?

It turns out Joyce Geyser, a Tempe Democratic activist, was in his office when Bob received a call from the American Council of Young Political Leaders (ACYPL). The ACYPL identifies young political leaders to visit other countries under the aegis of the State Department. They needed a Mexican American woman to complete the six-person delegation to Mexico City. Bob asked Joyce if she knew anyone. Joyce gave him my name. I told him I was interested, but I had to check with Elías. Andrea was ten and Marcos was six at the time. Ten days sounded like a long time, but Elías encouraged me to go, so I accepted.

Bruce Weinrod, the Executive Director of the ACYPL in D. C. called me. After confirming that I had a current passport, he told me they would book my flights and that I would be greeted at the airport by a welcoming committee. I asked for the name of the hotel and contact information for someone from the committee. He did not have the name of the hotel, or the name of the local contact. I told him my family needed to know how to reach me in case of an emergency. He said there would be no problem. I could call them when I arrived in Mexico City.

Arrival in Mexico City

On Saturday, November 13, 1976, I was on a flight to Mexico City. I was nervous because I had never traveled abroad by myself. Elías was uncomfortable because he had no contact information. When I arrived at the Mexico City airport, I looked for the welcoming committee, but no one stepped forward. I waited for about one-half hour, then tried to call the State Department contact in Washington, D.C. It was Saturday, so no one was there to answer the phone. I was in a panic. I did not know the name of the hotel, nor did I have any contact information for the host committee. I was on the phone with Elías when suddenly I heard my name over the intercom instructing me to report to a station in the airport.

When I told them I was Cecilia Esquer, they rudely said I could not be Cecilia Esquer and asked for I.D. I showed them my passport, but they asked for other forms of I.D. I think I showed them two or three additional documents before they would believe I was one of the members of the U.S. delegation. They were probably expecting a dashing blonde woman; not this short, brunette Chicana. They called someone from the host committee. About one-half hour later, one of the members came to greet me. They were pretty embarrassed. They had been at the airport but did not see anyone who looked like they might be from the delegation, so they left. Our delegation was from six different states, so we arrived on six different flights. They did not have a problem spotting the other five members of the delegation.

The Official Visit Begins

A member of the host committee picked me up. We arrived at the Hotel María Isabel Sheraton on the Avenida de la Reforma, a very ritzy hotel! We went to the bar, where the U.S. delegates and members of the host committee were getting to know each other. I was introduced to the group. The U. S. delegates included William Sweeney, Director of Research for the Democratic Congressional Campaign Committee; Katherine Wilt, Director of the Young Democrats of America; Bruce Weinrod, Executive Director of the ACYPL; Hal Rodgers, a Republican State Representative from Kentucky; and John Partridge, the Secretary of the Republican Party of Rhode Island. I was listed as a Democratic National Committee woman from Arizona. I was not given a list of the PRI host committee, but there is a picture of the group. The group was friendly and informal. Both sides were eager to exchange information about the incoming administrations.

After a half-hour or so, we went to our rooms to get ready for a reception at the U.S. Embassy. My room on the fifteenth floor was very luxurious. There was a fruit basket and a bottle of wine waiting for me. I was not used to this type of luxury. I was finally able to call Elías to let him know everything was going well and gave him the contact information. I could tell he was pretty worried, but happy to hear from me. All of a sudden my guilt for once again leaving my husband and young children returned. I felt like such an irresponsible wife and mother. But, there was no time to contemplate this further because I had to be downstairs to leave for the reception. The reception was hosted by Mr. and Mrs. Francis Starrs. Mr. Starrs was the Counsel for Political Affairs of the U. S. Embassy.

The reception at the U.S. Embassy was impressive and elaborate. It was attended by a broad spectrum of Mexican society, including artists, musicians, politicians and members of the opposition Partido de Acción Nacional (PAN). They cornered us every opportunity they had and asked for a meeting with us. When they saw this, our PRI hosts would come and interrupt our conversations and take us to meet someone else. We all agreed we were interested in meeting with the individuals from the PAN. Our hosts assured us they would arrange a meeting later in the week.

We had a pretty grueling schedule.[1] We started out early, usually by 9:00 a.m. and traveled in a large van with an interpreter and at least two members from the host committee. The main goal of the host committee was to showcase the modern campaign strategies adopted by then President–elect José López Portillo. They modeled the campaign after the John F. Kennedy campaign. López-Portillo was the first presidential candidate to use television extensively to get his message out. The first morning out, we met briefly with Porfirio Muñoz Ledo, the President of the PRI National Committee, who later was named to López Portillo's cabinet. We were treated to presentations by the various campaign heads. They showed us videos and gave us samples of the campaign materials: brochures, buttons, pencils, erasers, etc. As we drove around the City we could see numerous campaign signs painted on the walls of large buildings, on fences, anywhere they could place the PRI logo and

---

1   "Schedule of Activities for U.S. Democratic and Republican Leaders, November 13th to November 21st, 1976," Partido Revolucionario Institucional, Comisión de Asuntos Internacionales.

López Portillo's name.

We wondered why they ran such an extensive campaign. After all, the PRI, being the ruling party, had already named its candidate and there was no serious opposition. Yet López Portillo traveled the entire country, urban and rural areas. They explained it was important for the public to get to know López Portillo before he took office on December 1st, 1976.

The next few days were spent visiting PRI party offices and the offices of local elected officials. We were taken to a youth rally in the State of Querétaro. There were hundreds of participants, all enthusiastic and thrilled to be part of the political scene. We were hosted at small breakfasts with political VIP's and at huge luncheons, where we sat at the head table. Our activities were covered by the national press. Everywhere we went we were asked to describe how "grassroots" politics worked in the U.S.

As the days went by, the six of us got to know each other pretty well and established a good rapport. We also established a positive relationship with our hosts. Each day we would ask when we were going to meet with people from the PAN. Each day they would reply "mañana." One morning, one of the individuals we met at the U.S. Embassy approached us to remind us they wanted to meet with us. We told them our hosts were arranging a meeting. He told us it would never happen; that we needed to do this on our own because our hosts did not want us to hear about the opposition party views. Reluctantly, or foolishly, we agreed to meet them before breakfast the next morning.

We met with about five PAN representatives for about an hour. They told us they were tired of the PRI being in exclusive control of the country, and that they were mobilizing and winning some local elections around the country. It is ironic that the PRI's philosophy is very similar to that of the Democratic Party (liberal) and the PAN philosophy is similar to that of the Republican Party (conservative). However, we were told, the PRI had controlled the country for so many years that they had strayed from their lofty goals and had become a tyrannical force. So, the PAN saw itself as the "revolutionaries," the reform party. We would like to have visited longer, but we were already crossing the protocol line. We returned to the hotel about five minutes late and found our hosts waiting for us. They were very upset with us and felt we had betrayed them. They barely talked to us the rest of the morning.

That evening, over drinks, our hosts asked how it was possible for three Democrats and three Republicans to get along so well. It was difficult for them to understand that one could disagree on issues and still be cordial, even like each other. We were in their good graces again.

Ni Fu Ni Fa (Not one or the other)

In the van the next morning, one of the hosts asked about my nationality and how my parents got to the U.S. When I told him my grandparents were from Mexico, but lived in the Arizona territory from a very young age, he became irritated. He said my ancestors were traitors to Mexico, that they probably fled the country to avoid the Mexican Revolution. This was quite a surprise to me. I felt that, from the day I arrived, they did not see me as an equal to the other delegates. Now I knew why.

He then asked what I called myself. I told him I considered myself a Chicana. He told me I was a Yankee. Shocking! I always thought of Yankees as being Anglo. How could a Chicana be a Yankee? Then he told me I was a gringa; another amazing statement. I always thought gringos were fair skinned Anglos. All of a sudden I felt as if I had no identity. In Arizona, when politics got rough, we would be told to go back to our country (Mexico). But being a third generation American citizen, I considered the United States my country. In Spanish there is a phrase to describe this feeling: Ni fu, Ni fa (Not one or the other). It made me sad to feel that some individuals thought I didn't belong. Then I laughed at the idea of being a gringa and could hardly wait to get home to share the news with Elías.

International Intrigue - Los Desaparecidos - Argentina

On Friday, November 19, 1976 we visited the Center for Third World Studies. The Center had been established by President Luis Echeverría to bring scholars from all the Latin American countries. It was a beautiful Center with cultural exhibits from the different Latin American countries. The main auditorium reminded me of the United Nations. There were interpreter stations in soundproof booths in the rear of the room and all kinds of state-of-the art equipment. Echeverría hoped to run this Center after his term was over within a couple of weeks. From here, he could become an important player in Latin American circles. He hoped it would increase his chances to become the Secretary General of the United Nations. The PRI was ready to steer away from the third-world focus and looked forward to improved relationships with the United States. I ran into Alberto Noé, a sociologist from Argentina, and a researcher at the Center. I had met him at the Embassy reception. His name was not on the list of invitees. He said he was determined to get in so he could meet the Americans.

Alberto was Jewish and came from a prominent political family in Argentina. Unfortunately, on March 24, 1976 Argentina was taken over by a military junta who overthrew President Isabel Martínez de Perón.[2] The Junta began what is called "the dirty war" and began ridding the country of its political enemies. They especially concentrated on ridding the country of Jews. Legislation was passed that allowed the Junta to arrest individuals they determined to be a danger to the national interest. Individuals were kidnapped and taken to secret locations. Their families were given no information as to their whereabouts. Thousands were never accounted for. The individuals who had disappeared became known as los desaparecidos. Alberto Noé's brother, Victor Jacobo Noé, twenty-eight years old, and a prominent Argentine attorney, disappeared. Their mother was inconsolable.

Alberto asked if Katie Wilt and I would join him and some of his colleagues so they could brief us on the plight of los desaparecidos. His group picked Katie and me. They thought we had a lot of political clout in the U.S. because we were part of the Democratic National Committee, whose party had just won the Presidency. We could not convince him otherwise. In Mexico, high ranking PRI officials had that clout and did not hesitate to use it. We reluctantly told him that our schedule did not allow any time for this. He asked if we would at least contact Minnesota Congressman Don Fraser to ask him to intervene for his family. I told him I would do what I could, and then we exchanged contact information.

Someone from the U.S. Embassy joined us for lunch. When Katie and I told him about Alberto's invitation, he became very serious. He told us that under no circumstances were we to leave with anyone but our hosts because we could be kidnapped and held to convince the United States to get more involved in addressing the issue of los desaparecidos. This was a sobering reminder that we did not know too much about international politics.

---

2 "Argentine Dirty War", http://wikis.lib.ncsu.edu/index.php/Argentine_Dirty_War

Possible López - Portillo Cabinet Appointees

During the last day of our visit, rumors began to surface about López Portillo's possible cabinet appointees. Imagine our pleasant surprise when some of the names floating around were among the individuals hosting us.

We left Mexico City full of new information and with positive feelings that relations between the U.S. and Mexico were going to improve under the new administrations. We flew into Washington, D.C., where we were debriefed by someone in the State Department. They met with us individually, asked pretty detailed questions about what we heard and saw and were not too surprised that we had no "explosive" information. The next morning we all headed for our respective homes.

Los Desaparecidos - Ambassador Castro Steps In

Alberto Noé kept in touch with me. Minnesota Congressman Don Fraser had communicated with him, but unfortunately could not help his family directly. Congressman Fraser did send a letter of inquiry to the Argentine government through the American Embassy. He also spoke out against the actions by the military junta, but that was about all he could do. The following year, 1977, President Carter appointed Arizona Governor Castro to be the new Ambassador to Argentina. Castro had campaigned extensively for President Carter and was pleased to be returning to a diplomatic role. He had served as Ambassador to El Salvador and to Bolivia under President Johnson and was well respected in Latin America. I immediately received a letter from Alberto Noé begging me to ask Ambassador Castro to look into his brother's disappearance.[3]

Governor Castro was still the sitting Governor, so he really did not have authority to act until he had been sworn in as the Ambassador to Argentina. I did write a letter to Governor Castro,[4] that he answered on September 22, 1977 assuring me he would do what he could upon his arrival in Argentina. I ran into Governor Castro when he visited Arizona a few months after his arrival in Argentina.[5] He said living conditions in Argentina were difficult, especially for his wife Pat. They could travel only in an armored vehicle under heavy guard, so Pat mainly stayed

---

3   Noé, Alberto, Letter to Cecilia Esquer, 12 julio 1977.

4   Esquer, Cecilia, Letter to The Honorable Raul H. Castro, August 28, 1977.

5   Castro, Raul H., Letter to Mrs. Cecilia D. Esquer, September 22, 1977.

at the Embassy. It must not have been an easy diplomatic assignment either. President Carter represented a change in the U.S. government's attitude toward the Junta:

> More than nine months after the military junta deposed Isabel Peron and initiated the dirty war, Jimmy Carter assumed the presidency of the United States [January 20, 1977]. From the moment of his inauguration, the significance of human rights violations received a high place in American foreign policy.

> While Carter's foreign policy for the first time brought the issue of human rights to the forefront of American diplomacy, his approach was partly coupled with a desire to restore the American public's declining faith in the U.S. government following the Watergate scandal, public revelations of government involvement in overthrowing Allende in Chile, and the Vietnam War. Carter's revision of postwar foreign policy was made possible in part through the emerging appeal from the American public for an expanded focus on human rights in the mid-1970s.[6]

Ambassador Castro told me Alberto's situation was a tragic one and that there was little he could do to help find him, because there were so many desaparecidos. Then he commented: "Unfortunately, he is probably dead."

After the debacle over the Payne appointment, I did not know whether Governor Castro would even acknowledge my letter, much less act on it. I was truly amazed by his gracious treatment whenever I ran into him. Not long after the Payne appointment, I recall walking down a street in Washington, D.C. I was on my way to a Legal Services Corporation meeting, when all of a sudden I realized Governor Castro was walking in my direction with Senator DeConcini. I panicked a little and asked myself, "What should I do? Should I cross the street pretending I did not see them?" At that moment, Governor Castro called out my name and quickly walked over and gave me a big hug. I think Senator DeConcini got a big kick out of this.

I lost touch with Alberto Noé, so I do not know when Alberto

---

6 William Houston Gilbert, "From Condemnation to Conformity: Carter and Reagan's Foreign Policy towards the Argentine Junta, 1977-1982," Master's Thesis. http://etd-submit.etsu.edu/etd/theses/available/etd-1113105-173301/unrestricted/GilbertW120105f.pdf

learned that his brother had been assassinated. Through a Google check, I learned that Victor Jacobo Noé had been assassinated, along with thousands of attorneys and political activists.

I read a moving tribute by Alberto to his brother that he delivered at the inauguration of the Plaza Dr. Victor Jacobo Noé on August 30, 2002.[7]

The total dead is not known, but a 1984 report, *Nunca Más*, issued by the National Commission on the Disappearance of Persons (CONADEP) estimates that between 1976 and 1983 about 9,000 people were *desaparecidos*[8] . Human rights organizations estimate there were up to 30,000 deaths.[9] Apparently the United States State Department, led by Henry Kissinger during President Ford's administration, was aware of and tolerated these horrific policies:

> Washington, D.C., 4 December 2003 - Newly declassified State Department documents obtained by the National Security Archive under the Freedom of Information Act show that in October 1976, Secretary of State Henry Kissinger and high ranking U.S. officials gave their full support to the Argentine military junta and urged them to hurry up and finish the "dirty war" before the U.S. Congress cut military aid.[10]

It was easy to understand the desperation of the families of *desaparecidos* and their great expectations that things would change under President Carter. I felt helpless knowing there was not much I could do. However, Alberto expressed his appreciation of our efforts in the several letters he wrote to me.

---

7 Noé, Dr. Alberto, "Derechos Humanos y Justicia: Una plaza para Victor Noé," http://www.antroposmoderno.com/antro-articulo.php?id_articulo=241

8 Nunca Más, CONADEP, 1984. http://www.nuncamas.org/english/library/nevagain/nevagain_000.htm , http://www.nuncamas.org/investig/articulo/nuncamas/nmas0001.htm

9 "The Dirty War," http://en.wikipedia.org/wiki/Dirty_War

10 Carlos Osorio, editor, Assisted by Kathleen Costar, National Security Archive Electronic Briefing Book No. 104, The National Security Archive, Posted August 27, 2004

OFFICE OF THE GOVERNOR
STATE HOUSE
PHOENIX, ARIZONA 85007

RAUL H. CASTRO
GOVERNOR

September 22, 1977

Mrs. Cecilia D. Esquer,
1720 East Palmcroft Drive,
Tempe, Arizona 85282

Dear Cecilia:

On my return from a prolonged trip, I found your
letter reference problems faced in Argentina by
Victor Jacobo Nóe.

I am informed that the Department of State is
familiar with the case. The Human Rights
Division is well on top of most of these cases.

Be assured that on my arrival in Argentina, I
shall do whatever is possible to see that human
rights are implemented.

Sincerely,

Raul H. Castro
Governor

RHC:mmp

Letter from Ambassador Raúl Castro to Cecilia Esquer,
September 27, 1977, Phoenix, Arizona

Republicanos y Demócratas de EU en la Cámara de Diputados

JOVENES POLITICOS norteamericanos, de los partidos Demócrata y Republicano, estuvieron ayer en la sesión de la Cámara de Diputados, y recibieron el aplauso de los legisladores. (Información en la Página 12).

Top: U.S. Delegation Visit to the Mexican Congress (balcony)

Bottom: U.S. Delegation and Mexican Hosts Mexico City, Mexico, 1976. Courtesy of American Council of Young Political Leaders

9

FIRST JOB
ARIZONA ATTORNEY GENERAL

OW did I wind up advising the educational institutions I had hoped to reform when I decided to go to law school? I was impressed by Attorney General Bruce Babbitt's commitment to protect Arizona consumers and the environment, especially water. I met him when he was campaigning to become the Attorney General. Bruce would join us in our door-to-door efforts in South Phoenix or the West side. He showed a commitment to hiring women and minorities. I first worked as a law clerk at the AG's office while waiting for the Bar results.

In 1977, I was fortunate to be hired as an Assistant Attorney General and assigned to work on education issues. I was impressed by Bruce Babbitt's quick grasp of issues. My work consisted mostly of doing research and writing on legal questions presented in the area of education. I also reviewed some of the opinions from the various Arizona County Attorneys. It was not unusual for our Office to overturn the County Attorneys' opinions. Mr. Babbitt often told us that if we were working on a legal opinion and there was more than one conclusion that could be reached, he would like to be told so he could make the decision. When this happened, I would send him a short memo on the issues. When I went to meet with him he had actually read everything and understood the impact each conclusion could have.

Unfortunately, I did not get to spend too much time in the office. With Attorney General Babbitt's blessing, I accepted an appointment from President Carter to be one of eleven members on the national Legal Services Corporation Board of Directors. The Corporation funds most of the legal aid programs in the country. During the first year I attended more than one meeting a month – most for one of the two Board committees I served on, and three-to-four full Board meetings a year. It was difficult to keep up with my duties at work. However, I learned a lot about how our educational institutions operated. I enjoyed the challenges of the position and the contact with many of the administrators in the Department of Education. This experience was invaluable when I went into private practice. I also was privileged to work with one of the most outstanding Arizona Attorneys General. Bruce Babbitt had a vision for Arizona and fought hard to make it reality.

María Cueto and the Grand Jury

Even in the Attorney General's Office I could not escape from getting involved in political issues. One day, I received a call from Fernando Vender, one of my fellow Superiorites and a fellow undergraduate at ASU. María Cueto, one of our friends from undergraduate days, had been arrested for refusing to testify before a Grand Jury. She had to hire attorneys and needed help raising the funds to pay the fees. I agreed to help with the fundraiser.

But, that was not the end. María was being held even though the FBI knew she had not committed any crimes. She headed the Hispanic Desk for the national Episcopalian office located in New York City. One day FBI agents came to the New York headquarters to ask her questions about an individual who served on her advisory council. María and her secretary, Raisa, produced every file they had on the individual and answered every question asked. His service on the advisory council included translating some verses from old Spanish to modern Spanish. Who would have suspected that he was involved with the FALN terrorist group responsible for several bombings in New York?

When María arrived to work the next day, the Bishop who directed the office met her to let her know he had made a horrible mistake. He told her the FBI agents returned, knowing María and Raisa would not be at work, and asked to search their desks. They intimated the two women had not cooperated fully and that they had to make sure they had produced everything. Not only did they search María and Raisa's desks and files, they searched all the other desks: Women, Blacks, Indians, etc., a full fishing expedition. The women felt betrayed. Later that day, the FBI agents came to ask further questions. María refused to answer any questions and told them they had betrayed her trust. The agents had not found anything, but they still wanted to ask more questions. When the women refused, they were told they knew how to get them to testify. The next day they were served with subpoenas to appear before a federal grand jury. When they refused to answer any questions, the prosecutors offered immunity from prosecution, which meant that they were compelled to answer questions or face contempt of court charges. They had to hire attorneys but could not afford to pay for them.

I was horrified by this chain of events. It seemed unjust to be able to incarcerate individuals only because the FBI had the power to do this. We held a fundraiser and were able to get some publicity about María and Raisa's plights. This drew the attention of Bruce Babbitt. He asked to meet with me about this issue. He knew I was doing this volunteer work on my own time and not using State resources. We discussed María's case and the fact that the Episcopalian Church was going to continue to generate a lot of publicity about the injustices to two innocent persons.

At this time Bruce was lobbying the legislature to reinstate the State Grand Jury to provide a more effective vehicle to fight the many fraudulent land deals taking place in Arizona. He asked if there was anything he could add to the bill to meet some of the concerns we had about grand juries. I told him I was concerned about the fact that persons before a grand jury do not have the right to have counsel present when they are being questioned. He commented that it would be difficult to convince the legislature to provide the right to counsel and the right of counsel to cross-examine witnesses.

He asked if it would be acceptable to allow counsel to be present in the grand jury room, but without the right to participate or to cross-examine witnesses. It was clear the bill was going to pass. I thought it was a fair compromise, so long as the party could ask for a recess to consult with counsel. I don't know whether the bill that passed included this provision. Bruce Babbitt successfully prosecuted several major land fraud kings and set a model for prosecuting a crime that is difficult to investigate without a grand jury. To this day I worry that some overzealous prosecutor will misuse this powerful weapon.

State Board of Education,
President Schwada and Governor Castro

The Attorney General's Office serves as Counsel to the State Board of Education. Dave Rich, my supervisor, generally covered those meetings. He asked me to sit in for him one day. The State Board includes individuals appointed by the Governor and a President from one of the State universities. ASU President, Dr. John Schwada, was the university president that term.

I noticed that Dr. Schwada kept staring at me during the meeting. During the first break, he said:

"Young lady, may I speak to you please?"

I panicked thinking that he may have seen pictures of students picketing his inauguration and wanted to discuss that with me. When Dr. Schwada was hired in 1972, the press interviewed him before he came to Arizona. When asked about his stand on affirmative action, he mentioned, among other things, that he did not think there was one qualified minority professor at ASU. This did not set well with the minority student and faculty organizations who decided to picket Dr. Schwada's inauguration. I was teaching two Spanish classes at ASU that year (1972-73) and was hesitant to join the demonstration, but I decided it was important for us to let Dr. Schwada know we did not appreciate his comments.

During the early 1970s it was not unusual to have undercover law enforcement officers, state and federal, take pictures of the demonstrators. There were several "photographers" that day, plus a couple of television stations. My face made it into the evening news. I was sure someone had given Dr. Schwada copies of the photos taken that day.

When I went up to Dr. Schwada, he asked if I knew "a person by the name of Payne 'P – a – y – n – e'. I responded: "I vaguely remember the name." Then he said: "Young lady you have caused me a lot of pain 'P – A – I – N'." Now I really began to panic. Dr. Schwada then said that he was sitting in his office one day when Governor Castro called to tell him that one of his law students was using University equipment for political purposes. Dr. Schwada then "called that pointy-headed Dean of the law school" because he thought Dean Gellhorn would want to know that the Governor had called about one of his students. Angrily, Dr. Schwada commented: "Next thing I knew, I was being bad-mouthed at the regional hiring conferences. The Dean was urging prospective faculty not to come to ASU because the President did not respect students' First Amendment rights." I was relieved when it was time to get back to the meeting. I don't think I was able to concentrate the rest of the meeting, but I was happy to know it was not about his inauguration.

However, this is not the end of the story. About two weeks after this meeting I attended a meeting of the Board of the Legal Services Corporation in Washington, D.C. I had been appointed to the board by President Carter. Professor Bea Moulton, my clinical professor during law school, had been hired as the Director of National Support for the Corporation. We had dinner one evening. I told her what Dr. Schwada had said. She was furious and said she now had to tell me "the other side of the story. You were never supposed to know what happened!"

The day Dr. Schwada called Dean Gellhorn, the new law school Dean, the Dean called an emergency faculty meeting to discuss Dr. Schwada's call. The faculty voted to take no action on the allegation and also voted not to tell me about the Governor's call because they thought it would have a negative effect on my studies. She said the faculty was not getting along well with Dean Gellhorn, and that the Dean was not happy at the law school. In mid-semester he resigned his position and issued a letter stating he had accepted a position in another state. One of the reasons he gave for his resignation was Dr. Schwada's call, which he interpreted as a request to expel me from law school. He would not remain at a university where students' First Amendment rights were not respected.

I could not believe what I was hearing and was at a loss for words. Finally, I told Bea "You should know that at no time did I use University equipment to work on opposing the Payne nomination. Why should I, when Alfredo Gutiérrez set up an office for me in the basement of the Capitol?" We had a good laugh about that, but to this day, I am awestruck by the impact an ordinary citizen can have on our political process. It was hard for me to understand why the Governor saw me as such a threat.

Bruce Babbitt Becomes Governor

Bruce Babbitt was sworn in as the Arizona Attorney General in 1976. Most political pundits expected him to run for the U.S. Senate in 1980. However, fate took him in a different direction. When Governor Raul Castro resigned in October 1977 to serve as the Ambassador to Argentina, Secretary of State Wesley Bolin became Governor under the Arizona succession law. Five months later, on March 4, 1978, Bolin suffered a heart attack and died. Because there was no "elected"

Secretary of State after Bolin became Governor, the Attorney General, the next person in the line of succession, would become the Governor. So Bruce Babbitt became Governor on March 4, 1978.

Bob Allen – 9th Floor Invite

All of a sudden it felt like "Pledge Week" at the Attorney General's office as Governor Babbitt began to pick his staff. The Civil Division was located on the third floor of the old Motor Vehicles Building on Jefferson and Eighteenth Avenue. The doors would swing open, and in would walk Bob Evans who was serving on the Babbitt transition team. Rod McDougall, the Chief Counsel for the Civil Division, would join him, and they would walk down the hall. Many attorneys would stand in their doorways to see who was going to be asked to join the new Administration. One day Rod and Bob came to my door. Imagine my surprise. Rod said Bob would like to speak with me and gave me permission to leave the office.

We went to the cafeteria in the basement of the Capitol building for a cup of coffee. Bob said Bruce would like for me to join his team. However, he could not tell me the specific position I would have. Bruce wanted to get everyone together first; then decide what positions were appropriate for the Office. I told Bob I first had to check with Elías. Then I told him I came to the AG's Office to learn how to practice law. It might not be a good idea for me to leave with less than six months' experience. Then Bob said: "Bruce is waiting for you on the 9th Floor." I replied: "I don't think I can accept the offer." Bob replied: "No one says no!" As I got up to leave I told Bob: "Say hello to Bruce for me and tell him I feel honored to be asked."

Sometimes I wonder how my life would have changed if I had accepted Governor Babbitt's offer. He turned out to be a great Governor, one with a vision and a commitment to the environment.

As governor, Babbitt left a significant legacy of environmental accomplishment. He expanded Arizona's state park system and engineered passage of the comprehensive Arizona Groundwater Management Act of 1980. He also worked to create the Arizona Department of Water Resources and the Arizona Department of Environmental Quality.[1]

---

1 Http://www.absoluteastronomy.com/topics/Bruce_Babbitt

Sevilla, Spain – Elías Takes a Sabbatical Leave

Elías was granted a sabbatical leave for the spring 1979 semester. So in December 1978 I took a leave of absence from the Arizona Attorney General's Office. The entire family, Elías, Marcos, Andrea, and I went to Sevilla, Spain, where Elías attended the University of Sevilla. It turned out to be an incredible experience for all of us. Elías took three classes at the University of Sevilla and did research in the Archivo (archives) de las Indias. The archives included the New World records that contained more than 14 million original documents. These documents were from Mexico and Central America. Spain ruled those countries from 1519 until the early nineteenth century. Elías saw original letters from the Queen of Spain to some of the explorers: Hernán Cortes and Pizarro. He also read many of the logs from the various Spanish ships that landed in Mexico. They were incredibly detailed and included many treasures.

I home schooled Andrea and Marcos, which turned out to be pretty challenging when we covered topics unfamiliar to me. I remember one day trying to explain a math problem to Marcos after reading the instructions. Finally he said, "Do you mean this?" He had figured out how to solve the problem himself, but was enjoying my discomfort. We hired Spanish tutors for Marcos and Andrea so they could pick up the local vocabulary. Their tutors, Ángela and Nati, loved our kids and included us in their family activities, which gave us a special insight into life in Sevilla.

One of the most important events in Sevilla is Holy Week, which commemorates the Passion of Jesus Christ. Each night during Holy Week we would meet Nati and Ángela around 10:00 p.m. to watch the parade of the Christ and Mary floats from the various parishes. Some of the parishes were located many miles from the city center, through which all floats were required to pass. Nati and Ángela knew the history of each float and pointed out the ones that had been torched during the Spanish Civil War. They also made us laugh with stories about gossip surrounding different Mary figures.

There was severe competition among the parishes to have the best float, so they would disparage the reputation of any strong competitor. People from all over the world go to Sevilla to witness one of the oldest Holy Week traditions which dates back to the Fourteenth Century. This event was a big economic boon to Sevilla, not only for the tourist industry, but for local artists who were hired to work on the floats, including making the elaborate costumes for the Christ and Mary figures. We often returned home around 3:00 a.m.

A week after the end of Holy Week, the April Fair festivities Feria de abril began. Feria started around the Twelfth Century as a fair to trade horses and developed into quite a celebration. Locals would dress up in beautiful traditional costumes and would come riding beautiful Arabian horses. There were parades, horse shows and other competitive events. The general fair was open to the public; however, the tents where parties took place were by invitation only. We were privileged to be included in these celebrations one evening.

Ángela and Nati's families had their own tent. They also knew some of the union members whose union sponsored a tent, so they took us around from party to party into the late hours of the night. Most people were dressed in traditional Andalucian costumes. Everywhere we went, individuals were dancing traditional Sevillanas (flamenco style) dances. Brandy from Jerez de la Frontera, called fino flowed freely. Guests were handed a glass full of fino that was not allowed to be emptied. Before you knew it, someone had refilled your glass. There was food galore, and we were not allowed to pay for anything. There were typical games and rides for the young people, including a Ferris wheel. We would not have experienced either Holy Week or Feria as we did without meeting Ángela and Nati.

Top: Hon. Bruce E. Babbitt. Photo credit: http://en.wikipedia.org/wiki/Bruce_Babbitt

Middle and Bottom: Semana Santa 2002

✎ 10 ✎

HOW WAS I APPOINTED TO THE LSC BOARD?

You Must Be Kidding!

URING the fall of 1977, I was working as an Assistant Attorney General for Attorney General Bruce Babbitt. One morning I received a call from Andy Silverman, the Executive Director of Community Legal Services (CLS). Since I served as a CLS Board Member, I thought he was calling me on board business. He sounded upset and cut right to the chase. "Why didn't you tell me you applied for the Legal Services Corporation (LSC) Board?" I told him I had not applied for anything and asked "What LSC Board?" He became more upset: "You mean to tell me you do not know you are about to be named by President Carter to the LSC Board?" The Legal Services Corporation receives funding from Congress to fund more than 300 legal aid programs across the country. The programs provide free legal services in certain civil cases to those who meet the income guidelines. [More in Chapter 11]

The news about my potential appointment was news to me. Andy told me the Arizona legal aid programs were backing a Native American attorney from California for the Board. Andy just could not believe I did not know I was in the running. I told him I would make a couple of calls and get back to him. "You mean you don't know anything about this?" "Not a thing." I could not understand how this was even a remote possibility. I did not know anything about the Board, much less know there were five vacancies, and I had not submitted an application.

I called Joe Aragón, the head of the Latino Desk at the White House. I had met him when I served on the Democratic National Committee where he headed the Latino Desk. I lucked out. He was there and picked up the phone. Joe checked with Presidential Personnel and called back in about ten minutes to confirm that indeed my name was about to be sent to the Senate. He did not know who submitted my name. I could not believe how this could happen.

I called Andy Silverman to confirm his information. Then I asked him whether I should withdraw my name and join them in supporting their Native American candidate (call me naive!) He was incredulous about my offer to withdraw and finally believed that I truly did not know about the impending nomination. He was excited about the prospect of having someone from Arizona on the Board.

I called my husband with the news. He asked if this was something I wanted to do. I told him it sounded like a great opportunity, even though I did not know exactly what was involved. He said he was very proud of me and that he would support me if I was chosen. How could we be so fearless?

Then I spoke with my Chief Counsel, Rod McDougall, to see how it would affect my job. He was so thrilled and insisted that I let Bruce Babbitt know immediately. Rod walked me over to Bruce's office so I could tell him in person. Bruce congratulated me and assured me that I should consider the work on the board as a professional activity. It would not affect my job. I called around trying to find out who submitted my name to the White House. No one knew, but they were all thrilled about my potential nomination. I never received "the call" from whoever submitted my name telling me they were happy they were able to be of service.

I then called Karen Scates. I met Karen when she was an aide to Alfredo Gutiérrez, a Democrat, who became the Arizona Senate majority leader in 1974. Karen now worked for Arizona Congressman Mo Udall in Washington, D. C. She was very excited about the nomination and asked me to keep her in the loop as things developed. A few days later, Karen called to tell me my name had been taken off the list by the White House. "I don't know why, but you better call Ron Ober in DeConcini's office. Dennis should be able to straighten things out." I did not want to do this because I knew I would "owe" Ron. Karen insisted.

It turned out this nomination was subject to confirmation by the U.S. Senate. I called Ron Ober who said he would check on it and get back to me. A few hours later, Ron called and told me I was back on track. It was my good fortune that Senator DeConcini was the Chair of the oversight committee for the Legal Services Corporation.

Senate Confirmation Hearing

Some weeks later, I received a letter from the White House telling me about the nomination and that they would let me know the date of the Senate Confirmation hearing. The Senate recess came up before the confirmation hearing could be set, so President Carter made five recess appointments to the LSC Board. I was one of the five!

The confirmation hearing was set for February 7, 1978, before the Senate Committee on Human Resources. Karen Scates called: "Congressman Udall is hosting a small reception for you following the confirmation hearing. Send me your resume and call Ron Ober right now to ask if Senator DeConcini would introduce you to the Committee. Another chit for Ron.

Ron said the Senator would be thrilled to do so. Again, profuse thanks were in order. Ron asked me to meet at Senator DeConcini's office so the Senator could walk me to the hearing room. My husband did not go to D.C. with me because I told him it was "no big thing." Senator DeConcini graciously accompanied me to the hearing room. I was pretty nervous about this because I did not know him very well. He escorted me to my chair at the table to join the other four nominees. Then he asked the Chair, Senator Harrison A. Williams, Jr., for the privilege of introducing the nominee from Arizona. Senator DeConcini proceeded to give a long flowery introduction.[1] I was so embarrassed at being the only nominee introduced by a Senator. The other nominees: Steven Engleberg, a Washington lawyer-lobbyist; Hillary Rodham, a litigation attorney from Arkansas; Dick Trudell, the Native American from California, and Josephine Worthy, a legal services client representative.

The LSC staff had briefed us individually on the process the day before the hearing, so we had some idea about the questions that would be asked. It was a friendly exchange for the most part. Hillary Rodham and I had the most difficult questions. Her husband, William Jefferson Clinton, had been the Attorney General for Arkansas. His office represented state agencies in lawsuits brought by legal aid programs in Arkansas.

Senator Williams: [To Hillary Rodham] "Don't you think this presents a conflict of interest?"

Ms. Rodham: "This does not raise a legal conflict of interest at all. If you are asking whether my husband would influence my actions on

1   Dennis DeConcini, Statement of Hon. Dennis DeConcini, A U.S. Senator from the State of Arizona, record of Nomination Hearing before the Committee on Human Resources, United States Senate, February 7, 1978, U.S. Government Printing Office, Washington: 1978.

the LSC Board, let me assure you that I am an independent thinker and capable of making my own decisions!"

Because legal aid programs often sue state agencies, and I represented some of these, I had to explain the process we had for dealing with this type of conflict. I would not be assigned to any cases filed by any legal aid program. Finally, I had to assure the Committee that this "adversarial" role of the Attorney General would not affect any funding or other decisions I made as a Board member.

The Committee voted to send our names to the Senate floor with the recommendation that the Senate vote to confirm all five nominees.[2] The hearing ended with smiles and congratulations. The group chatted for a few minutes after the hearing. Even though we shared a commitment to legal services for the poor, it was difficult to break the ice. Dick Trudell and I seemed to have more in common and visited longer. He directed the Indian Lawyer Training Program based in Oakland, California. I had taken an Indian Law class in law school and was very interested in Indian issues, especially since Arizona has 21 recognized tribes. Dick was thrilled when I invited him to the reception in Congressman Udall's office. Congressman Udall was the Chair of the House Committee on Interior and Insular Affairs, which includes Indian Affairs. Dick lobbied on Indian issues.

Reception by Congressman Udall

We walked into a reception room filled with about 200 people. I only knew the Congressman and Karen. Congressman Udall gave a warm welcome, and then these 200 individuals came through the reception line and congratulated me telling me what a great job I would do. I don't think I ever saw any one of them again. Dick Trudell had Congressman Udall's ear for at least 20 minutes. It finally dawned on me that this was a "big thing." I regretted that my husband and children were not there to share in this once-in-a-lifetime experience.

Dinner at Ethel Kennedy's Home!

As we left the reception, Dick Trudell asked if I would be interested in going to dinner at Ethel Kennedy's house.[3] Dick served on the Board

2 All five nominees were confirmed by the Senate on March 20, 1978, Daily Digest, Congressional Record, March 20, 1978, D378.

3 Ethel Kennedy is the widow of Robert F. Kennedy (RFK), the brother of John F. Kennedy, Jr. RFK was assassinated on June 5, 1968. He was running for President and on that date, it appeared he would be the

of the Robert F. Kennedy Foundation. The Foundation was having the annual dinner to recognize media individuals for their commitment to and protection of the First Amendment. I could not believe I would be going to Ethel Kennedy's house that evening!

Off we went to McLean, Virginia – pretty heady stuff. We were greeted by Ethel Kennedy. As we walked in we saw Walter Cronkite, Roger Mudd, Bob Graham, Robert and Margaret McNamara, and other prominent individuals. Ethel Kennedy was very familiar with the Legal Services Corporation and immediately peppered us with questions, many of which we could not answer: i.e.: How many lawyers nationally? How many programs? What types of cases are accepted by the programs? How many clients are served each year? How many are turned away each year? Then Senator Ted Kennedy came to greet us. Once again, more questions, but also a strong statement about his support for legal services for the poor. He displayed a detailed knowledge of some of the workings of the Legal Service Corporation and urged us to call his staff whenever we needed his assistance. I was overwhelmed by the entire thing: the famous people we met, the setting, and the realization that the Legal Services Corporation really stood for something I deeply believed in: making the legal system accessible to poor people. It seemed unreal. How could all this be happening to me?

Reflections

As for Hillary Rodham, who could have guessed what lay ahead for her? She was an outstanding board member. In fact, we elected her as the first Chair of the "Carter Board" in recognition of President Carter's commitment to appoint women to policy making positions. Although shy at first, Hillary took that gavel and ran with it.[4] She was a great spokesperson for the corporation and the legal problems facing poor people in the United States. On a personal side, I had many conversations with her, got to hold her daughter Chelsea as an infant, and got to meet Bill Clinton. He accompanied Hillary to Washington, D.C. from time-to-time to attend Democratic Council meetings and would join us for the Board dinner on Friday evening. At this time, he was beginning his quest

party's nominee.

4   The sitting six Board members included Roger Crampton, who had served in President Nixon's Office of Legal Counsel and who was then the Dean of Cornell Law School; Robert Kutak, the founding partner of Kutak Rock, which at that time was the biggest law firm in the country; Bill McAlpin, at that time the Secretary of the American Bar Association. The LSC President was Tom Erlich, former Dean of Stanford Law School.

for the Democratic nomination for President. When Hillary first told us about this, all of us around the table broke out in laughter. He seemed so young and, anyway, how many of us knew anyone who would run for President? When I relayed the news to Bruce Babbitt, who was now the Governor of Arizona, he said: "Tell Hillary that I am running for President." Bruce Babbitt's wife, Hattie, was also an attorney, so the four of them had become pretty good friends through the Governors' Association.

Looking Back – How did my name surface?

My three days in Washington, D.C. and the flurry of activities, day and evening, left little time for me to digest the significance of the events. I took a shuttle from the Mayflower Hotel to Dulles International Airport. On the flight back to Phoenix, I began to reflect on the incredible chain of events that resulted in this Presidential appointment. Perhaps "it was written."

It took me a year to find out that no one had submitted my name to President Carter. So, how did my name get to President Carter's desk? My friend, Eliza Carney, was one of the individuals who headed President Carter's Arizona campaign. She also campaigned for him anywhere she was needed, particularly in her home state of South Carolina. President Carter appointed Eliza to the National Advisory Council on Women's Educational Programs that focused on compliance with Title IX, equality for women, particularly in athletics.

One month in 1979, our boards met on the same days, so Eliza set up a lunch meeting with Peggy Rainwater, the Associate Director of White House Personnel. She brought her assistant, Roberta Adams. Peggy complimented Eliza and me for our work on our respective boards. She was proud of the changes taking place in the Legal Services Corporation. The conversation flowed easily, so I garnered up the courage to ask how I came to be appointed to the LSC Board. Roberta insisted she tell me.

During my tenure on the Democratic National Committee (DNC), Jimmy Carter, the Governor of Georgia, and one of the Governors on the DNC, began to gather support for his nomination. The DNC Women's Caucus made him promise to appoint women to policy making positions if he got elected. He agreed. Harriet Cipriani was the head of the DNC Women's Caucus. The Caucus then purchased a computer and created a database of resumes of women from all over the country. Governor Carter agreed to check the computer whenever a policy-making position came up. I did not run for a second term on the DNC in 1977 because of a prohibition from holding any partisan position while working as an Assistant Attorney General. Harriet asked for an exit interview with me and insisted I input my data into the computer.

When the five vacancies for the LSC Board came up, White House Personnel received many letters of interest and had winnowed the list to five to present to President Carter. However, a woman attorney working for White House Personnel thought the slate of names did not meet the promise President Carter had made to the DNC Women's Caucus. Before they sent the list over to the Senate, they remembered they had not checked the computer. They entered several identifiers and only one name surfaced: mine!

"Then what? That was it?"

"Of course not. We had to check you out. So we called Bob Strauss" [the former Chair of the DNC].

"What did he say?"

"He said you would be 'wunnerful'."

I was surprised to hear that because the Latino caucus had had some pretty hostile discussions with him behind closed doors accusing him of not doing enough to ensure Latino representation.

They then called Arizona Governor Raúl Castro, who told them I would do a "magnificent" job. I could not believe this either. I thought Governor Castro was very unhappy with me because of my efforts to block one of his nominees to the Arizona Board of Regents.

"Then we called Alfredo Gutiérrez", the Senate Majority Leader at the time. "He spoke very highly of you.

"And that was it?"

"No! We became suspicious. If all these políticos thought you were great, you might not be a good advocate for the poor. So we called our grassroots sources. They also spoke highly of you." It dawned on me that Presidential appointments are rare for Arizona, a small state that tended to vote Republican, so everyone was excited about the prospect of my appointment.

"Why didn't you call me?"

"There was no time – and, anyway, who would say no to a Presidential appointment?"

I was elated! I didn't owe anyone any political chits for submitting my name – just to a computer that did its job, and a thoughtful attorney I never met who made an extra effort to carry out her President's wishes.

Howard Sacks
West Hartford,
Connecticut

Robert J. Kutak
Omaha, Nebraska

Hillary Rodham
Little Rock, Arkansas

Steven L. Engelberg
Chevy Chase,
Maryland

F. Wm. McCalpin
St. Louis, Missouri

Josephine Worthy
Holyoke,
Massachusetts

Richard Trudell
Oakland, California

Cecilia D. Esquer
Tempe, Arizona

Ramona Shump
Topeka, Kansas

Michael Kantor
Pacific Palisades,
California

Revius O. Ortique, Jr.
New Orleans, Louisiana

Dan J. Bradley, ex officio
Washington, D.C.

Above: Legal Services Corporation Board of Directors, 1980 LSC Annual Report, Washington, D. C.

OPPOSITE PAGE PHOTO CAPTIONS:
Top: President Jimmy Carter and Cecilia D. Esquer, Washington, D. C., 1982

Bottom: Certificate of Appointment, Washington, D. C., March 22, 1978

Best wishes to Cecilia —

BY VIRTUE OF THE AUTHORITY VESTED IN ME AS PRESIDENT OF THE UNITED STATES

UNDER THE PROVISIONS OF THE LEGAL SERVICES CORPORATION ACT OF 1974,

I HAVE NOMINATED, AND, BY AND WITH THE ADVICE AND CONSENT OF THE SENATE,

DO APPOINT

Cecilia Denogean Esquer, of Arizona,

A MEMBER OF THE BOARD OF DIRECTORS OF THE LEGAL SERVICES CORPORATION

FOR

a term expiring July 13, 1980,

SUBJECT TO THE CONDITIONS PRESCRIBED BY LAW.

The White House
March 22, 1918

Jimmy Carter

⬧ 11 ⬧

THE LEGAL SERVICES CORPORATION BOARD

A Learning Experience

Iknew next to nothing about the Legal Services Corporation, much less the Board. It turns out there are only eleven Board members. Appointments to the Board are highly coveted by members of the American Bar Association, especially by attorneys in the large law firms. Apparently my name was taken off the list because more than a few people thought I was not a "highly experienced" attorney. They were absolutely right. I was admitted to the Arizona Bar in 1977 and nominated to the Board in 1978. However, President Carter was committed to appointing women and minorities to policy-making positions. The challenge was over when Senator DeConcini spoke with Tom Erlich, the Legal Services Corporation President, to tell him he would like to see me on the Board. What do you say to a ranking Senator who chairs the oversight committee for the Corporation?

So I went forward with great trepidation hoping things would work out. The Board was responsible for a budget of more than three hundred million dollars, which supported more than three hundred local legal aid programs in every State, Washington D.C., and Puerto Rico. More than three thousand attorneys, plus paralegals and other support staff, provided direct services to legal aid clients. In addition, there were twelve national support centers that provided research and litigation assistance to the local programs. The programs were overseen through nine regional offices. How was I going to get my arms around this?

I attended about twenty-five meetings during my first year on the Board. Not only did the five new Board members have a lot to learn; but, with the election of President Carter, the work of the Corporation was taking off in a new direction. The staff was very helpful and provided written materials. They made themselves available for questions in person or over the phone. I developed a great respect for the advocacy efforts by the senior staff. They worked many hours beyond what is expected of them to protect our funding and to address issues raised by Senators or Congressmen. They also worked closely with the national support centers, the regional offices and the local programs. Most of them had worked in local legal aid programs and were very committed to improving the plight of poor people.

President Carter was very supportive of funding for legal services, so we were able to make some strides in increasing the number of clients served by legal services. We secured increased funding from Congress and developed plans to meet the goal that "all poor persons in this country have some access to quality legal representation."

My First Legal Services Corporation Board
Unofficial Meeting

I arrived in Washington, D.C. a few days before our confirmation hearing to meet the staff and for a briefing on the confirmation process. Mary Bourdette, the LSC Government Relations Director, did an excellent job of preparing me by giving me an overview of the work of the Legal Services Corporation, the members of the confirmation committee, and possible questions the committee might pose.

The Budget Committee of the LSC Board was meeting in the afternoon and Mary suggested I attend. Roger Cramton, a President Gerald Ford appointee, Chairman of the Board, and Dean of the Cornell Law School, was the Budget Committee Chair. They were discussing options for investment of LSC funds. At this time, LSC received its annual appropriation from Congress in one payment. The Corporation disbursed those funds throughout the fiscal year, so the practice was to invest the funds reserved for future disbursement. This actually resulted in a substantial increase to the annual appropriation because the funds were placed in interest-bearing accounts. Remember, this is 1978. The economy was good and the Ford-appointed board had good support from Congress, so the annual appropriations were gradually rising.

The LSC controller, Fabio de la Torre, recommended that some funds be placed in various banks, including a Latino owned bank. The banking industry was experiencing changes in the form of the establishment of non-traditional banks: i.e., women and minority-owned banks. One of the committee members spoke against investing LSC funds in the

Latino-owned bank because he said it was too risky. I raised my hand and asked if I could ask questions even though I was just an observer and had not yet been confirmed. Yes, I could.

I asked whether the funds invested would be FDIC insured. The controller confirmed they would be. "Are you proposing investing funds that exceed the amount FDIC can insure?" "Absolutely not." I then suggested that the committee should consider Fabio de la Torre's recommendation seriously, since the clients served with these funds included a substantial number of women and minorities. The committee approved the Controller's recommendations, which included making relatively small investments in women, Native American, and Latino-owned banks. Bernie Veney, the Executive Director of the National Clients Council, introduced himself after the meeting and commended me for asking the questions about the banks. Fabio de la Torre was beaming as he came over to introduce himself and thanked me for supporting his recommendation. I did not realize this type of question was somewhat unusual in this Republican-appointed Board.

Internal LSC Politics

I soon discovered that the politics within the legal services community was intense. I also discovered that the Board and staff needed to learn a little more about the special needs in Indian Country and in the rural areas of the country. The thing that stood out vividly for me is the fact that there were few Latino or Native Americans in the D.C. office and the regional offices. I raised the issue with Tom Erlich, the LSC President. There was some defensiveness on his part. Finally, I told him "You do not need color TV here; everything is in Black and White." There was good representation from the African American community.

When it came time to hire a new legal counsel for the Corporation, I was pleased to learn that Tom Erlich had hired Mario Lewis, a Latino attorney from Texas. Next thing, they announced the hiring of Bea Moulton, my former Clinical Professor at the ASU College of Law, to be the Director for National Support. Although not a minority, Bea brought her extensive experience in legal services, was creative and fearless, and already had the respect of the people in the field.

Challenging the Funding Formula

Legal aid programs had traditionally been set up in large urban areas because more people could be served in densely populated areas.. Coming from Arizona, which has a large rural population and twenty-one recognized tribes, I was approached by migrant and Indian program directors to rectify what they considered unequal funding for migrant and Indian programs. I met with two senior staff for a briefing on the funding formula. It turned out they each had a different understanding about how it worked.

At the next Board meeting, I raised the issue about the disparate funding formulas. When the President denied this existed, I asked the two senior staff to explain to the Board how Indian funds were calculated. It soon became clear that little attention had been given to this issue and that there had been little communication between senior staff.

I moved for a change in the funding for Indian programs. The motion failed six to five votes. The five minorities on the Board voted in favor of the motion, the rest of the Board members voted against. When the meeting was over, they came to congratulate me on my good work and told me I had made some valid points. Well, it wasn't over yet! I heard Hillary Rodham express to Tom Erlich, the LSC President, her concerns over possible inequities. Before the next board meeting, I received calls from the field telling me the funding formula had been changed pretty much in the manner I suggested! It took me a while to realize that the majority vote was to show support for management, not against the idea, and concluded that the results were the most important factor.

I approached the migrant funding formula in a different manner. Senator DeConcini was Chair of the Oversight Committee for the Legal Services Corporation. I met with him to brief him on the lack of funding for rural areas and for the migrant programs. Apparently he called Tom Erlich to see if he had any solutions. Next thing I knew, there was a study to determine how to meet the needs of the rural populations, followed by the establishment of new programs to serve the rural poor. This took place over the strong objections of the Board members and staff who had been involved in the establishment of the original legal services programs. "It was never anticipated that there would be enough funding for everyone. Extending the programs to rural areas will dilute the services in the urban areas. The plan was to concentrate the funds where they will get the biggest bang for the buck," was their argument.

Peterson Zah,[1] the Executive Director of the DNA Legal Services Program, invited the Board to hold a meeting in the Navajo Nation. One

---

1 Peterson Zah was elected Chairman of the Navajo Nation in 1983.

of the board committees accepted the invitation. Dan Bradley, the new LSC President, and several of the senior staff attended the meeting. We were taken to visit several of the DNA branch offices, where we met staff and many clients. Most of the board members and staff had never been on a reservation, so they had not been able to appreciate the challenges that faced DNA Legal Services. We all left with a new awareness of the special needs in Indian Country. In the end many creative ways of delivering legal services were established. Of course when the administration changed and big funding cuts were made, everyone suffered.

The Reginald Heber Smith Program
(The Reggie Program) – A Hot Item

Prior to the establishment of the Legal Services Corporation, President Lyndon Johnson created the Office of Economic Opportunity to administer the funds for his War on Poverty. The Office of Legal Services was created to provide civil legal services for the poor. The Reginald Heber Smith Community Lawyer Fellowship Program (Reggie Program) was established in 1967 through an LSC grant to the University of Pennsylvania.[2] In 1969, the Program was moved to Howard University due to the need to increase the number of minority Fellows. The annual grant was approximately three million dollars. This program included 255 one-to-two-year fellowships to recent law school graduates. The fellowships were highly coveted. In the initial years of the Program, graduates from Ivy League schools fought to become Reggie Fellows. Reggie Fellows generally represented the best in the legal profession: highly motivated attorneys dedicated to public service and to improving the plight of poor people by targeting systemic practices in the private as well as the government sectors.

Because the Office of Legal Services was part of the Executive Branch, local legal aid programs soon became the subject of political interference.

As its designers had intended, the new program soon resulted in major changes in the legal circumstances of low-income Americans. Major Supreme Court and appellate court

---

2   Reginald Heber Smith, a Harvard Law School graduate, was known as the father of poverty legal services. He wrote Justice and the Poor (1919), a groundbreaking study of how the economically disadvantaged fare in U.S. legal systems that led to the establishment of the first legal aid programs across the country.

decisions in cases brought by legal services attorneys recognized the constitutional rights of the poor and interpreted statutes to protect their interests in the areas of government benefits, consumer law, landlord-tenant law and access to health care, among others.[3]

To protect the programs from political interference, the organized bar and the legal services community succeeded in having the Nixon Administration propose legislation to form the Legal Services Corporation as an independent agency whose board would be appointed by the President, with the advice and consent of the senate. The bill passed the House and the Senate and President Richard Nixon signed the legislation on July 25, 1974. The first board was appointed by President Gerald Ford because, by that time, President Nixon had resigned.[4]

At one of the LSC Board meetings during my first year on the Board, the funding of the Reggie Program was on the Agenda. I had been lobbied by various field-office representatives to demand a "clean up" of the Program. They presented some serious concerns: the Director of the Program was a full-time law professor and at the same time was being paid for being the full-time Director of the Reggie Program. This resulted in poor administration and little or no oversight of the activities of the various managers and employees of the Program. They told me that Reggie recruiters were involved in unprofessional practices across the country, including asking for sexual favors in return for becoming a Reggie. They also said that Howard University was paid very high overhead costs, but provided few services to the Program, not even office space.

I was not too familiar with the politics surrounding the Corporation and Howard University. When we got to the Reggie Program on the Agenda, Tom Erlich, the President of the Legal Services Corporation, introduced Wiley Branton, the new Dean of the Howard University Law School. Then I began to ask questions. Tom asked for a recess. He immediately pulled me aside and asked if I knew what I was doing; he seemed upset.

"What do you mean?" —I asked.

"Do you know if you continue to ask this type of question, you will

3   History of Civil Legal Aid, National Legal Aid and Defender Association, Washington, D.C., (2003). http://www.nlada.org/About/About_HistoryCivil

4   Ibid.

be called a racist?"

"What do I care? This is taxpayer money we are talking about. It is our duty to ensure it is not being wasted."

When we resumed the meeting, Dean Branton asked for permission to address the Board. He acknowledged there were legitimate concerns about the Reggie. However, since he was new, he would like to invite me and any Board member to visit with him to discuss our concerns. The room was pretty silent. Thank goodness I understood the signal. I thanked the Dean for the invitation and told him I would arrange to meet with him very soon.

John Davis, the Reggie Program Director, arranged for the meeting with the Dean, which took place a few months later. John and I spent about a half day discussing the various problems. He acknowledged he did not have sufficient time to run the Reggie and teach full-time. He had spoken with Dean Branton, and they were in the process of selecting a full-time Director. The meeting with the Dean went smoothly. Dean Branton reassured me he had received the message and that we would see some immediate changes.

Tom Erlich decided to ask for an evaluation of the Reggie Program. The evaluation was conducted by James Robertson from Wilmer, Cutler & Pickering, a highly respected Washington, D.C. law firm. The report was submitted to the Corporation on May 26, 1978. It was not an in-depth report, but did result in a fair assessment of the strengths and weaknesses of the Program. No mention was made about the sexual favors allegation; however, that was discussed informally and steps were taken to prevent this type of behavior. There were major changes to the Reggie Program: the next contract was for one, not three years. A national advisory board was created, and increased monitoring procedures were implemented.

The lesson from this political encounter was not too pleasant. I concluded that "White liberals" never want to be called racist by African Americans. They are willing to overlook flaws in the use of taxpayer money to avoid raising the issue. I do not find the same reticence when it comes to Chicanos, perhaps because at that time, Eastern "White liberals" had not had a lot of experience dealing with the history of discrimination against Chicanos. They were acutely aware of the legacy of slavery and discrimination against African Americans.

Attitudes of Elected Officials toward the
Legal Services Corporation

Apparently elected officials do not like to be named defendants in a lawsuit. When Ronald Reagan was Governor of California he worked to take funding away from the California Rural Legal Assistance Program (CRLA), a program that predominantly served farm workers.

> Like two knights locked in endless combat, Ronald Reagan and legal services lawyers are undying adversaries. During his eight years as Governor of California, Reagan constantly urged the Nixon Administration to end all federal support for free legal services for the poor in civil cases. In 1970, the Governor vetoed a $1.8 million grant to California Rural Legal Assistance (CRLA) because a Reagan-requested inquiry had found 135 apparent incidents of misconduct by the group's lawyers. CRLA survived that threat when a three-judge commission declared the charges "unfounded and without merit." [5]

CRLA had filed successful challenges to some of the governor's welfare and Medicaid policies. Governor Reagan did not think federal funds should be used to sue government agencies, plus he did not like to lose. Since legal aid is the last resort for poor people who cannot afford a lawyer, who could they turn to when they have been wrongfully denied services?

When he was elected President in 1980, President Reagan submitted a budget to Congress with a zero appropriation for the Legal Services Corporation. The Congress did not accept this figure, but they did vote to cut the budget by 25 per cent – from $321 million to $241 million.

Another example of elected officials' attitudes toward Legal Services took place in Arizona. I was at a function at the ASU College of Law. Dean Alan Matheson began to introduce me to his brother, Scott Matheson, the Governor of Utah. Governor Matheson extended his hand as Dean Matheson proudly introduced me as "Cecilia Esquer, appointed by President Carter to the Board of the Legal Services Corporation." Governor Matheson quickly pulled his hand back so we did not complete the handshake. When Dean Matheson[6] and I looked

---

5 Bennett H. Beach, "One More Narrow Escape," TIME, Inc., November 23, 1981.

6 I have always admired Alan Matheson. He was a founding professor of the ASU College of Law and has been the "glue" that has kept the college on track. He is always willing to step forward to serve as

at him with puzzled looks, he said "I don't appreciate being sued by your organization." Other individuals came by to greet Governor Matheson, so that was the end of our encounter.

The idea that poor people could sue the government with federal funds did not sit well with those on the losing end of the lawsuits. This included elected officials and large corporations. Even though the Legal Services Corporation was an independent body, funding for the Corporation came from the Congress. There were extensive efforts to include provisions prohibiting many types of lawsuits and many calls for the reduction of the funding. When the Republicans had a majority in Congress, many restrictions were placed on the types of lawsuits programs could file.

Initial Reagan Appointees – Not too bright!

When President Reagan was elected in 1980, we knew there would be changes in the Legal Services Corporation. Elías and I began remodeling our house in 1981, a huge do-it-yourself project. I think it was December 30, 1981, when the phone rang and rang. Elías and I were carrying a three-foot- by-four-foot quarter-inch solid plate glass window to install at the front entryway. When I laid my side down to answer the phone, the window cracked.

The caller identified himself as William Olson, the new Chairman of the Legal Services Corporation Board. I was stunned. I asked him under what authority he was using this title. He said President Reagan appointed him and six others to replace seven Carter Board members.[7] All of our terms had expired, so we were holdovers because President Carter had not made any new appointments. Since Congress was not in session at that time, the Reagan appointments were recess appointments. Mr. Olson then told me he was calling to invite me to attend a special meeting of the Board at 10:00 a.m. the next day. It was so unreal. I told him there was no way I could get from Arizona to D.C. in time for a meeting the next day. His solution: he had arranged

interim Dean or in whatever capacity he is needed. He has always expressed an interest in students. Even in the Emeritus status, he is actively involved with the law school and with mentoring students.

7   The seven recess appointees were: Howard H. Dana, Jr., Verrill & Dana; Marc Sandstrom, San Diego Federal Savings & Loan; William F. Harvey, Indianapolis University Law School, Board member, Pacific Legal Foundation, William J. Olson, Smiley, Murphy, Olson & Gilman, George E. Paras, Johnson, Greve, Clifford, and Diepenbrock, Robert Sherwood Stubbs II, Executive Assistant A.G., Georgia, David E. Satterfield III, Cook, Purcell, Hansen and Henderson. They replaced: Robert J. Kutak, Richard Trudell, Howard Sacks, William McCalpin, Michael Kantor, Ramona Shump, and Revius O. Ortique, Jr. Remaining on the Board: Hillary Rodham, Steven Engleberg, Josephine Worthy and Cecilia D. Esquer.

for me to participate by phone. I objected to the short notice, but he said they had posted a notice of the meeting at the entry of the Legal Services Corporation offices as required by statute. I tried to ask more questions, but he cut me off saying he had other calls to make.

I called Clint Lyons, the Field Offices Director for the Corporation. There was no answer. Then I tried Mario Lewis, the legal counsel's office; again no answer. The receptionist told me that most everyone had taken off for the holidays. I reached Mario Lewis at his home in Texas. He was shocked! He did not know about the meeting and told me he would get back to me as soon as he reached Clint Lyons. I then called Steve Engelberg, a Carter Board member in Washington, D.C. He was in his office! Steve did not know about the meeting and said he would make sure he attended. I was furious. I did not even know the names of the Board members who had been replaced. Mario Lewis called back about two hours later and verified that a meeting was scheduled the next morning. He advised me the meeting was not lawfully called, and that I should object to proceeding with the meeting when Mr. Olson called the meeting to order. He was trying to reach Linda Perle, the Associate Legal Counsel, to see if she could attend the meeting. I told Mario Steve Engelberg said he could attend, so Mario called Steve.

When the meeting was called to order at 10:00 a.m. the next morning, I objected to proceeding with the meeting and said it was not a lawfully called meeting. Steve Engelberg also objected. Mr. Olson took our objections into consideration and proceeded to read the agenda. The agenda was basically a one-item agenda. The Reagan appointees wanted to stop the distribution of the 1982 grant monies to the field programs. I almost started laughing. When I told them the monies had been distributed to the field many months before, they would not believe me. I reminded them the Federal fiscal year was from October 1 to September 30. I could feel the anger. Mr. Olson insisted the fiscal year was the calendar year. Steve told him it was not. Each time they raised an item on the agenda, I objected to the discussion. Finally, Mr. Olson told me that my objections were already on the record, and asked for me to stop interfering with their meeting. The meeting was very brief.

President Reagan had been sworn in on January 20, 1981. Even though eliminating federal funding for the Legal Services Corporation was one of his top priorities, he had not submitted any names for Senate confirmation. So now they faced the reality that they could not impact the 1982 budget. This is a good example of the ignorance of the private sector about the federal bureaucracy. This came into play again and again during the first year of the Reagan Board.

So where was Clint Lyons? Clint called me later that day to apologize for his oversight. He said he saw a notice of a Board meeting for December 31, 1981, but assumed it was a joke. Apparently they had been playing tricks on each other in the D.C. office since President Reagan was elected. Clint said "I tore down the notice, crushed it up and threw it in the trash. Who would call a meeting on December 31?" To his credit, Clint stayed on for several years. The Reagan board had to keep someone on board who knew how the Corporation functioned. It was a challenging period for Clint Lyons.

Retrospect – Tenure on LSC Board 1978-1982

There are more examples of the political issues that came before the Board that provided me opportunities to express my opinions. My tenure on the Legal Services Corporation Board of Directors turned out to be an incredible learning experience. Even though I had served on the board of the local legal aid program, we dealt primarily with local issues and setting priorities for the types of cases the program would accept. Serving on the national board was a totally different experience. We had to deal with a Congress who was supportive of providing legal services for the poor. But there was a huge difference in philosophy among the members of Congress on the types of legal services the programs should provide.

Because the Corporation received funding from Congress, we had to be cognizant of the political issues that might affect our funding levels. During the late 1970s and early 1980s, legal aid programs across the country were bringing about social changes through class-action lawsuits on behalf of poor people. Many of the legal aid lawyers were graduates from Ivy League law schools who committed two to five years of their lives to serving the poor. They were among the "best and the brightest" in the legal profession and were largely young, idealistic men and women. Some of the successful class-action lawsuits resulted in legislation that extended protections to all consumers, not just the poor. The Federal Truth-in-Lending Act is an example.[8] Buyers now had

8 Sellers of consumer products who extended credit in connection with the sale now were forced to disclose in "conspicuous language" the actual terms of the contract, including the true interest rate to be charged, the number of years of the contract, the actual sales price and the total amount to be paid upon >

specific rights in connection with a credit sale; the penalties for sellers/lenders were huge.

This success brought a firestorm of protests from the business sector that sent lobbyists to plead their case to their elected federal officials, officials to whom they had made significant campaign contributions. This led to legislation that placed restrictions on the rules for class actions, changes that made it more difficult to proceed with these types of cases.

After other successful lawsuits challenging segregation practices in public schools, a woman's right to an abortion, and denial of military benefits to military personnel, the Congress was forced to pass legislation that prohibited legal aid programs from providing representation in these types of cases. There were legal aid programs on tribal reservations that challenged the federal government's practices in Indian Country. In addition special migrant programs were created to push for the rights of migrant farm workers. These programs were very successful and incurred the wrath of elected officials. However, the Congress was not too successful in eliminating these programs.

The task for the LSC Board and staff was to advocate against the proposed restrictions. However, we soon learned that if we insisted on blocking or eliminating these restrictions, the funding levels for our programs would suffer significantly. It was heart wrenching to realize that we were powerless to stop the imposition of many of these restrictions. However, we were proud of the fact that we were able to keep the Indian and migrant programs alive.

When the Reagan Administration came into power, one of President Reagan's priorities was to totally eliminate federal funding for legal aid programs. He began by nominating individuals who supported his goal and who would work for more extensive restrictions on the work performed by legal aid lawyers. Funding for Indian and migrant programs was greatly reduced.

I was one of the last Carter appointees to be replaced. In a sense, I was relieved that I would not be a part of the dismantling of an outstanding program. Funding for legal aid continues to date because there is a fear in Congress that if federal funds were totally eliminated, poor people would have no access to the legal system and might take their grievances to the streets. However, the restrictions have so

completion of the contract and any warranties made in connection to the sale. In certain types of sales, the buyer was entitled to a 3-day "cooling off" period during which he could cancel the contract.

limited the type of representation a legal aid lawyer may provide, that it became more difficult to attract lawyers to legal aid programs.

Arizona Legal Aid Involvement

Several years after serving on the national board, I became the Director of the Arizona Statewide Legal Services Project, which provided support services to the seven legal aid programs in Arizona. After that, I worked for two years as a staff attorney for Four Rivers Indian Legal Services, a legal aid program in the Gila River Indian Community.

I am proud to have been part of a movement that worked for empowerment of the poor by working for equal access to the justice system. I look forward to the day when once again legal aid programs across the country can provide legal services to their clients with minimal political interference. That day may be a little closer as a result of the new political make up of the Congress, and the fact that we have a President who seems to share our goal of equal access to justice.

Top: Cecilia D.
Esquer, Dan
Bradley, Gerry
Singsen, Senator
Dennis DeConcini
Washington, D. C.,
March 1980. Photo
courtesy of Senator
Dennis DeConcini

Bottom: Letter
from Don Wharton,
Portland, Oregon,
January 13, 1981

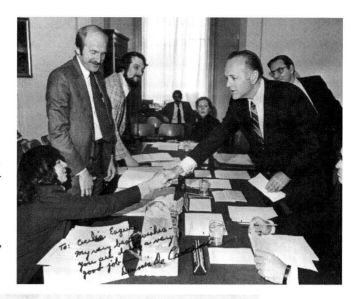

NATIONAL ASSOCIATION OF INDIAN LEGAL SERVICES

2386 N.W. Hoyt Street
Portland, Oregon   97210
(503) 223-9483

13 January 1981

Ms. Cecilia D. Esquer
Arizona State University
College of Business Administration
Department of Administrative Services
Tempe, Arizona   85281

Dear Ms. Esquer:

We are writing to express our gratitude for your excellent service on
the Board of Directors of the Legal Services Corporation. Your clear
dedication to assuring access to justice for all Americans aided the
legal services community and our clients immensely during your tenure.

We especially appreciated your concern for and sensitivity to the
minority and Indian concerns the LSC Board faced in recent times. You
have left a record, personally and as a board member, which will be
difficult to equal.

With all best regards.

Sincerely,

Donald R. Wharton, Chairman
for the National Association of
Indian Legal Services

DRW:bkn

Top: Richard Trudell, Willard Nez, Cecilia D. Esquer, Navajo Nation, Window Rock, Arizona, September 9, 1980. Photo Courtesy of Hon. Peterson Zah

Middle: Martha Blue (DNA Staff Attorney), Dick Trudell, Cecilia D. Esquer, Dan Bradley, (LSC President), Hon. Peterson Zah, Nevy Jensen, Navajo Nation, Window Rock, Arizona, September 19, 1980. Photo Courtesy of Hon. Peterson Zah

Bottom: Cecilia D. Esquer and Hillary Clinton, Washington, D.C., 1993

12

CITIZENS ORGANIZED FOR AN UNBIASED PRESS (COUP)

A S I look back, I wonder: How did we do it? To this day I still have trouble saying NO when I am asked to take on a new project. Elías spent the spring 1979 Semester on sabbatical leave at the University of Sevilla, Spain. Andrea, Marcos, and I tagged along. We returned in early June. I decided not to return to the Office of the Attorney General, so I started looking for possibilities in private practice. I wound up in a partnership with my former law school classmate, Manuel Silvas. It was a scary prospect for me – just two lawyers, no capital. Anybody would think that starting a new practice would require all of my time. It should have.

I was still serving on the national board of the Legal Services Corporation. That required frequent out-of-town trips. I also served on the local board of Valle de Sol, a non-profit corporation dedicated to serving the Chicano community. And, I had two young children and a husband at home. Andrea was now thirteen and Marcos was nine.

In mid-September 1979, Alfredo Gutiérrez, then the Minority Leader in the State Senate, asked to meet with me. He was furious about a series of articles that appeared in the Arizona Republic, and wanted to do something about it. He felt the paper was unfair and untruthful in covering a sensitive family situation.

One of his nephews had been kidnapped and was being held for ransom in a dispute over drugs and money. The paper accused Alfredo of using his office to pressure the Phoenix Police Department into providing the one hundred pounds of marijuana requested by the kidnappers. Although the charges had been proven false, the paper did not retract its story. Instead, it published an editorial calling Alfredo a "moral" criminal.[1] The New Times, an alternative newspaper at that time, investigated the incident and published an article stating the Arizona Republic knew their story was not truthful at the time they ran

---

1 Editorial, "Misguided Loyalty," Arizona Republic, September 6, 1979.

it.[2]

We discussed calling a meeting of some Chicano activists to explore the options available to address this issue. We decided the issue was more than this particular incident and thought this would be a good time to challenge the paper on its negative treatment of the Chicano community. I became the spokesperson for the group. We held a community meeting at St. Anthony's church on September 18, 1979. Twenty-eight persons showed up. Alfredo discussed his situation. Others began to discuss the Republic's negative treatment of our community. The consensus was that we needed to do something. The following Saturday, September 29, we held another meeting, this time at Friendly House, another non-profit corporation serving the Chicano community. Twenty-two persons attended.

Another meeting was held on October 6, 1979 at Friendly House. We agreed to develop a plan of action and formed committees to explore the possibility of initiating a subscription boycott of the Republic. We also discussed the possibility of challenging the granting of a cable license to Camelback Cablevision. The Arizona Republic owned a five per cent interest in this company. The application to the City of Phoenix included a provision allocating three of the cable channels to the Arizona Republic. We objected to the expansion of this monopolistic enterprise. The Arizona Republic and Phoenix Gazette (R&G) had no competition in the print media. Now they wanted to be the only newspaper that had control of 3 cable stations, including a twenty-four-hour news station. Imagine the lucrative ads from the business community. The R&G already had the market on ads in the print media. In fact, the story goes that they successfully forced at least two newspapers to go out of business: The Evening American, whose publisher was Evan Mecham,[3] and the Arizona Journal. Apparently the R&G warned their advertisers that if they ran ads in the competing newspapers, the R&G would not carry their ads. In 1979 the newspaper was the main advertising venue for businesses in the Valley. No newspaper can operate without ads. Finally, we agreed on a name for our group: Citizens Organized for an Unbiased Press (COUP).

We also began to expand our base. On October 10, four of us made a presentation to the Metropolitan Phoenix Indian Coalition.

2 Michael Lacey, "The Press: 'My stories were accurate," – Republic Reporter John Winters," New Times Weekly, Sept. 19-25, 1979, p. ll.

3 John Hebers, "Arizona Publisher Says Papers In His State Dictate to Politicians." The New York Times, July 14, 1967, p. 41:2. http://en.wikipedia.org/wiki/Evan_Mecham

The panel included Rev. Robert Chew, from the Black Ministerial Alliance; Sra. Julieta Bencomo, a community activist and member of the State Board of Education; and Felix Moreno, a member of IMAGE, a national organization concerned with government employment for Hispanic Americans. The Coalition voted to join COUP. The Black Media Coalition, Statewide MEChA, LULAC, and the Interdenominational Ministerial Alliance also joined our efforts. Individuals from the business community, unions, and women's groups also joined COUP. Others provided support anonymously because they were afraid of repercussions to their company or their jobs. These groups felt their particular communities were badly treated by the R&G.

We held our first press conference on October 16 at the Phoenix Press Club. I was elected to be the spokesperson for the group. We did not expect great attendance. But, to our surprise, every TV station was there, along with National Public Radio and a couple of other radio stations. The Spanish language press was very visible, both TV and radio. We did not realize that other media organizations did not particularly care for the R&G. They felt the R&G basically controlled what companies could run ads, not only in the R&G, but in other media outlets. The R&G had a statewide readership and it had the largest circulation of any newspaper in the State of Arizona. With today's technology, the R&G is not so powerful. At the press conference we announced the formation of COUP and presented our plan of action: the boycott of the Phoenix Newspapers, Inc. – the R&G.

Following the press conference, KTAR Radio interviewed Bill Shover, the Director of Community and Corporate Services for the R&G. Although he admitted on the air that they had made a mistake in saying that Senator Gutierrez exerted great pressure on the Phoenix Police Department, and that they had discussed doing something about the editorial calling Senator Gutiérrez a "moral" criminal, they never printed a retraction. COUP received extensive coverage. Gloria Ybarra, an attorney, and I appeared for TV and radio interviews. Art Mobley from the Black Media Coalition was tremendously helpful in securing resources. He recruited Allen Black from the NAACP Legal Defense & Education Fund to provide legal advice. In addition Mauricio Méndez, from KIFN radio, subsidized the expenses around our first press conference, including hiring a public relations firm. The rest of our expenses were covered from small contributions by community people.

On December 15, 1979 we held an "Informational Picket" at

the R&G offices on Van Buren Street in Phoenix. Pepe Martínez, a community activist, contributed greatly to the strategies we adopted. The "Informational Picket" was a light-hearted event. Parents brought their children. We had colorful balloons and handmade picket signs. The MEChA students turned out in force. Again, we received great press. There were individuals taking photographs of everyone, which was commonplace in the 1970s and 1980s. Sometimes it was the local police department, other times it was the FBI. The City of Phoenix also sent some undercover officers; of course we knew who they were immediately!

During the demonstration John Winters, the R&G reporter who covered the Gutiérrez incident, came to meet us. He stood by his story. Jack Mayne, one of the editors, also came to visit with us. In fact, he shook our hands. During this period of time, the Newspaper Guild was organizing and recruiting new members. They were striving for improved working conditions and salaries. One of the reporters, Bonnie Bartak, became the President of the Guild. The Guild's efforts were proving very successful. Too successful, so Bonnie, who had been covering the coveted City Council beat, was reassigned to cover the night police beat. She filed a complaint with the Department of Labor accusing the paper of unfair labor practices.[4]

Jack Mayne, her supervising editor, testified on Bonnie's behalf. He did not feel the transfer was warranted. We heard that the Monday morning after our "Informational Picket" on December 15, Jack walked into his office. His boss was waiting for him with a blown-up picture of Jack shaking hands with some of the demonstrators. Jack was asked to clean his desk immediately and leave. Jack wound up filing a lawsuit against the R&G, and eventually reached a monetary settlement.

Bill Shover, the R&G Communications Director, agreed to meet with me. We met on December 21. I told him I wanted to explain how COUP worked and wanted him to know a number of things we were discussing, among them a discrimination charge with the EEOC. As an organization we would ask for a "Commissioner's Charge" to investigate discrimination in employment and recruitment practices. He said "Well Cecilia, we have troublemakers like that here at the paper. I don't know if you know Bonnie Bartak, but she's filed an EEOC complaint against us." Then he said something to the effect they knew how to take care of troublemakers, "but we are not afraid of the EEOC." After the meeting

4 "Federal suit, New Labor Charges Filed Against R&G," New Times Weekly, June 4-10, 1980.

I called Bonnie to tell her about Mr. Shover's comments. She called her attorney, who thought my testimony would be helpful in her case in the Department of Labor. I told her I was willing to testify.

I was served with a subpoena to appear before the Federal Labor Relations Board on February 23, 1980. When I arrived, Mr. Shover was testifying. Since I was the next witness, his lawyer asked him to tell the Administrative Law Judge a little bit about me. He said I was a radical, and then proceeded to tell them about COUP. In his hand, he had a stack of subscription cancellation cards. I was so excited when I saw the cards! In our haste to get the cards printed, we failed to provide two cards, one to send to the R&G, and one to send to COUP. So, until then, we had no idea how many people had canceled their subscriptions. He had quite a stack, so we declared victory!

R & G Cable License

We had been monitoring the City of Phoenix cable licensing process since November 20, 1979. It was a complex, confusing process, beyond a lay person's understanding. There were two main applicants for a license: Camelback Cablevision, in which the Phoenix Newspapers owned a five percent interest. Then there was American Cable Television Company. In addition there were two or three smaller companies. Camelback Cablevision was the clear favorite; however, the City Council was forced to look at multiple licensing. American Cable was having problems getting its financing together. The City pushed them hard to meet deadlines. We knew from the beginning that Camelback Cablevision would get their license, but we were able to put a kink in the process.

The City provided us with a copy of each application and a copy of the application guidelines. In reviewing Camelback Cablevision's application, I noticed that some required information was missing from their application. The Council planned to act on the application at its February 1980 meeting. Several COUP members appeared to testify on behalf of their organization: Ruben Vasquez, MEChA President, appeared for MEChA. Earl Wilcox and Gloria Ybarra spoke for the community organizations. I appeared to represent COUP. In addition to the obvious conflict of interest when a monopoly print media wants to go on cable, I pointed out that the Council had failed to properly review Camelback Cablevision's application. It was missing some key required documents: a copy of their corporate charter, an ownership disclosure statement, and a financial report. Why was the Council insisting that American Cable meet every requirement, yet overlooked some major flaws in Camelback Cablevision's application?

When Frank Fairbanks, the City Manager, heard me say this, he appeared shocked and looked directly at the staffer responsible for those details. The Mayor asked Mr. Fairbanks for an explanation. Mr. Fairbanks said he would have to get back to the Council. It took three more months before the item was on the agenda again. Again, we felt victorious. We had made our point.

COUP's Success

The real success of COUP was the fact that we were able to coalesce a variety of interest groups in a very short period of time. Blacks, Chicanos, Native Americans, women, unions, clergy and business people joined with us to stand up to a giant bully. We did force some changes: the R&G hired its first woman editor and started a weekly bilingual section. The Department of Justice offered to mediate a meeting with the newspaper. They also offered to sponsor a one-day conference on working with the media and to provide facilitators. They even offered to cover expenses for two national speakers. I do not recall whether this ever came to fruition.

Real life took over. I had to get back to my practice, which was not going so well. During this time I was also traveling to Washington, D.C. and other places for Legal Services Corporation meetings or legal aid conferences. My clients were very patient, but they needed my attention. And my family? How did we do it?

OPPOSITE PAGE PHOTO CAPTIONS:
Top: Republic and Gazette Building, Phoenix, Arizona, December 15, 1979

Bottom: Hon. Mary Rose Wilcox, Gloria Ybarra, Nancy Jordan, Phoenix, Arizona, December 15, 1979

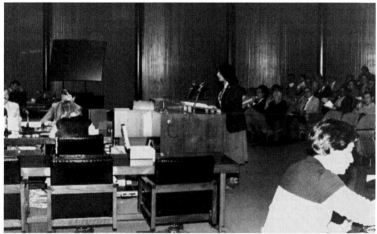

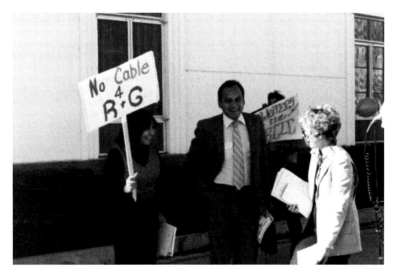

OPPOSITE PAGE PHOTO
CAPTIONS:
Top: Demonstrators,
Phoenix, Arizona,
December 15, 1979

Middle: Cecilia D. Esquer,
Phoenix City Council,
Phoenix, Arizona, 1980

Bottom: Cecilia D.
Esquer, Reporters
Sal Quijada and Rita
Pearson, Phoenix,
Arizona, December 15,
1979

Top: Jack Mayne, John
Winters, Phoenix,
Arizona, December 15,
1979

Bottom: Demonstrators,
Phoenix, Arizona,
December 15, 1979

13

MINORITY LAWYERS
IN THE LEGAL COMMUNITY

EVEN after I successfully passed the bar exam, I quickly realized that many Anglo attorneys did not see me as an equal. Like some in the general public, many assumed I had been admitted to law school only because I am a Chicana. They failed to recognize that I took the same classes as other students did – there were no classes for minorities – and that I successfully completed law school. I even "wrote the book" [got the highest score] in one of my classes. I also passed the same bar exam: there is no minority bar exam.

During law school, El Grupo, the Chicano law student organization, advocated for the hiring of a Hispanic law professor. It was not easy. The Dean would tell us they could not find any "qualified" applicants. A "qualified" applicant was one who graduated in the top ten of his class, served on law review - and preferably a graduate from an Ivy League school. We finally threatened to go to EEOC and to call a news conference in the rotunda of the law school to decry what we considered a discriminatory hiring practice. In less than a month, Dean Pedrick found an applicant who came to interview. Subsequently, they made him an offer, which he accepted.

Professor Richard Delgado graduated in the top ten of his class and served as the Notes & Comments Editor of the California Law Review, University of California at Berkeley. When one of my professors heard Professor Delgado had been hired, he stopped me in the rotunda. He told me that, even though Professor Delgado met the academic criteria, he did not think Professor Delgado would fit into their social circle. Professor Delgado turned out to be a great Prof. However, he only stayed one year. It was clear he was not comfortable in this law school setting, and he apparently had several options. He accepted a position at the University of Pittsburg School Of Law. He is an outstanding scholar:

> One of the leading commentators on race in the United
> States, Richard Delgado has appeared on Good Morning

MINORITY LAWYERS IN THE LEGAL COMMUNITY | 153

America, the MacNeil-Lehrer Report, PBS, NPR, the Fred Friendly Show, and Canadian NPR. Author of over one hundred journal articles and fifteen books, his work has been praised or reviewed in The Nation, The New Republic, the New York Times, Washington Post, and Wall Street Journal. His books have won eight national book prizes, including six Gustavus Myers Awards for outstanding book on human rights in North America, the American Library Association's Outstanding Academic Book, and a Pulitzer Prize nomination.

Stanley Fish described his career and book, The Rodrigo Chronicles in the following terms: "Richard Delgado is a triple pioneer. He was the first to question free speech ideology; he and a few others invented critical race theory; and he is both a theorist and an exemplar of the importance of storytelling in the workings of the law. This volume brings all of Delgado's strengths together in a stunning performance." [1]

I guess the law school was not ready for this discipline. If someone like Professor Delgado was not considered an equal, imagine what some of the law professors and some practicing attorneys thought about me. Even the "White liberal" attorneys had their doubts.

The Big Firms Weren't Hiring In-State
Minority Law Graduates

When we returned from Spain after Elías's sabbatical, Alfredo Gutiérrez told me Dino DeConcini's law firm was opening a Phoenix office, and they were interested in hiring minority attorneys. He insisted that I call Mr. DeConcini to have coffee and to discuss possibilities. He was sure Dino would want to hire me. I knew Dino pretty well from political campaigns. He was also Governor Castro's Chief of Staff during the Payne nomination fiasco. We all considered Dino DeConcini to be a liberal, more liberal than his brother, Senator Dennis DeConcini. Dino and Elías got along famously, and we had mutual friends and mutual interests, so we saw each other often

The coffee started out very congenially. We caught up on events. I then mentioned Alfredo told me the DeConcini firm was recruiting

1 www.law.pitt.edu/faculty/profiles/delgador

minority attorneys. Dino's demeanor changed dramatically. He became all business. He said they generally did not hire minority attorneys from an Arizona law school. They only hired minority attorneys who graduated from an Ivy League school. The reason: I was probably specially admitted to the law school, but, more importantly, their clients did not think that a minority law graduate from an Arizona school was qualified to represent them. He went on to say that I probably did not do well in law school and that they generally recruited from the top of the class.

I was flabbergasted. In other words, I was considered a second class citizen in the legal community. It took what seemed like ten minutes to respond to Dino. I told him he probably did not know that I had earned the highest grade in one of my classes, and that I had scored among the top of the class in a couple of other classes. I told Dino I would never have thought of applying to his firm, but that Alfredo insisted he would be open to hiring me. He became uncomfortable, probably very embarrassed. He had been exposed! He did not have to verbalize his assumptions about me.

Dino said he did not ask Alfredo to help him recruit, and that I was the second person Alfredo had sent to see him. To this day I wonder why Alfredo would subject me to this. There was a brief exchange of niceties and our meeting was quickly over. I felt humiliated, but as a minority woman in a non-traditional field, I would never let "them" see me cry. Dino knew he had lost face and had lost a friend. Since I first met Dino, he presented himself as an advocate for minorities. He devoted a lot of time and resources to minority issues. But, "business is business." Our relationship was never the same after that. We basically avoided each other. Sadly, this was the general attitude in the large Arizona law firms.

In recent years, there have been some successful efforts to convince large law firms to hire minority law students from Arizona law schools. This is due in large part to the efforts of Los Abogados, a Hispanic Bar Association, some of the Latino lawyers working in the large law firms, and other minority bars. They convinced Dean Patricia White to initiate a program that would expose the large law firms to minority law school students. The reports so far are that there has been an increase in the hiring of minority law graduates from Arizona law schools. The experience with Dino DeConcini is not the only experience I had to endure.

During our first year of law school, non-minority students would comment to minority students they knew they were going to pass because the minority law students were their "buffer." After some of us earned grades as good or better as theirs, that died down.

Then, too, there were the comments about any recognition I received: "You got this because you are a Chicana." While that might have been one of the factors in some instances, I don't think so many incredible things would have happened to me if I had not been so involved, or if I had not succeeded in the positions I attained. As late as 2003, I had to put up with this type of comment. However, I do have to mention that two individuals, one at Phoenix College and one at the Attorney General's office, apologized for their remarks some time after and told me they were wrong. Hopefully they learned not to judge so quickly.

Events like this keep reminding me that too many individuals do not consider me an equal. Some days it is hard to ignore so I always have to be on guard. As Frank, one of Barack Obama grandfather's war buddies told Barack:

"You can't blame Stan [Barack's grandfather] for what he is," Frank said quietly. "He's basically a good man. But he doesn't know me. Any more than he knew that [black] girl that looked after your mother. He can't know me, not the way I know him. Maybe some of these Hawaiians can, or the Indians on the reservation. They've seen their fathers humiliated. Their mothers desecrated. But your grandfather will never know what that feels like. That's why he can come over here and drink my whiskey and fall asleep in that chair you're sitting in right now. Sleep like a baby. See, that's something I can never do in his house. Never. Doesn't matter how tired I get, I still have to watch myself. I have to be vigilant for my own survival."[2]

As I write this memoir, I become very emotional at times and even shed tears thinking of the many slights I have had to endure. And then I cry some more thinking of the many more affronts my husband, our main source of income, had to endure to keep the job he loved at Mesa Community College. Despite all this, Elías had a big impact on the hiring of minorities in the community college district. He also garnered the

2 Obama, 1995, 2004, p. 90

respect of most of his students, many who decided to become foreign language teachers because "Professor Esquer" was such a great Prof.

14

I FILED A COMPLAINT AGAINST TWO JUDGES?

Background – Law Practice of Esquer & Silvas

IN 1979, Manuel Silvas, a law school classmate, and I opened a small law office in Tempe, Arizona. It was a general law practice. Manuel handled most of the criminal law cases; I handled many of the civil law cases. We were fortunate in having individuals seek our legal advice. Manuel had worked for Governor Castro. I had been pretty visible as a community activist. However, neither of us had much legal experience.

This small practice provided some great court experiences. While I handled some very interesting cases, one particularly stands out.

Complaint against two Judges

Challenges come at the most unexpected times. On June 30, 1982, I had a matter before a Maricopa County Justice Court – a trial on a Motion to Dismiss. I was representing Rubén and Faustino Hernández, officers of the Hernández Trucking Company. The matter involved a citation for non-registration of a forklift.[1] The Justice of the Peace (JP) from that precinct had previously granted my Motion to Dismiss a previous non-registration citation because the law was clear registration was not required. He granted that motion over the phone without a hearing.

---

1   The Arizona Department of Transportation [ADOT] was trying to get Hernández Trucking to voluntarily register its forklifts. At this time, "implements of husbandry [agriculture]" were exempt from the registration requirement.

Hernández Trucking was a hay-hauling company, so the forklifts qualified as an "implement of husbandry." The company owned several forklifts. Ruben's company was a family owned business. Ruben's grandfather had founded the company. Tino Hernández, the company president and Ruben's brother, took a firm stand against registering the forklift: "My grandfather never registered a forklift, my father never registered a forklift; the law doesn't require us to register; I'll be damned if we are going to register our forklifts."

In a period of about two months, Hernández Trucking received about 16 citations for non-registration. In most cases, I was able to secure a Motion to Dismiss without a hearing because the law was very clear they were not required to register the forklifts. I later learned that ADOT had targeted Hernández Trucking; other hay-hauling companies had voluntarily registered their forklifts.

I think he set this citation for trial because Faustino had filed a civil rights complaint against him. Since the complaint was still in process, I filed a Notice of Change of judge, which automatically removed the JP from the case.

When I appeared for the trial on June 30, 1982 the Prosecutor for the Maricopa County Attorney told me the judge wanted to talk with me in chambers before the trial. The visiting judge was Fred Ackel,[2] the Tempe JP.

Judge Ackel was at the judge's desk. The Prosecutor and a third individual were also present. No one identified the third individual; I assumed he was the Prosecutor's associate. Judge Ackel stated the reasons he was going to deny my motion. Before I had an opportunity to state why he should grant the motion, the third individual interrupted. He started saying disparaging things about my client and that my client had received numerous citations for refusing to register the company's forklifts. I told Judge Ackel that all but three matters had been dismissed or resolved without a trial. One was this case before Judge Ackel; the other two were pending in Phoenix Justice Court.

Judge Ackel asked me if I had ever been in this JP's court. I indicated I had represented my client in several matters prior to the current one in this court. However, I told Judge Ackel, I had never met the JP because he had granted my Motions to Dismiss over the phone. Imagine my surprise when Judge Ackel introduced the third individual as the JP from that precinct.

I objected to the JP's presence in the courtroom. He was recused from this matter, and here he was – testifying against my client and stating some things that were not true. Judge Ackel did not ask him to leave. The Prosecutor refused to make a comment when I asked him to advise the judge about the law. It was a trying situation.

The JP continued participating in the pre-trial conference. He stated several times that my client was flaunting the law by refusing to register the forklifts. He said this was an especially serious matter because my client was refusing to register the forklift even after losing an appeal to the Superior Court. My client had never appealed the issue to the Superior Court. I asked Judge Ackel to require the JP to produce evidence that there had been an appeal. Judge Ackel did not grant my

---

2   At this time, all complaints before the Commission were confidential. The judges' names and the proceedings before the Commission could not be discussed with anyone. I mention Judge Ackel's name because a reported case, discussed in this chapter, makes his name public.

request. I did not ask Judge Ackel to order the JP to leave the room because I was afraid it would hinder the outcome of my client's case.

During this proceeding, Judge Ackel had addressed me as "darling" when I entered the room. Toward the end of the hearing he stood up, looked over the desk and made a comment about my legs – something to the effect that I had good-looking legs. The three men laughed. I found the entire proceeding very intimidating. I was disappointed the Prosecutor went along with this type of conduct. As I left the hearing, I told all three of them this was not the end of this matter.

The Commission on Judicial Qualifications

When I returned to my office, I immediately called Sherman Bendalin, the Executive Director of the Commission on Judicial Qualifications [now the Commission on Judicial Conduct.] I told Mr. Bendalin that I was considering filing a complaint against two JPs with the Commission. What I needed to know was whether the Commission would take my complaint seriously. There was a feeling at this time that the Commission was not doing a good job enforcing the Judicial Code of Conduct. I needed that reassurance from Mr. Bendalin because I knew I would probably be appearing before these judges in the future. On July 6, 1982, after receiving Mr. Bendalin's reassurance that the Commission would take my complaint seriously, I filed a written complaint.

On November 9, 1982, I received a letter from the Commission advising me of the action taken on my complaint by the Commission at its October 15, 1982 meeting. With that, the case was closed. I was satisfied with the decision.

Another Complaint against Judge Ackel

Four years later, on December 2, 1986, I received a call from Ms. Edith Croxon, who was now the Executive Director for the Commission, telling me my complaint against Judge Ackel had been reopened. Judge Ackel had filed a Motion to Dismiss my complaint. My testimony was needed to show he had been formally warned about his conduct in the past.

The hearing before the Commission took place on January 9, 1987. I was one of the witnesses called to testify. Following the hearing, the Commission issued its recommendation to the Arizona Supreme Court. On October 27, 1987, after reviewing the proceedings of the Commission, the Arizona Supreme Court issued its decision. The case involved a written complaint about Judge Ackel's sexist conduct toward a female attorney and some pretty egregious conduct on the Judge's part. The Court agreed with the Commission that the judge's conduct in this matter constituted "wilful [sp] misconduct."[3] The Commission had recommended that Judge Ackel be removed ". . . from his position as Justice of the Peace . . . ."[4]

> Instead of removal from office, the Court held:
> We hereby formally and publicly censure Fred S. Ackel for reasons given herein. We adopt the Commission's recommendation that Ackel be assessed attorneys fees and costs in the amount of $2207.07. . . .[5]

The decision was reached in part because the Court found a prior written complaint (my complaint) had put the judge on notice. Apparently there had been five other complaints about Judge Ackel's behavior, but none of the five individuals filed a formal written complaint. However, five witnesses testified at this hearing as to Judge Ackel's " . . . . use of endearing terms toward and physical contact with women." The Court then amended the Commission's findings of fact to eliminate all references to the oral complaints to the Commission, and then stated:

> We agree with the Commission that item 5 [my complaint] can be considered as an aggravating factor. We would add as an aggravating factor (In the Matter of Fred S. Ackel, Justice of the Peace, Tempe Precinct, Maricopa County, State of Arizona) Ackel's repeated use of endearing terms toward and physical contact with women.[6]

In explaining the reason for censure rather than removal, the Court observed:
> By publicly censuring Ackel rather than removing him,

---

3 In the Matter of Fred S. Ackel, Justice of the Peace, Tempe Precinct, Maricopa County, State of Arizona, 155 Ariz. 34, 745 P.2d 92 (1987). The Court said "By no stretch of the imagination, though, can we deem Ackel's sexist conduct towards Randall the product of ignorance, carelessness, or thoughtlessness. If Ackel's comments concerning prophylactics and oral sexual practices, his invitation to Randall to join him in an out-of-court nocturnal setting, and his embrace of Randall do not constitute willful conduct, then we are unable to envision what type of conduct falls within the rubric of the term. P. 8

4 Ibid.

5 Ibid.

6 Ibid.

we in no way discount the seriousness of Ackel's conduct. If he fails to mend his ways and finds himself again before this tribunal on similar charges, the above consideration will not save him twice. p 11

In the Commission's "Summaries of Arizona Cases," we learn "[t]he judge later resigned and agreed not to seek appointment or election to judicial office again when new allegations involving sexual harassment came to light."[7]

As for the other JP, it appears he learned his lesson. I appeared before him when I was working at Four Rivers Indian Legal Services. I was apprehensive as I stood before the Judge, but I had no problems being heard. He treated me in a very professional manner.

Lessons Learned

It takes a lot of courage to file a written complaint against a judge. If the charges are not proven to the satisfaction of the Commission, appearing in court, especially with the judge in question, will be very difficult. In my case, I think one of the reasons I was treated so poorly by these two judges and the Prosecutor is the fact that they did not think a Chicana would do anything about their egregious conduct. This made me feel that minorities must always be on guard when appearing before judges. However, attorneys have a duty to protect the integrity and reputation of the legal system. They must find the courage to file complaints against offending judges.

As to the operational aspects of our practice, perhaps the most important lesson I learned was that it was difficult for me to practice in a small law firm. The overhead costs are tremendous. Too many clients are slow to pay their fees. Since we started with almost no capital investments, we experienced terrific pressure when it came time to pay our bills.

The most difficult part was not having other attorneys around to mentor and support us. As inexperienced attorneys, Manuel and I had many issues come up where we needed someone who could answer our questions. It was not like the Attorney General's office, where there were many attorneys I could rely on. Manuel thrived in this type of

---

7   Summaries of Major Cases, Handbook, Commission on Judicial Conduct, p 27.
http://www.supreme.state.az.us/ethics/Handbook/Major CaseSummaries.pdf (Conduct)

setting. I did not. I lost a lot of sleep wondering if I had made some crucial error that would hurt my client's case.

In addition, I still was active on the Valle del Sol Board and the Legal Services Corporation Board, which involved a great deal of travel. Then there were the hot political issues which took me away from my practice. I soon discovered this type of practice setting was not suitable for me. Manuel, on the other hand, became a very successful sole practitioner representing criminal defendants. I learned a lot in a short period of time. I enjoyed working with my clients, especially those who had suffered as a result of someone's fraudulent practices. However, I soon found myself making another transition.

15

ARIZONA STATE UNIVERSITY FACULTY – 1981-84

How I was Hired at ASU

FATE has a way of stepping into my life when least expected. I was leaving Probate Court one morning when I saw Dr. Gloria Natale, my Communications professor at ASU. I had not seen her in years. She told me she was on her way to the courtroom to testify in the Kevin Rutledge trial. Frank Kush, the ASU football coach was being sued by one of his former football players after Coach Kush punched him during football practice.[1] Kush was known for being pretty tough on his players. Rutledge had been Dr. Natale's student, so she was asked to testify as a character witness for Rutledge.

Dr. Natale asked me if I missed teaching. I told her I would always miss the classroom. She told me there was an opening in the Department for a Business Law professor and urged me to apply. Unfortunately, the next day at 5:00 p.m. was the deadline for applications. I told her I would think about it and let her know if I decided to apply, but that it would be difficult to get everything done because I had a hearing the next morning. I got home early that afternoon and told my husband about the possibility. Elías thought it would be great if I would return to teaching. It was difficult for us to get away when I was on a twelve-month calendar, and we missed traveling. I told him I did not think I could get everything together by 5:00 p.m. the next day.

Elías took care of everything. He picked up an application form that afternoon and I filled it out. We gathered the different documents requested. Elías said he would make copies and hand-deliver everything the next day – and he did. As usual, I did not have high expectations of being hired. The ASU College of Business had a dismal record in hiring minorities. To my surprise, I was called in for an interview the next week. A few days later, I was offered the position. Elías really wanted me to accept the offer. If I did, I told him that, even though the position

---
1 "Frank Kush," http://en.wikipedia.org/wiki/Frank_Kush

was a tenure-track position, he should understand there was no way the College of Business would grant me tenure. I would be gone after three years. He said it was worth the risk.

Teaching with Former Profs

In my case, it was not a good idea to teach with some of my former professors. Dr. Lohnie Boggs was the department chair. He had been my professor and adviser in undergraduate school, where I majored in Business Education. Dr. Robert Gryder, another one of my professors, was also in the department. It took me a while to get used to being their colleague. Dr. Boggs made it clear that he expected me to be a very visible member of the department and the college. I soon realized that I was the only minority woman in a tenure-track position in the College of Business. I was expected to serve on a department committee, a college committee, and a university committee. In addition I was strongly encouraged to serve on the Tempe Community Council. I was also told I would be the coordinator for the Revlon Project beginning October 1981.

The Revlon Foundation had made a $25,000 grant to the College of Business to assist in the recruitment of Hispanic students. The funds had been lying dormant for some time because no one was willing to take on this project. Dean Glenn Overman was fearful that Revlon would withdraw the funding. Dr. Boggs assured me they would provide a research assistant if I was successful in getting the funding, but that the Department budget did not have the funds to cover any released time that semester. Dr. Boggs said he understood that I would need some time for winding up my law practice. I told him I planned to resign from the Legal Services Corporation Board because of the amount of travel involved. Dr. Boggs insisted I remain on the Board because it would bring recognition to the College. I was also completing a term as Chair of the Board of the Valle del Sol Corporation, a local non-profit. We were in the middle of selecting a new Chief Executive Officer, which of course required a lot of meetings.

Ethan Locke, another attorney, had also been hired to teach Business Law that fall. He also was in a tenure-track position. It was clear he had strong support. Ethan was told he could not serve on any committees and was given a light load so he would have time to do research. Like other universities, ASU had a policy of "publish or perish" when it came to getting tenure. When Ethan found out I had a higher salary and was also a first-year Prof, he came to complain to me. I told him he should not be complaining and that he should be thrilled he was on the tenure track. Also, I told him, I had prior teaching experience, although not at the university level, and I was merely filling a number for the college and would likely not get tenure. When would I have the time to do research with the extraordinary schedule I was required to accept? Ethan would not believe this. But after I left ASU, he told Dr. Mary Jane Dundas, one of our colleagues, that I was right. And, Ethan Locke became a tenured professor. On another note, Dr. Robert Gryder, my former professor and now my colleague, was aware of my plight.

Dr. Gryder had been one of my most outstanding professors at ASU. He took a special interest in each of his students and often helped us resolve difficult dilemmas. Dr. Gryder did his best to be my protector. He let me know he knew the game the College was playing and that he did not like it. He offered to help me in any way he could. Dr. Gryder was pretty upset when he found out I had to coordinate the Revlon Project, but would not receive released time. Yet he recognized there was little either of us could do.

The Revlon Project

I had to devote an extensive amount of time to making the Revlon Project a reality. I wanted to build a successful program, one that could be institutionalized. During that first semester I had to rewrite the original proposal and budget. This required that I meet with key individuals throughout the campus to find out what things were possible and what resources were available to assist with the project. The college could not provide enough information on the procedures to implement the project, so I had to set up meetings to learn the process (requisitions, hiring student help, legal requirements, proposal submissions, etc.) The promised clerical assistance did not materialize, so I had to personally do the clerical chores associated with the program: room reservations, equipment reservations, scheduling high-school visitations, and so forth. I also became the co-sponsor of the Hispanic Business Students Association because I felt they would become invaluable to the success of the Revlon Project.

I worked many evenings and weekends to get the project on track and to keep up with my teaching schedule. I had never taught Business

Law before. An upper-division course takes many hours of preparation. In addition, the class had a required written project that, with seventy-five students in each of my three classes, took many hours to grade.

Despite my heavy schedule, I was able to attend all of the Department and College faculty meetings and to assist with academic advising of General Business and pre-law students in the College of Business. I attended seminars for new faculty members concerning student advising and research and writing. I also represented the College at several functions. In addition, I presented two papers at professional conferences. I was successful in getting a renewed commitment from the Revlon Foundation, so I asked to be released from the coordinator position due to my impossible schedule. Dr. Boggs was aware of this schedule and still insisted that I work on the Revlon Project because it was important for the department, the college, and the university. He assured me that I would be recognized for my efforts. He also promised clerical help, which did not materialize until the middle of the spring semester.

During the spring semester I was released from one class preparation. However, the time was devoted to recruiting students and businesses for the Revlon Project. I visited seventeen high schools, appeared on media talk shows and made presentations to various organizations. There was no time to do scholarly research. During the summer I directed the Revlon Summer Program and collected the data to submit the Annual Report to the Revlon Foundation. We brought thirty students to spend one week on campus so they could get an idea what it would be like to attend ASU. The program was very well received.

As we approached the 1982-1983 academic year, I told Dr. Boggs I could not continue with the Revlon Project because I was falling behind in research. He indicated that perhaps not continuing with the Revlon Project would be just as bad as not doing research because the project was important for the department, the college, and the university. I was disappointed, but not surprised, that my former professor and advisor was not looking out for my best interests. The grant for the following summer was increased to $40,838. Roger Shelley, the President of the Revlon Foundation, insisted that I direct the project. The College of Business also had a new Dean. William Seidman came from Wall Street and had no administrative experience in a university setting. The faculty was apprehensive about his lack of academic experience.

I met with Dean Seidman to brief him about the Revlon Project. Before I could begin, he told me he did not think I was qualified to teach at a university! I smiled at him and told him we must be even, because the word on campus was that he was not qualified to be Dean, so we should just plod forward and do our best. At the end of the briefing I told him about the need to hire a director for the program, because I could not handle the program, my teaching assignment, the expected community service, and the research requirement. He said he would look into it.

Despite the many requests I made to be released from the project, I was not allowed to withdraw. Repeated promises were made about giving me released time and providing a research assistant; all promises were broken. Instead I was given a full teaching load with a new class preparation. I was familiar with the game. When I was in private practice, I had counseled a few ASU faculty who were having similar problems. I felt for them because they did not have many options should they not get tenure. I was fortunate that I could go back to practice law, something I knew I would enjoy. I was successful in getting Dr. Christine Wilkinson and Bea Meza, who worked recruiting students for the University, to provide some assistance with the Revlon Project. The HBSA students had become an integral part of the program. They assisted with high-school visitations. I hired some of them to work during the summer when the students were on campus. They also were very vocal with their concerns about the program.

We had agreed to recommend a retention component to the program, so we could retain the students we had recruited to enroll in the College of Business. Dean Seidman told me he did not believe that anyone deserved special treatment. Students had to "sink or swim" on their own. He asked me to cut the $100,000 grant proposal to $85,000. Roger Shelley, the Revlon President, came to negotiate the new grant. A few days prior to his arrival, I called a meeting with Dean Seidman and the administrators who were involved with the Revlon Project to prepare for the meeting with Mr. Shelley. Dr. Wilkinson and Bea Meza also attended. We thought we were ready for any questions that might come up.

Imagine our surprise when Dean Seidman started the meeting telling Mr. Shelley he did not think we had a very good program, and that he would like to start off reducing the amount requested to $65,000. He had not informed any of us he would do this. Mr. Shelley indicated that he and the Revlon Foundation felt the Revlon Project was one of their most outstanding, if not the most outstanding program they funded. The purpose of the meeting that day was to finalize the 1984 program and try to resolve any questions once and for all. He said Revlon was interested in having the 1984 proposal serve as the model that was to be followed from now on so that we would not have to be renegotiating the contract every year. The Revlon Foundation was committed to the program and wanted to ensure there were sufficient funds to do what needed to be done. Mr. Shelley asked me if $85,000 was sufficient to do what needed to be done. I brought up the retention component idea and told him $85,000 was not sufficient to include that. There was an extensive discussion of the retention component. Dr. Wilkinson and Bea Meza were extremely helpful in convincing Mr. Shelley that the cultural differences of the Revlon students were of a degree to warrant special attention in the form of the proposed retention program. At the conclusion of the meeting there was an agreement that the proposal would be rewritten for approximately $100,000. At a cocktail reception at Dean Seidman's home that evening, Dean Seidman congratulated me for doing a good job.

The proposal included funds for a full-time director and for released time from one class for me to continue working on the follow-up study of the Revlon students. Again, the promises were broken. When the funding was awarded, Dean Seidman declared that no funds could be used to cover my released time; the funds had to come from the Department. Dr. Boggs said the Department did not have the funds to cover the released time. Dr. Boggs continued to have problems with my released time. He told me if I felt Dean Seidman was not supportive of minorities, if he were in my place, he would consider leaving. He also said if he were in my place, he could not go through one more year of this. Even from where he stood, he felt he could not take one more year of this.

Roger Shelley became concerned about the lack of commitment from Dean Seidman. When we spoke on the phone I convinced him that pulling the grant would be a great disservice to the Hispanic community. In fact it would be detrimental to our students. So the grant remained. Dean Seidman was not happy about my conversation with Roger Shelley.

At this time I concluded I no longer had Dr. Boggs's support and never had Dean Seidman's support. I requested a one-year leave of absence so we could all assess where the College stood in regard to my tenure. When Dr. Jack Kinsinger, the University Academic Vice-President, heard about this, he called me in to discuss my situation. He said they did not want to lose me, and offered me a position as an Assistant Vice-President. I responded that I came to ASU to teach, not to be an administrator. I also told him I had other options as a lawyer; I did not need ASU – ASU needed me more than I needed them. I gave him a copy of a letter from Senator Manuel Peña to Dean Seidman congratulating Dean Seidman on the $100,000 grant for the 1984 Revlon Program and commending me for my efforts. Senator Peña wrote, in part:

> My congratulations to your College for being the recipient of Revlon's $100,000 grant for the 1984 Hispanic Program . . . . Let me also take this opportunity to express my sincere congratulations to Cecelia [sp] Esquer. . . No doubt, without her keen interest, supportive role and as author of the proposals for the past two years, the financial grants could have been difficult to achieve. To my knowledge, no other Hispanic Professor in your college or within the universities in Arizona have singularly been responsible for authorship of proposals totaling $145,000. Cecelia [sp] is one of the most influential and highly respected professionals among Hispanic Business and political communities. You are most fortunate to have the skills, dedication and knowledge in education that a person like her possesses. She will, without a doubt, continue to bring prominence and excellence to your College and Arizona State University.[2]

Dr. Kinsinger then asked what it would take to keep me. I told him I would stay if there was a written signed contract concerning released time, committee assignments, and a research assistant. He said he could not do that, so I renewed my request for an unpaid leave of absence. I was granted the leave, never to return to teaching at ASU. Instead, I went to work for legal aid.

In my August 12, 1985 letter of resignation, I told Dr. Boggs the reason I would not return to ASU: "Unfortunately, as I indicated to you over the three years I was at ASU, I do not feel that there is sufficient

2 Letter to Dean L. William Seidman from Senator Manuel Peña, Arizona State Senate, Phoenix, Arizona, December 23, 1983.

commitment in the College of Business to the retention of minority faculty."

The Revlon Foundation continued to fund the Revlon Project for several years. It became a model for other minority recruitment programs at ASU and other colleges and universities. To this day, I come across individuals who participated in the Revlon Summer Program. Many are serving in high-level positions in the public and private sectors. They tell me the Program was instrumental in helping them realize their potential.

Despite the hardships I endured, I enjoyed teaching, the contact with the students, and working with many dedicated professors and student services personnel across campus. Another project I worked on at ASU was the development of the first Hispanic Convocation.

First ASU Hispanic Convocation

The idea for a Hispanic Convocation came from a trip to the University of Southern California (USC) by some HBSA students, and a few faculty members who attended the ASU-USC football game. They went to the traditional tailgater where Hispanics from both universities gathered. The USC people were telling them about the USC Hispanic Convocation and invited them to attend the upcoming Convocation the next spring. The invitation was accepted. When they returned from the Convocation, they decided to explore the possibility of having one at ASU.

The HBSA students asked Dr. Louis Olivas, one of my colleagues, to be the faculty sponsor of the group. He suggested they ask me because he did not have time. I had learned the HBSA students were pretty dependable and generally followed through with their commitments. I agreed to be their sponsor on the condition that I would be an advisor and they would do the work.

At our first planning meeting the suggestion was made to hold a potluck and invite the graduates and their families. I asked "Do you intend this to become a tradition at ASU or a one-time event?" I had to convince them they needed a strategy that would institutionalize the convocation. ASU President Russell Nelson would be very willing to support their efforts, but they had to have a workable plan to present to him. I also told them they would have to bring in other Hispanic organizations if they expected this to be a university-wide event.

As we discussed the framework for the convocation, it was obvious

HBSA did not have the resources to carry it out. I convinced them to make an appointment with Dr. Nelson, present their plan, and ask him to get a commitment from each of the academic deans in the various colleges to pledge monetary or in-kind support. The students did not understand why Dr. Nelson would be interested. When I reminded them that ASU did not have a very good reputation for serving Hispanics, they agreed they would be well received. One of the students volunteered to call Dr. Nelson and asked if I was going to the meeting with them. I told them I would not be going because it was a student project. Dr. Nelson needed to see they were committed and capable of carrying out this endeavor. Their meeting with Dr. Nelson was very successful. He not only said he would get the Deans to cooperate, he also committed to participate in the convocation.

Now the students had to get the other Hispanic organizations involved. They were uneasy about approaching the MEChA leadership. Many of the HBSA members thought MEChA was too radical. However, one of the HBSA members was friends with the MEChA president and offered to approach them. To everyone's surprise, every Hispanic student organization agreed to participate. President Nelson was successful in getting the Deans to provide support for the convocation. The first ASU Hispanic Convocation was held on May 12, 1984 in the Town of Guadalupe. Dr. Nelson led the procession. The thirty-four graduates who participated were joined by family members, anywhere from four to ten relatives per graduate. In many instances this was the first-ever college graduate in their family. The student convocation committee was very proud of the results and committed to continue this new tradition. Today there is a fall and a spring convocation, with more than 200 graduates participating each semester. In May 2009 the convocation was held at the Phoenix Convention Center to accommodate the thousands of graduates, families and guests.[3]

The Maricopa County Community Colleges, through the Arizona Association of Chicano Educators (AAChE), began their own Hispanic convocation. My husband, Elías Esquer, was the AAChE president and instrumental in the establishment of this convocation to honor community college graduates. At ASU the Native American and African American students began their own convocations. It was an honor to have been the faculty advisor to that group of young Hispanic leaders who began such a successful tradition.

---

3 http://www.asu.edu/vppa/hispanicconvocation/about.html

Top l to r: Dr. Louis Aranda, Dr. Cecilia D. Esquer, Regent Edith Auslander; ASU President Russell led procession, First Hispanic Convocation – Arizona State University, Guadalupe, Arizona. 1984

Bottom: ASU Hispanic Convocation 2005, Arizona State University, May 20, 2005

The A.S.U. Convocation Committee
cordially invites you to the

First Annual Hispanic Convocation
of
Arizona State University
Saturday, May 12, 1984
at five in the afternoon at
"El Tianguis" (The Mercado)
9201 South Avenida Del Yaqui
Guadalupe, Arizona
Dinner 6:00 p.m.

R.S.V.P.
April 20, 1984

Top: Invitation to
the First Hispanic
Convocation – Arizona
State University,
Guadalupe, Arizona.
1984

Bottom: ASU Students
– Revlon Project,
December 18, 1982,
Tempe, Arizona

REVLON PROJECT REUNION
Class of '82
December 18, 1982

Top: José Ronstadt, Dr. César Chávez, Dr. Lattie Coor, ASU President, Andrea Esquer (Master of Arts), ASU Hispanic Convocation 1991

Bottom: Hon. Peterson Zah – Inauguration, Navajo Nation, Window Rock, Arizona, January 11, 1983. Photo courtesy of Hon. Peterson Zah

The Navajo Nation
requests the honor of your presence
and participation in the Inauguration of

PETERSON ZAH

as Chairman of the Navajo Tribal Council

EDWARD T. BEGAY

as Vice-Chairman of the Navajo Tribal Council
and

THE NAVAJO TRIBAL COUNCIL

on

the morning of Tuesday, the Eleventh of January,
Nineteen hundred and Eighty-three
at Eleven O'Clock
in
Window Rock, Arizona

Invitation to Inauguration

⁓ 16 ⁓

LOS AMIGOS DE TEMPE

Pioneer families from the Barrios of Tempe

ONE of our most rewarding and enjoyable activities was becoming part of a group called Los Amigos de Tempe. They were a group of old-time friends, many who knew each other since childhood, others who met in grammar school, and some who met at Tempe High School, including Elías T. Esquer. I was impressed with the strong bonds between these individuals, bonds that developed because many lived in the old barrios of Tempe, where families knew each other for several generations.

Many of these families had been living in Tempe since the 1870s and had settled around the "A" Mountain in a community they named San Pablo. "In the 1950s, a rapidly expanding Arizona State University wanted the land that housed Tempe's distinct Mexican-American neighborhoods."[1] The City of Tempe also took some of the properties to develop downtown Tempe. Because the families refused to sell their property, the University resorted to the power of eminent domain to acquire most of the properties in San Pablo, where the university built dormitories, Sun Devil Stadium and other facilities needed to sustain the rapid growth of the University.[2] The barrios were destroyed and the families were scattered, some settling in West Tempe and others going to different places in Maricopa County.

Reuniting the Families from the Old Barrios

In early 1982, three of Elías's high school classmates decided to try to reunite the families from the barrios of Tempe. At the time, Clara Yutze Urbano was living in California, Irene Gómez Hormell was living in Florida, and Rachel Burgos Arroyo lived in Tempe. Rachel Arroyo was our chair. With the help of our small group, she managed to coordinate the first reunion of the barrios held at the Mesa Holiday Inn in 1983.

---

1 Scott Solliday and Chris Marin, "Tempe's Hispanic Heritage, Arizona Stories," Arizona Public Broadcast Station, http://www.azpbs.org/arizonastories/seasontwo/hispanicheritage.htm
2 Ibid.

We expected 250 to 300 people, but word got around quickly, and we wound up with more than 700 people in attendance. "Our Amigos danced between the tables, on the dance floor, couples danced anywhere they could find an opening. The music was fantastic . . . People shed tears of happiness while greeting old friends. There was a lot of hugging, kissing and remembering old times."[3] The event was so successful that we decided to hold the reunion every three years. By the next reunion, Clara and Irene had moved back to Tempe and lent their energy and spirit to this incredibly touching and successful event. Through the dinner-dances held every two or three years, we were able to reconnect many of the families from the original barrios in Tempe. We also asked the families to bring their photos and stories to share. These were displayed at each reunion. The contributions kept growing until we did not know what to do with all the materials.

The Tempe Tardeada is Born

The Tempe Historical Museum invited some of Los Amigos to join a Hispanic Advisory Committee. From this came the Barrios Exhibit, the first time the Tempe Historical Museum included in its programs some of the Hispanic contributions to the City of Tempe. Joe Soto, a local artist and barrio resident, added to the exhibit by showing his paintings depicting the barrios as they existed in the late 1940s. The reunions of the families from the barrios evolved into the annual event called the Tempe Tardeada that is sponsored by the City of Tempe. Councilmen Ben Arredondo and Dennis Cahill were instrumental in garnering the votes needed to approve this event. The Tardeada provided the badly needed resources to include the greater community in celebrating our Hispanic culture. Clara Yutze Urbano, Rachel Burgos Arroyo, and Irene Gomez Hormell were deeply involved in each activity. The mission of the Tempe Tardeada is "To identify and recognize the Hispanic historical roots of Tempe and educate the community with a celebration of the Hispanic culture."[4]

Since the first Tardeada in 1999, the Tempe Historical Museum has opened its doors to the public on the day of this event, and displays the family albums created through a project sponsored by the Museum.

---

3   Clara Yutze Urbano, The Heritage of the Tempe Barrios, City Lights, City of Tempe Office of Volunteer Services, June/July/August 1993, Issue 2.

4   http://www.tempe.gov/Tardeada/advisory.htm

Today, the Tempe Tardeada attracts more than 12,000 attendees.[5] I feel privileged to be part of this special group of friends who have enjoyed such close bonds since childhood. Although we do not hold the reunions anymore, our group still gets together at the annual Tardeada festival and to celebrate holidays, birthdays, or just our friendship.

Tempe Historical Museum
Hispanic Oral History Program

Los Amigos had an impact on the work of the Tempe Historical Museum. The three Amigas, Clara, Irene, and Rachel, at the urging of Scott Solliday and John Akers, former Tempe Historical Museum employees, recruited volunteers and began compiling oral histories to further document the Hispanic contributions to the City of Tempe. The Tempe Historical Society had started an oral history program more than 30 years ago, but few if any Hispanics or other minorities were included. The Hispanic oral history program expanded to include a Hispanic family album project. Many Hispanic families brought their photos and memories to the workshops offered by the Museum and created their own family album. The family album project was so successful that other community groups began their own.

Lunch with a Legend

In 2004, I inadvertently became involved with the Museum. As Elías and I went out the door for a short trip to Tucson, Arizona, I picked up the day's mail, which included a newsletter from the Museum. As I took the mail inside, I noticed an article "Lunch with a Legend," a Tempe Historical Society fund-raising event in which attendees would sit at a table and have lunch with a "legend," someone who had played a role in Tempe's history. When I read the list of the "legends" I noticed there were no Hispanics on the list and, from what I could tell, only one minority. I was furious. I made Elías wait while I sent an email to the Council expressing my objections. Then we left for our three-day trip.

When we returned I had many voicemails, all having to do with my email to the Council. I returned a call from Virginia Tinsley, a member of the Society. Apparently Will Manley, the City Manager, decided to ask the Tempe Historical Society to cancel the fundraiser. All I wanted to do was to raise the issue of exclusion and demanded a more diverse

5 http://www.tempe.gov/tardeada/tardeadabooth.pdf

group of "legends." I told Virginia there were many Hispanics who had been in Tempe much longer than some of the "legends" on the list. She said they did not include Hispanics because they did not know anyone in the Hispanic community who fit their criteria. Mrs. Tinsley had been a member of the Tempe Union High School Board for many years and was a longtime Tempe resident.

I called Will Manley to ask why they had canceled the luncheon. He thought that is what I wanted. He was very relieved when I told him all I wanted was a more diverse participation. Everyone was pleased with the outcome. Hispanics and other minorities were asked to participate. As it turned out, the luncheon had a bigger attendance and raised more money than previous years' luncheons.

The Tempe Historical Museum's New Interpretive Framework

Dr. Amy Douglass, the Museum Director, asked to meet with me to make sure I understood the Society was an independent group that raised funds to support the Museum. She thanked me for raising the issue. Dr. Douglass became the Director of the Tempe Historical Museum in 1988. Perhaps the success of the Hispanic Advisory Committee efforts prompted the Museum Board to revise its priorities. One of the board's new priorities was to present a more complete history of Tempe. The museum adopted an interpretive framework that presents ". . . four aspects of Tempe as a 'desert' Southwest urban community."[6]

- Surviving in the desert -- looks at how Tempe residents interact with and affect the environment
- Building our community -- tells the more traditional story of how Tempe was founded and developed
- College town - addresses how Arizona State University affected and was influenced by the city and vice versa
- Living together - analyzes the city's different communities and how they interact

"We want to make history more accessible so we can connect with it," Douglass said. "We want people to be able to identify with the stories."[7]

The new interpretive framework prompted the Museum Board to

---

6 Elisabeth Arriero, "New name, themes for Tempe History Museum," The Arizona Republic, August 12, 2009. http://www.azcentral.com/news/articles/2009/08/12/20090812tr-museum0812.html

7 Ibid.

change the name of the Tempe Historical Museum to the Tempe History Museum. The new name symbolized the change in the Museum's direction. We wanted to "... show a diverse story," not just "... showing a lot of objects without the context of a story."[8] In December 2000, the National Endowment for the Humanities awarded the Tempe History Museum a grant that provided a course to assist the staff in developing ways to present history, an effort " . . . which took us the better part of 2001 to implement."[9]

As a result, new projects and activities were launched. The City of Tempe is one of the few Arizona cities that has a paid holiday in honor of César Chávez. One of the first exhibits developed was one honoring the farm workers' organizer, which opened the week of the César Chávez holiday. The opening included a panel of individuals who had been active in the farm workers' movement.

James Burns, the Museum Curator, formed an Oral History Advisory Committee. I accepted his invitation to become a member of the committee, in part because of the bedlam I created over the Society's luncheon. New efforts were undertaken in expanding the scope of the museum. The Museum partnered with two other organizations, 1in10 and Q Speak Theater, to develop an oral history of the gay community titled: "All of Us: Documenting Lesbian, Gay, Bisexual and Transgender History in the Valley of the Sun." James Burns ". . . trained youth and community members to do oral history interviews and they went out and conducted 30 interviews."[10] A visiting playwright was added who "used stories from the oral histories and created dramatizations that resulted in a series of performances."[11] This group also started an album project.

At the urging of the African American community, the museum now has an African American Advisory committee that works with Curator Burns to collect oral histories of Tempe's African American community. A special exhibit, "A Proud Journey Home: Cambodian, Laotian and Vietnamese Communities in Arizona," was created through the joint efforts of the Tempe Historical Museum with Arizona State University, with partial funding from the Arizona Humanities Council. An exhibit advisory committee that included representatives from the three Asian

8   Ibid.
9   Dr. Amy Douglass, August 17, 2009.
10 James Burns, August 17, 2009.
11 Ibid.

communities featured in the exhibit participated in the preparation and presentation of this successful exhibit.[12]

Another important exhibit was developed with the assistance of a Muslim Advisory Committee. The exhibit, entitled "Jewel in the Desert: Getting Acquainted with our Muslim Neighbors . . . exhibited at City Hall from October 2008 through April of 2009."[13] Dan Miller, the Museum's Exhibit Coordinator led these efforts.

We are proud of our involvement in increasing the awareness of the positive contributions of the families from the barrios of Tempe and congratulate Dr. Douglass, her staff, and the City of Tempe for supporting these successful events.

---

12 "A Proud Journey Home, Cambodian, Laotian and Vietnamese Communities in Arizona, Timelines, http://www.tempe.gov/museum/Newsletters/timelines%20July05%20COLOR.pdf

13 Dr. Amy Douglass, August 17, 2009.

Proclamation

WHEREAS, The City of Tempe is blessed with a rich and diverse heritage, as demonstrated by the many Tempeans who were born and raised in the barrios of San Pablo.

WHEREAS, These residents played a pivotal role throughout our history in the growth and prosperity of Tempe.

WHEREAS, In a desire to maintain their friendships, fellowships and place in the history of our City, many of these residents formed "Amigos de Tempe."

WHEREAS, The "Amigos de Tempe" were instrumental in founding the annual "Tempe Tardeada," which celebrates our community's Hispanic heritage and maintains the friendship and fellowship of our founding residents.

WHEREAS, The Tempe City Council voted to formalize this annual celebration to assure its place in Tempe culture and history with the formation of the Tempe Tardeada Advisory Board, which is comprised of many of the original members of "Amigos de Tempe;" and

WHEREAS, On the eve of this first Tardeada created under the new Advisory Board, it is appropriate to acknowledge the roots of this celebration, the roots of our community and the efforts of those residents who have worked to remind us of this rich heritage.

Now, therefore, I Hugh Hallman, Mayor of the City of Tempe, Arizona do hereby declare:

October 6, 2006
as
Dia de San Pablo
in Tempe, Arizona

IN WITNESS WHEREOF, I hereunto set my hand this 6th Day of October, Two Thousand and Six

_____
Mayor

🛉 City of Tempe

Above: Tardeada Proclamation, Tempe, Arizona, October 6, 2006

Top: Dedication
– Clara Urbano
Boat – Tempe Town
Lake, Los Amigos
de Tempe, Tempe,
Arizona

Middle and
Bottom: Los Amigos
de Tempe, Tempe,
Arizona

Top: Los Amigos de Tempe, 3rd Reunion, at the Centennial Hall, August 12, 1989, Mesa, Arizona

Bottom: Musicians - Tempe Tardeada, Tempe, Arizona

17

ARIZONA LEGAL SERVICES EXPERIENCE

Arizona Statewide Legal Services Project

WHEN word got out that I had left ASU, I received a call from one of the legal aid program directors, asking if I would apply to become the Director of the Arizona Statewide Legal Services Project. It had been several years since I completed my term on the national Legal Services Corporation Board, so I did not have a conflict of interest and was free to work for a legal services program. I applied, went through the interview process, and was hired. I looked forward to working with the Arizona legal services program directors.

The Arizona Statewide Legal Services Project (Statewide) was a support center serving the seven Arizona legal aid programs. The focus of Statewide was on organizing and presenting training programs, developing a desk manual for legal services attorneys and publishing a statewide newsletter. A yearly survey of employees in Arizona legal services programs was conducted to determine the training needs of the different staff: attorneys, paralegals, support staff, project directors, and supervisors. Training was provided in the most needed areas: generally trial advocacy, support staff, farm worker issues, tribal court advocacy, and substantive training on family law, the Indian Child Welfare Act (ICWA), and on government benefits including the Arizona Health Care Cost Containment System (AHCCCS). Other areas were in administrative law, employment law, housing, and consumer law. Most of the trainers came from the local programs.

There were some regional training programs that usually involved Arizona, Colorado, and New Mexico. John Vail, Project Director for the New Mexico Statewide program, and I worked closely on the Indian law programs. Indian law became a priority for all of the directors in the region, because there had not been too many offerings in the Indian law area in recent years.

I hired Lawanna Durbin for the Training Coordinator position. She turned out to be an excellent choice. She was responsive to the local programs, knew how to plan and organize training events, and carried them out smoothly. A third-year law student, Anita Estupinian, became the newsletter editor.

The IOLTA Program

My first meeting with the Board of Directors turned out to be quite interesting. I had been on board about two weeks. I was pretty surprised when they asked me for Statewide's mission statement and action plan. I reminded them I had just arrived and would get to that with their advice and consent. However, I asked them: "What role are we going to play in securing funding for our programs from the new Arizona State Bar Interest on Lawyers Trust Accounts (IOLTA) program. A couple responded they did not want to waste their time on that, because they did not expect IOLTA to generate a lot of money .[1]

My experience on the national Legal Services Corporation Board told me they could be very wrong. I told them we needed to be involved from the very beginning because there was a possibility IOLTA could generate a lot of money. Until we knew, we should be directly involved. The directors reluctantly agreed and asked me to represent the legal services programs at the IOLTA meetings. One or two of the directors also attended. As it turned out, IOLTA generated about one million dollars in its first year. The next challenge was convincing the IOLTA committee to allocate a fair share to Arizona's legal aid programs.

This proved to be difficult because some of the State Bar committee members thought the monies should be used to establish legal aid programs that would compete with the existing programs. Many of these attorneys represented entities that had been sued by a legal aid program. They thought legal aid programs should be providing legal services for such things as divorces, food stamps, welfare program issues, and landlord-tenant matters. They did not think the legal aid programs should be filing the large class-action lawsuits or suing State and Federal governments. During one of their early meetings the committee went into executive session to discuss the alternatives. Apparently, the discussion got pretty heated. One of the committee

1 IOLTA "... is a unique and innovative way to increase access to justice for individuals and families living in poverty and to improve our justice system. Without taxing the public, and at no cost to lawyers or their clients, interest from lawyer trust accounts is pooled to provide civil legal aid to the poor and support improvements to the justice system. http://www.iolta.org/grants/

members, a former State Bar President said that "over [his] dead body" would any money go to the legal aid programs, and especially not to the Indian programs. Things seemed pretty dismal at this point. What happened next shows the commitment, dedication and political savvy of the legal aid attorneys.

We concluded the private practitioners did not understand what it took to run a legal aid program, and told them there were not enough funds to set up competing programs. They also were not very familiar with the day-to-day work of the legal aid attorneys, paralegals, and support staff or the incredible training they received to make them so effective for their clients. We invited the committee to visit the programs across the state and to allow us to make presentations on the mission and the work of the programs. To their credit, they accepted.

This delayed the distribution of the IOLTA funds for a while, but we thought this needed to be done. The committee members took their work seriously and made the time to hear us out. Not only did we make group presentations, but we also met one-on-one with the members of the committee. It quickly became clear to the committee members that the IOLTA funds were not sufficient to create new programs or to provide the training needed to be effective advocates. The result? More than 90% of the first year IOLTA funds went to the legal aid programs, including funding for the Indian and migrant programs. We also learned from them.

Legal aid programs were initially set up to serve the urban poor, despite the fact that the rural populations would not have access to their services. We agreed to explore ways of providing legal services to the rural populations. This resulted in new, innovative programs that involved both the legal aid programs and private practitioners, to provide legal services to a larger segment of the poor populations. There was increased respect and collegiality between the two groups. Some of the committee members even became strong advocates for the legal aid programs, which helped protect the funding from Congress.

The board members had high praise for my insistence that we become involved from the very beginning.[2] This took the better part of a year for me, but the core work of Statewide continued at an unprecedented level, thanks to our great staff. During my second year

2 "Every state in the U.S. operates an IOLTA program. Between 1991 and 2003, IOLTA generated more than $1.5 billion nationwide to ensure justice for our country's most vulnerable residents." http://www.iolta.org/grants/

with the program we devoted time to reviewing the mission and goals of the program, especially in setting priorities for the types of training to be conducted.

1985 and 1986 were exciting, productive, and rewarding years. My mother became quite ill mid-year, so my time and attention was pretty split. She died from cancer in November 1985. I finally decided that I needed to spend some time at home, so I resigned my position in 1986. But this would not be the end of my involvement with legal aid.

Four Rivers Indian Legal Services

In May 1987 I received a call from Eric Dahlstrom, the Director of Four Rivers Indian Legal Services (Four Rivers or FRILS), a legal aid program located in the Gila River Indian Community, located approximately 34 miles south of Tempe. Eric told me they were having a tough time filling an attorney position and wondered if I would be interested in working with them, even for a brief period. I told him I was waiting to hear from a potential employer, but that I would be available for the next three months and would be happy to help out. So, with some excitement and trepidation, I went to work for an Indian legal aid program. Although I had taken an Indian law class during law school, I had never practiced in the area; however, I looked forward to this learning experience. I enjoyed this so much that I soon made a two-year commitment to the program.

I was well received by the staff, but a little overwhelmed by the case load turned over to me. Fortunately, many of the cases dealt with consumer law issues. I was pretty familiar with this area. I suspect there is a standard "welcome to Indian Country" initiation for new staff attorneys at Four Rivers. I was assigned to do case intake during my first week. There is always a steady stream of people seeking legal advice. The case intake process involves gathering as much information from the potential client and presenting the requests for legal representation at a weekly Friday staffing meeting.

I looked forward to presenting my cases. As I presented each case, I was continually interrupted with questions like:

Q. "Is this person Indian?"
A. "Well, yes."
Q. "Is this person a tribal member?"
A. "Not sure."

Q. "Does this person live on the reservation?"

A. I could generally answer this question.

If the case involved a contract:

Q. "Was the contract signed on or off the reservation?"

A. "Not sure."

Q. "Is the other party Indian?"

A. Usually no.

If the case involved an auto accident:

Q. "Did this take place on or off the reservation?"

A. "Not positive."

And so on. The answers to these questions are vital to know whether the matter belongs in Tribal, State, or Federal Court. I had my work cut out for me. I needed to gather the missing information from each individual. Unfortunately, in 1987 tribal members did not have telephones in their homes; several lived in remote areas of the reservation. I had no choice but to write a letter asking them to call me (from the pay phone at the grocery store) or to come to the office. Not everyone responded. I was reassured by the staff I was not the only new attorney who learned about jurisdiction in this manner.

They were right. Potential clients would come to Four Rivers after being served with legal papers. Some of the attorneys in the large, prestigious law firms were not too familiar with service on the reservation. The mailing address made it more difficult to spot the problem because the address was usually to a P.O. Box in Laveen, Arizona, or a street address in Scottsdale, Arizona. Attorneys new to Arizona did not recognize the fact that these addresses were on tribal lands. At that time, service of process would only be valid if the documents were first presented to the Tribal Court, which would stamp the documents. Imagine my joy when calling the attorney to say we were filing a Motion to Quash because the attorney did not follow the correct service of process procedure. I could feel the embarrassment on the other end. It is very expensive to send a process server to the reservation.

Another fact unique to Indian Country: Most tribal courts do not require that an individual be an attorney to represent someone in tribal court. In fact, some tribal courts do not allow attorneys to appear in civil matters. The cases in tribal court from our program were handled by our tribal court advocates. The attorneys provided some legal research and feedback on the pleadings and legal memoranda. The cases in

State or Federal courts were handled by the attorneys. I soon learned that the Tribal Court Advocates were excellent litigators. They also were able to quickly gain the trust and confidence of the client because of shared cultural values. Most tribal court judges were not attorneys, but they became skilled from the training programs offered to tribal court judges. Finally, tribal courts are courts of limited jurisdiction dealing with misdemeanors in criminal matters. However, they have broad jurisdiction in civil cases.

In addition to consumer issues, the program provided representation on Social Security Disability matters and Indian health issues, which generally dealt with the denial of payment for emergency medical services provided to indigent Native Americans. No one wanted to be responsible for the costs involved: the State would say the BIA or the Federal government was responsible, while the BIA would say the State was responsible because Indians are residents of the State. This resulted in the providers billing the patient. When the bill remained unpaid, they would turn it over for collection, despite the fact they knew the patient was indigent. Another area of representation involved the denial of Public Benefits, including Aid to Families with Dependent Children (AFDC), unemployment compensation and food stamps. School issues were also part of our caseloads: fraudulent school loans, discipline, special education placement, and the right to attend school outside of the district of residency. Indian probate and Indian land leases provided interesting experiences.

Again I was impressed with the skill and dedication of each legal worker. Training was one of the great successes in the legal aid movement. When the Reagan Administration came into power, training support centers and specialized training in Indian and migrant law were the first to be eliminated or severely cut back. The defunding of Indian law training had an immediate impact in Indian Country. The administration of justice suffered greatly when tribal court advocates or judges had no legal training.

I enjoyed working in this new environment and the fact that I was able to get some real litigation experience. I appreciate the warm treatment by my fellow staffers and the community at large. My tenure at Four Rivers ended at the end of my second year.

During the first six months at Four Rivers, I had received a call from a friend in Danny Ortega's law firm. Danny wanted to know if I was interested in joining the firm. Ortega & Moreno was an outstanding law firm providing representation in areas of great interest to me. I told her I had made a two-year commitment to the program and would be happy to visit with Danny at the end of two years.

Leaving Indian Country

As the two-year period was coming to an end, Danny called to ask if I was still interested in discussing possibilities of working with Ortega & Moreno. I agreed to meet with him and his partner, Mario Moreno. Their main concern about me was the frequency with which I changed jobs. I explained this had to do with being free to be at home when needed, but that my children were now old enough, so I could now make a five-year commitment to the firm. They were not willing to make that commitment to me. I think Danny and Mario were a little apprehensive about my "activist" past and were not sure I would be a good fit for the firm. They wanted to see how we did the first year before making a longer commitment. After a lengthy discussion, I accepted their offer to join the firm.

Arizona Statewide Legal Services Project staff member Barbara Benavides (left) and Project Director Cecilia Esquer (center) welcome new employee Anita Estupinan to the Project's offices located at the Phoenix Indian Center, 1337 North 1st Street.

Top: Barbara Benavídez, Cecilia D. Esquer, Anita Estupinian, Phoenix, Arizona, 1985

Bottom: Dave Williams, Arizona State Bar, Cecilia D. Esquer, Rosalind McClanahan, Administrative Assistant, DNA Legal Services, David Frank, Litigation Director, DNA Legal Services. Navajo Nation, Window Rock, Arizona, c1986

Top: Andrea and Marcos Esquer, Arizona Legal Services Conference, Gold Canyon, Arizona, 1985

Middle: Front Row – Gail Apodaca, Cecilia D. Esquer, Lucy Hoyema; Back Row – Angie Carlos, Diana, Sherry Harvier, Becky Webb

Bottom: Jon Vail, Cecilia D. Esquer Albuquerque, New Mexico, February 24, 1985

18

ORTEGA & MORENO, P.C.

I joined the firm of Ortega & Moreno, PC, on August 1, 1988. It was a six-attorney law firm that provided legal representation in the areas of business, commercial litigation, corporations (non-profit and for profit), government agency representation, domestic relations, personal injury, and other civil matters. The firm had contracts to provide representation to three school districts and to more than five non-profit corporations. I looked forward to getting experience in these two areas.

For the first time, I did not have to worry about the second-class treatment issue. The firm was unique because all of the staff was bilingual. Danny Ortega, the senior partner, felt this created an obligation to provide representation to clients who did not speak English. To make our services more affordable, the firm offered a reduced hourly rate to Spanish-speaking clients for representation in family law matters. There were very few firms that offered representation in family law matters, much less in a bilingual setting. We were also expected to provide some pro bono representation. My agreement with Danny and Mario was that I would take a lower salary, on the condition that I could limit the number of cases assigned to me, and that I would have a voice in what cases were assigned to me. I don't think Danny anticipated I would strictly hold him to these terms.

One of the reasons I was interested in working at Ortega & Moreno was to develop my litigation skills. Danny had a reputation for being a successful litigation attorney. I was not disappointed. I learned a lot from Danny in the short time I was with the firm. My husband and I had met Danny when he was a senior in high school. I was teaching at McClintock High School then, so I was a few years older than Danny. Danny's mother made sure he was polite and respectful to women, especially older women. I was treated very well. I don't think Danny realized how little litigation experience I had and how serious I was about learning from him.

Initially, I think he got a big kick out of our new relationship. He was the teacher and mentor. I often went to him for advice when I had a court hearing or came across something I had never done. At first, I think he thought I was kidding, but he soon learned I was very serious and really needed his help. On the other hand, he also learned I was serious about limiting the number of cases I would accept.

Ortega & Moreno was a well-known law firm and had many requests for legal representation. Sometimes, he could not find a lawyer for a case, so he would try to assign the case to me. Imagine his chagrin when I would tell him I could not accept the case. To this day, I am proud of the agreement I worked out with Danny, and that I stood by our agreement. As it was, I was working late hours and many weekends on the cases I already had.

I thrived in this fast-paced challenging environment. I was on a fast track doing things I had never done before. I worked with school district administrators providing legal advice. I soon learned that, like other elected officials, school board members and school administrators did not want to be named-defendants in lawsuits. They worked hard to settle issues before they went to court, issues that in some instances lacked merit. I could not convince them that winning a lawsuit of this type could deter others from filing frivolous claims.

Working with Non-Profits

I enjoyed working with the various non-profits who contracted with Ortega & Moreno for legal services. In one instance, I conducted a legal check-up on one non-profit and found that some of their procedures were not in compliance with state or federal law, something that could affect their funding. I worked with the administration to make the appropriate corrections and assisted in the training on the revised procedures.

Providing legal services to a non-profit corporation is very different from serving on the board of directors, something I had done for quite some time. There are many details not shared with board members. It was satisfying to know that I had helped to get the non-profit on the right track and to see firsthand the deep commitment most employees had to serving the community.

Recall Election Case

One of the most challenging cases I handled was representing Rubén

Hernández, the Mayor of the Town of Guadalupe, when there was an effort to recall him from office. They wanted to recall the Mayor because he used the "F" word in one Council meeting. They also added a litany of charges concerning financial mismanagement. Mayor Hernández specifically asked that I be his attorney. When I told him I had no experience in handling this type of case, he responded: "It's time you learned. If you won't take my case, then I will just resign."

Danny Ortega sat in on this conference and assured me he would be there to help me. Danny had extensive experience in election law. I reluctantly accepted and was grateful that Danny assigned a paralegal to assist me in this matter. These matters move very rapidly because it involved petitions for injunctive relief. If we were successful in getting the court to grant our petition for a temporary restraining order, we would have to immediately prepare for a hearing to request a permanent injunction to stop the recall attempt. Everything would take place in about 90 days or less. The hearing on the petition for a permanent injunction was in effect a trial where we had to present witnesses and evidence to prove to the court there was no merit to the recall attempt. If successful, the court would grant a permanent injunction that would end the recall effort.

We were successful in getting the court to issue a temporary restraining order. We had to immediately prepare for trial. It turns out that many judges love to handle cases involving political issues. In this case, Judge Michael Dann, the Presiding Judge, decided he would hear the case. Judge Paul Katz, who issued the temporary restraining order, was disappointed when he was replaced. We had about 60 days to gather our evidence. This involved getting copies of the recall petitions, checking them for invalid entries, finding witnesses who would be willing to testify at the hearing, and preparing a legal memorandum outlining our case. We worked many late hours and on weekends. We were confident we could prove that some of the signers were not registered voters and that some of the signatures could not be counted because they were illegible. Most importantly, entire petitions should be invalidated because they did not comply with State law.

Arizona law requires the person who signs the affidavit as the circulator of the petition actually circulated that petition. The circulator must affirm that each person who signed that petition personally signed in front of him. In fact, the petitions had been left at various places in the community, including the grocery store and the community action program reception counter. When the petitions were gathered, various individuals signed as the circulator, despite the fact they had not actually circulated some of the petitions they signed as circulator. Arizona law states that this action would invalidate the entire petition. In addition, there were criminal penalties for violating this law. This alone would invalidate enough signatures to bring the number of valid signatures below the required number to go forward with the recall.

Since we did not know how Judge Dann would rule on these issues, I felt we needed to make sure we had an alternative argument. Virginia Herrera-Gonzales, the paralegal working with me – now a practicing attorney, brought in a county elections manual and pointed to the provision in the manual that said the only offices subject to recall were elective offices. We found this specific requirement in the Arizona Constitution. Now we had an alternative argument. In the Town of Guadalupe, as in many Arizona towns, the Mayor was not "elected" by the voters. The voters elected the council members and then the council members would meet to "select" one of them to be the Mayor.

During this time, I was at a fundraiser for a non-profit agency and was seated next to John Frank, a founding member of the law firm of Lewis & Roca, and a nationally renowned expert in constitutional law. When he asked me what interesting cases I was working on, I told him about the recall action and mentioned that we had sufficient evidence to disqualify enough signatures to stop the election, but we were not sure how the court would rule. However, I mentioned to him, we thought we had another winning argument based on the Arizona Constitution, since the Mayor of Guadalupe was not elected by the voters. He told me there was no way the Constitution had this provision, that he had filed at least 30 lawsuits in this area and knew the provision was not there. I insisted it was. He was so baffled that he told me he would pull out the Constitution when he got home and would call me if I was right.

I arrived at the office about 8:30 a.m. the next morning and found a message from John Frank, stating I had an appointment with him at his office at 10:00 a.m. He also asked me to bring the pleadings in the case. My experience when I arrived at his office is unforgettable. His secretary walked in with me and remained for instructions. He asked her to prepare a file for the case and to have David Cantelme, one of the firm's partners, come to his office immediately. When David arrived, John declared his amazement at this provision. How could he have missed this phrase all these years?

He quickly looked through my pleadings, told me they could be better, but they were adequate. Then he told David I needed a case to support my argument, and that I needed it by 11:00 a.m. because my motion was due that afternoon. David said he would get on it right away. John's secretary came in with the file. This ended our meeting. John wished me luck. All of this took place in less than 20 minutes! I left the office awestruck. When I arrived at my office, David had already faxed the case I could use to support my argument. I really appreciated John's generosity and his willingness to help a fellow lawyer. And where was Danny Ortega? He had little time to work on the case with me because he was working on two other election issue cases. Thank goodness I had Virginia, a great paralegal, working with me.[1]

At the hearing I presented our witnesses and the proof that the petitioners did not have a sufficient number of signatures for the action to go forward. Then I presented the argument that all of the petitions should be declared invalid because the petitioners were recalling the "Mayor," an office that was not subject to recall. Virginia went to the hearing with me and sat next to me so she could keep track of the issues covered and to hand me the documents I needed. I couldn't have done it without her. There were three attorneys on the other side: one representing the petitioners who wanted to recall the Mayor; one representing the Maricopa County Recorder; and one representing the Town of Guadalupe.

Who could guess how Judge Dann would rule? At the end of the hearing he declared how he would rule, and that he would issue a written opinion within the next few days. While we had presented evidence that the petitioners did not have sufficient valid signatures for the recall to proceed, he declared that he would not invalidate the petitions, because he felt the individuals who signed as the petition circulators came from a community (Guadalupe) where they lacked the education to understand the significance of an affidavit. In addition, he said the circulators would not understand that there were criminal penalties for falsely stating in the affidavit that each person personally signed in front of the circulator.

Judge Dann's comments brought loud objections from the

---

1 Virginia Herrera-Gonzales is now an attorney and served as Chief Counsel of the Civil Rights Division in the Arizona Attorney General's office while I worked there as the Chief Counsel for the Public Advocacy Division.

petitioners, who objected to the judge's claim about the lack of education. One person yelled out she had a college degree; another yelled out she was a manager where she worked. Judge Dann called for order and declared that his ruling would be that all the petitions were invalid because they did not comply with the Arizona Constitution. Several days later he issued a detailed opinion. There would be no recall.[2] Imagine the relief I felt at winning the case on the merits, but I also was perplexed and disappointed at Judge Dann's stereotypical views about a minority community. How many other judges felt this way? How did this affect their rulings in other cases?

When word of the court order got out, I received calls from various lawyers asking about the case. Some were city or town attorneys, others were representing someone who was being recalled. They used our case to convince the court that the recall actions in their respective cases could not proceed. Several recall lawsuits were dismissed in Maricopa and Pinal County.

When things settled down, I recalled something Bill Canby, my constitutional law professor, mentioned in class one day. He said there was nothing more rewarding than finding a word or a phrase in the constitution that had never been interpreted. I felt especially proud of our accomplishment, especially since Mayor Hernández was one of the individuals who had encouraged me to go to law school. He even had enough confidence in me to hire me to represent his trucking company when I was in private practice.

School Redistricting Case

Other significant cases I participated in included a lawsuit in Federal District Court against the Phoenix Union High School District in Maricopa County. The plaintiffs asked the court to order the creation of individual districts for the election of school board members. The basis for the lawsuit was to increase the chances for minority candidates to be elected. The legal team included attorneys from five law firms, including attorneys from the National Association for the Advancement of Colored People (NAACP) and the Mexican American Legal Defense and Education Fund (MALDEF), two large law firms and Ortega & Moreno. I participated more to learn how this type of case is handled. There were enough lawyers to do the legal research and writing. I got

---

2 Brent Whiting, "Guadalupe recall try blocked," The Arizona Republic, 1989 [date missing].

a firsthand look at the role of expert witnesses in this type of case and the incredible fees these experts charge. Our expert was a renowned "numbers cruncher." We were lucky to retain him before the school district had time to contact him. He had every possible statistic we would need to support our lawsuit and could provide information in a comprehensible vocabulary. I was impressed with the involvement of the attorneys from the large law firms. We were all providing our services on a pro bono basis. The school district quickly expressed an interest in settling the case without going to trial. The case settled after some serious discussions. Although single member districts were created, ironically, no minority candidate was elected at the next school board election.

The experience of working with various law firms on a case has been invaluable. Not only did it provide a great networking opportunity, but I was able to get a pretty close view of the way large law firms operate. Ortega & Moreno was very special in this regard because Danny Ortega was highly respected, not only in the minority community, but also in the larger community, for his political involvement and community service.

There were always interesting cases to work on. The down side of private practice was the fact that sometimes we had to personally call clients who were not paying their bills. Even though we had worked hard for the clients and knew we had earned the fees, it was difficult to have to speak to clients about past-due accounts.

I haven't said much about Mario Moreno, Danny's law partner at the time, because Danny was the managing partner and he ran the firm. Mario was a great resource and was always available for questions.

Big Personal Injury Cases

Since Danny Ortega was well known and respected in the community, many cases came to the firm, including personal injury cases where the injuries were severe and were worth well over half a million dollars. At my request, I did not work on any personal injury cases, but I learned a lot from just being part of the firm. Danny would brief us at our weekly staff meetings.

One of the cases dealt with a woman from Mexico, living in Arizona, who suffered severe permanent injuries when a fourteen-wheeler rear ended the pickup truck in which she was a passenger riding in the truck bed with her head against the rear gate. Instead of rendering assistance, the driver of the fourteen-wheeler was busy "cooking" his time log. He had to account for twenty-four hours he had spent with a woman who was not his wife. He was driving more hours without a rest than the law allowed. The case was probably going to go to trial, and the potential damages were around two million dollars. Danny decided to bring in outside counsel to handle this big case in federal court. Chuck Roush, a retired superior court judge who had joined a small law firm, agreed to serve as co-counsel and to be the lead attorney at trial.

The trucking company attorney made some ridiculous settlement offers, so the case was set for trial. Just before the trial began, Danny and Chuck made an offer of settlement in the amount of about two million dollars. The offer was turned down. At the end of presenting the plaintiff's case, Danny and Chuck again made a final offer not much higher than the original offer. This offer was also turned down. It was clear the trucking company was liable, but their attorney was confident he could get the jury to award a lower amount of money damages.

During his closing argument, the company's attorney stated that, if the jury found the trucking company liable, they should take into consideration the fact that this woman came from Mexico, and might be in the country illegally. In addition, he said, Mexicans have a lower standard of living and do not have access to the type of medical facilities found in the United States. So the jury should not award the amount of damages they would award an American citizen. Finally, he said the plaintiff was not used to a high standard of living since she was only a secretary. How could he not have noticed there were several minority jurors on the panel? And, how could he discount the smoking guns presented to the jury, including a memorandum from the company president telling their drivers if they were ever in a situation where their logs might come into question, they should make sure their logs showed the proper information – in other words, fix the books.

The company was aware the driver had numerous speeding citations and had a radar detector in the truck at the time of the accident, one the company had paid for. It was against the law in Arizona to have a radar detector. Finally, the attorney was disrespectful and insensitive when questioning our client, making her cry during her testimony. What a contrast to Chuck Roush, a perfect gentleman and superb litigation attorney.

The jury's verdict awarded our client $2.5 million in compensatory damages and about $7.5 million in punitive damages that, at that time was the largest award for punitive damages in Arizona for this type of case.

Insurance companies have their own insurance companies (re-insurers), so what followed was amazing. We heard something to the effect that the insurance company attorney had not informed their insurance company about the final offer of settlement. The insurance company is supposed to inform the re-insurer about any offers of settlement. When the re-insurer learned about the final offer of settlement, they told Danny and Chuck that they would work out a settlement with our client so they could proceed to dealing with their insurer, the law firm representing the company.

Even though I did not work on this case, I learned a lot about handling a big case and a little about how insurance companies operate. I was able to observe the questioning of some of the witnesses and was there for the closing arguments. Again, the paralegals were invaluable, not only in managing and organizing the documents, but in responding to the many calls from the client and her family. I clearly understood why Danny was able to attract this type of case.

Leaving the Firm

Shortly after this case, I received a call from Myrna Harrison, the President of Phoenix College, asking if I would be interested in applying for a faculty position in the Legal Studies Department. This was totally unexpected. I did not know President Harrison very well and wondered why she would call me. I told her I was nearing the end of my commitment at Ortega & Moreno. I would have to speak with Elías and then with Danny and would get back with her.

Elías immediately said I should apply. He was concerned about the many hours I spent at the office, and the fact that we could not get away for long periods of time during the summer and semester breaks. I knew I would enjoy being back in a classroom, but I was torn because I was practicing in areas of law I enjoyed and was learning so much.

Danny immediately blamed himself because he had not accepted my offer of a five-year commitment with the firm. He told me I could be a great litigation attorney and should seriously consider whether I wanted to forego this opportunity. I told him it was not a done deal because there were many applicants for faculty positions in the community college district. I then told him I would go ahead with the application to which he responded: "You know you will be offered the position." It turned out as he predicted.

Guadalupe recall try blocked

By Brent Whiting
The Arizona Republic

A Maricopa County judge on Monday blocked the attempted recall of Guadalupe Mayor Ruben Hernandez, saying the recall was "fatally flawed" because it was aimed at Hernandez's job as mayor and not at his elected post as a member of the Town Council.

B. Michael Dann, presiding judge in Superior Court, ruled that because the Guadalupe mayor is chosen by the council from among its members, recall petitions should have sought Hernandez's removal as a councilman.

"The plain reading of these documents is that recall is being sought of the 'mayor,' not of a councilman, and that the recall effort presumably would not affect his position on the council," Dann ruled.

"This likely reading could have misled petition signers who wished to retain plaintiff (Hernandez) as a council member but who favored his removal as mayor."

The judge issued his decision in an Oct. 27 lawsuit filed by Hernandez seeking to stop a recall election that had been set for mid-February. The recall was launched by Guadalupe Councilman Leonardo Lozano, who has accused Hernandez of improper conduct during council meetings.

Cecilia Esquer, a Phoenix lawyer for Hernandez, said that her client is pleased that Dann has stopped the recall and that he is gratified that the judge has upheld his position that the post of mayor is not subject to recall.

Neither Lozano nor his Phoenix lawyer, Joel Erik Thompson, could be reached for comment. Thompson had argued that the term "mayor" was merely a title for a council member.

Brent Whiting Article, Arizona Republic, October 1989

19

PHOENIX COLLEGE: THAT'S NO WAY TO START!

A Cool Reception

AFTER a screening process that included an interview before the screening committee and a mini-teaching session, I was offered the faculty position and told I would be teaching paralegal classes. There had been some department reorganization before I arrived. The paralegal program had been in the Business Department. The law enforcement program was a separate department. When I arrived the two programs had been placed in a new department, the Department of Justice and Legal Studies. Tom Thackery was the Department Chair and gave me a warm welcome. The same was not true for the other members of the department; in fact they were pretty cool and less than friendly.

One of my colleagues accused me of plagiarizing her study guides for the Introduction to Law Class. I was not told she had prepared the study guides. In fact the Legal Assisting (LAS) Program Director gave me a set of the study guides and told me I should use them and provide copies to my students. I could not understand the hostile manner in which I had been accused, so I went to the LAS Program Director. She apologized profusely for the misunderstanding. In the past these study guides had been shared in the department. She said she would explain to my colleague that she had given me the study guides.

Then she proceeded to tell me this was not really the reason for my colleague's behavior. Apparently she was unhappy I had been hired because she thought an attorney who had taught on a one-year only contract the year before should have been hired. Once I understood the unfriendly welcome, I made it a point to go out of my way to speak with my colleague. I sought her advice on how to handle certain issues in class. She had no choice but to speak with me.

The atmosphere continued to be stressful in the department. Finally, Tom Thackery, my Department Chair, told me the attorney who was not hired for the position, had filed a reverse discrimination complaint with the District, and that my colleague was helping him through the process. Tom went out of his way to make me feel welcome.

I loved Phoenix College and being back in the classroom. And, I loved the diversity of the student population. I was not going to let negative attitudes force me out. Dr. Virginia Ramos Foster, the Chair of the Foreign Languages Department, came to welcome me. She was good friends with Tom Thackery, so she had an idea what was going on. She invited me to lunch and, from then on, we became very good friends. If Virginia had not come along when she did, I don't know whether I would have continued at Phoenix College for thirteen years. We became lifelong friends – "cuatas."

Legal Assistant Program Evening Coordinator

One of my contractual duties was to be the Evening Coordinator for the Legal Assisting Program. Apparently no one else would take this job. Even though it took quite a bit of time, I thoroughly enjoyed it. I was able to meet the adjunct faculty who taught in the evening, and I was in charge of hiring and evaluating them. I met many evening students when I visited their classes. Many of these students worked in law offices and had great suggestions for making the classes more relevant for paralegals – more "hands-on" assignments was the term. In addition to being the Evening Coordinator, I served on campus committees, which brought me in touch with other faculty and administrators. I was spending many hours at Phoenix College. Often I did not get home until 9:00 p.m. One of the reasons I decided to leave private practice was the stressful nature of the work. I thought teaching at Phoenix College would involve a less stressful experience.

Justice & Legal Studies Department Chair

Apparently everyone noticed I did not mind the extra work involved. The following year, Tom announced he would not continue as Department Chair after the school year, so we had to select a new chair. I was shocked when I was asked if I would be willing to become the Department Chair. I agreed to serve on the condition that I would only be required to serve one three-year term. Of course, I soon realized this was another position no one wanted to take. It involved too much work and attending many meetings. It was a great experience for me. As a relatively new faculty member, I worked with the senior administrators and all department chairs at Phoenix College. The department chair position is probably one of the most powerful positions in the Maricopa Community Colleges, especially when it comes to hiring faculty.

Diversity Issues – Screening Committees

My husband Elías was serving as the Department Chair in the Foreign Languages Department at Mesa Community College at this time. He was a great mentor and knew how to get things done. I learned a lot from him, especially about the lack of diversity in the faculty in many departments across the district. In most instances, college presidents defer to department chairs' hiring recommendations. Many chairs were not supportive of hiring minority faculty. However, there was a lot of pressure on the District from internal and external minority organizations to diversify the faculty.

In fact one of the main reasons I was hired at Phoenix College is that the student organization, Movimiento Estudiantil Chicano de Aztlán (MEChA) had picketed the president demanding she hire more minority faculty at Phoenix College. Apparently there was a lot of press coverage on this issue. Other community organizations expressed their support of the students' demands. The biggest obstacle in the hiring process is the screening committee.

A screening committee screens the employment applications of the faculty who meet the job description qualifications. The department chair generally selects the members of the screening committee. Predictably there were few minority faculty on these committees. At the urging of minority faculty organizations, some of the presidents began to require that the screening committees include members from minority groups. And, some made the screening committee members subject to the president's approval. If the committee was not affirmative, some of the presidents would add an additional member.

Initially I was asked to serve on several screening committees. However, when the word got out that I challenged some of the committees' actions, I was not asked to sit on many faculty screening committees. However, since the college president named the members of the screening committees for administrative positions, I did get to serve on screening committees for the Phoenix College President, the Dean of Instruction, and several other senior level positions. The work of the screening committee requires a lot of time, but I felt an obligation to serve when asked.

Probably the most memorable experience was serving on the screening committee for a faculty position in the English Department during the spring 1995 semester. Even though Phoenix College was established in 1920, the Department did not have a Hispanic faculty member, despite the fact that there were many Hispanics with master's degrees in English. The committee started out amicably. However, by the time it came time to make our recommendations, we came to an impasse and actually called in President Myrna Harrison to help us find a solution, which she did. So, the first Hispanic faculty member in English was hired at Phoenix College. Although the department chair had not favored hiring a minority, he became a mentor for the new faculty member, who turned out to be a good fit in the department. I was never again asked to serve on a screening committee for the English Department.

Legal Assisting Program Changes

In 1992 I became the Director for the Legal Assisting Program because I wanted to change the direction of the program, from a "mini-law school" instructional approach to a more hands-on approach that would actually focus on the type of work common to paralegals. One of the first changes was requiring our students to become computer competent. The Legal Assisting Program had an advisory committee that welcomed the proposed change in approach. The committee members included practicing paralegals, paralegal managers, and law office managers who came from small to large law firms and the public sector. They were thrilled with this proposal and worked very hard to make specific suggestions for the various classes. In addition, I began to hire paralegals to teach some of the skills classes.

Scott Hauert became the Evening Coordinator when I became Department Chair. Scott was an adjunct faculty member from the public sector who happened to be very skilled in computer technology. In fact, he also taught a computer class for the Business Department. Scott had great ideas for expanding the role of computers in our program. When a one-year-only faculty position became available, he agreed to fill the position and left his position at the Maricopa County Attorney's office.

As luck would have it, the President announced the library was going to undergo major renovation. The Library Department Chair asked for input from the departments about any special needs they might have that could be included in the renovation. Scott and I drafted a proposal requesting a computer classroom and the relocation of the legal collection so it would be next to the new classroom. Our proposal was accepted. Scott worked with the Library Department Chair on the details for the computer classroom, including the purchasing of new computers for the classroom.

At the grand opening of the renovated library, now twice the size of the original library, the Library Department Chair pointed out the "lovely new classroom for the Justice & Legal Studies students." There were cries about "how about our department?" from other faculty members. The Librarian pointed out we were the only department that submitted a proposal. This classroom helped us tremendously with the American Bar Association (ABA), the body that approves (like certification) legal assistant programs across the country. ABA approval is vital to the success and growth of the program.

Before the initial ABA approval of the Phoenix College program in 1988, there were fewer than 300 students enrolled in the paralegal program. Linda Edwards, a member of our Department, devoted many hours to preparing the application for initial approval. The year after the program was approved by the ABA, the enrollment shot up to more than 600 students. That led to the creation of the faculty position I filled.

American Bar Association Approval Commission

When the Phoenix College program came up for review the year before, we had less than a successful visit and received conditional approval. I concluded the only way to change this quickly was to have Phoenix College involved at the national scene. The ABA Approval Commission was looking for minority members. I was appointed to what turned out to be a powerful commission. I quickly learned the ins and outs of getting programs reapproved. So when we submitted our report with all the changes we had made, and after a follow-up visit, our program was fully approved again. The Commission involved much travel time and work.

Not only did I attend Commission meetings, but commissioners were expected to participate in two site visits per year. The site visits involved legal assistant programs that were up for initial approval or re-approval. There were extensive materials to read before the site visit; a visit that generally took two to three days. It was a good investment of time. Not only did I provide service to the profession, but I was able to get national recognition for the Phoenix College program. It was one of the biggest programs in the country. The program had great resources, from state-of-the-art computers in a dedicated classroom, to a rather complete legal collection. In fact, members from the private bar often came to do legal research at the Phoenix College library.

Tribal Court Advocacy Program

After many requests from Indian legal services programs to develop a program for tribal court advocates, I assembled a planning committee that worked for almost two years developing program goals and objectives and a full curriculum. The planning committee included individuals from various tribes who were familiar with the work of tribal court advocates. Some were tribal court advocates, others were tribal attorneys, and the rest were adjunct or full-time faculty and administrators. Dr. Peterson Zah, the former President of the Navajo Nation and a special assistant to President Lattie Coor, was very supportive of our efforts and attended some of our meetings.

When I sought approval for the tribal court advocate program, the understanding with Dr. Marie Pepicello, the PC President, was that this program would probably not pay for itself and should be treated as an important service to the community. When the Legal Services Corporation cut the funds for Indian law training, there were no affordable training programs for tribal court advocates. Justice in Indian Country was suffering. Dr. Pepicello committed resources to the program. We hired a Program Coordinator and began to recruit students. The program was very successful in its first two years. We began with an enrollment of twenty-five students. Many had to travel great distances to attend classes. The program received national recognition, but after I left Phoenix College, the enrollment fell tremendously. Around 2004, the program was placed on moratorium for lack of enrollment.

Sabbatical Leave:
University of Guanajuato Law School

I was granted a sabbatical leave for the fall 1996 semester to attend law school at the University of Guanajuato in the state of Guanajuato,

Mexico. My goal was to learn about the Mexican legal system and to develop my legal vocabulary in Spanish. I hoped to develop a course in Spanish legal terminology. I was allowed to audit classes at the University of Guanajuato law school. In addition, I was privileged to observe legal proceedings from the lowest to the highest courts in the State of Guanajuato. I visited with a judge at each level for about three weeks at a time. This turned out to be a great learning experience.[1]

Mexican law is based on a Civil Law system, while U.S. law is based on an English Common Law system. The difference in the courtroom is dramatic, especially the roles of the judges and the lawyers. Lawyers in Mexico present their legal arguments totally in writing. If the judge has questions for the lawyers or the parties, the judge calls them into the courtroom. The judge asks the questions. There is no jury trial as we know it, so forget Perry Mason. The judge alone decides the case. A "jury" in Mexico consists of a panel of judges, generally three to five, who decide issues of law only when asked by the trial judge. They are not used very often. There are efforts in Mexico to allow opportunities for oral arguments, similar to those in the United States. This would help to provide some transparency and to gain the confidence of the general public.

Upon my return, I developed a Spanish legal terminology course that became popular with attorneys, paralegals, and legal secretaries. I am grateful for the opportunity to expand my knowledge of the legal profession and to live in a foreign country for an extended period of time.

Phoenix College – A Great Place to Work

There are many more details I could discuss about my thirteen years at Phoenix College, but I will limit the discussion to the reasons I loved teaching at Phoenix College. Not only did I gain confidence in my administrative skills, but I was able to develop a new program for tribal court advocates and a new class in Spanish legal terminology. There is a cadre of faculty and staff who are deeply devoted to the students and community and strive to make Phoenix College an integral part of the community. They were very supportive of my efforts. Finally, I became

---

1 The judges included: Lic. Concepción Méndez Zárate, Juez de Juzgado Menor [like J.P. Court]; Lic. María Raquel Barajas Monjaraz, Juez de Juzgado de Primera Instancia [like Superior Court]; Magistrado Gabino Carbajo Zúñiga [State Supreme Court]; Court of Lic. José Juan Bracamonte Cuevas, Juez de Segundo Distrito – visited with his Secretario: Lic. Alejandro Vega [like Federal District Court].

involved in many of the political issues that affected faculty and staff and was able to help develop useful strategies for dealing with these issues. Having Elías as a mentor gave me quite an advantage, as he had been teaching and active in the system since 1970.

As the Legal Assisting Program Evening Coordinator, I developed procedures and forms that helped provide consistency to the program. As the Department Chair, I was a strong voice for our department and gained support from the Phoenix College President in getting needed resources for our programs. As the Legal Assisting Program Director, I was able to change the direction of the LAS Program, which resulted in making the program more relevant to paralegals. I could not have done this without the support of a very active advisory committee.

Stress Takes its Toll – Leave of Absence

On the home front, we were confronted with the reality that our families and friends were aging. We found ourselves attending more funerals than baptisms and weddings. My tendency to take on too many responsibilities continued. I soon found the stress taking its toll. Anytime I am in charge of something, I feel tremendous pressure to be successful. I neglect everything else to make sure I am successful in my job. At Phoenix College, I preferred being in the classroom, but it seemed I was needed to run things.

Our two children, Andrea and Marcos, were grown, but Marcos still needed more of my time, something he thought he lost out on when I went to law school and got so involved in politics. I decided to take a leave of absence to explore retirement possibilities. I was not sure I was ready to retire. But during the one-year leave, I discovered I could handle retirement very well. It was time to focus on the home front. I resigned from Phoenix College feeling I had contributed something during my thirteen-year tenure. There certainly were individuals who were willing to take over and move the program forward. My only disappointment is the loss of minority faculty and the lack of a strong commitment by the Department Chair to hire minority faculty in the program.

After leaving Phoenix College, Elías and I went to Spain for a month in 2002. We rented a car and kept a very flexible schedule. We stayed mainly in hostales (bed and breakfasts). We met families who received us warmly and gave us some great tips on where to go and what to see. Upon our return, the real world immediately came into play.

No More Political Campaigns?

Upon returning from Spain, I had to make a choice: spending time on the home front or saying yes to another invitation to get involved. Our friend Jim Walsh had decided to run for the Arizona Corporation Commission and asked me to Chair his campaign. I had sworn off working on political campaigns many years before, but when a good person and long time friend asked, I could not turn him down. This is not exactly what I planned to do during my leave from Phoenix College. Elías cautioned me about getting too involved, but he agreed Jim needed my help. Jim Walsh was one of the last candidates to file, so we had a lot of catch up. I was soon devoting eight hours to this campaign and stressing over the many challenges that come with the territory.

We finally hired a field coordinator, who turned out to be very talented and gave me a lot of hope for the future. Tom Reade was about nineteen years old, yet he was a natural field coordinator and soon had dozens of young people campaigning for Jim Walsh. To my surprise, Marcos volunteered to help me track the monies received. He input most of the data and prepared the bank deposit slips. He was a lifesaver. This was his first voluntary and active involvement in a campaign. Marcos was soon into discussing the issues of the day. However, like his mother, his other obligations took him away the last couple of months. But he helped at the most crucial time.

Terry Goddard, the former Mayor of Phoenix, was running for Attorney General, so we all worked very closely. In the end Terry was elected. Jim ran a great race, but came in second. However, both campaigns had just spent about eight months working in the same building, helping each other and attending many of the same political events, so we got to see each other in action. Apparently Terry Goddard was so impressed with Jim and me that he asked us to become part of his senior staff.

Top: Guanajuato, GTO, Mexico, 1996

Bottom: Contracts Class - Students and Professor J. Jesús Zárate Lujano, Guanajuato College of Law, Guanajuato, GTO, Mexico, November 1996

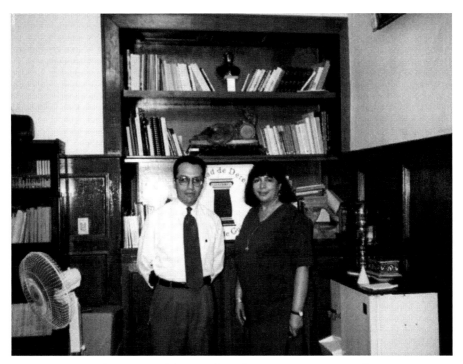

Top: Dean Manuel Vidauri Aréchiga and Cecilia Esquer, University of Guanajuato College of Law.

Bottom l to r: Rebecca Valenzuela, Cecilia D. Esquer, Dr. Virginia Ramos Foster, Phoenix, Arizona. Photo courtesy of Rebecca Valenzuela

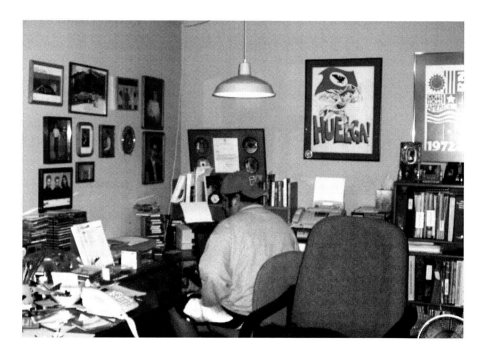

Top: Marcos Esquer, Tempe, Arizona, 2002

Bottom: Cecilia D. Esquer, Dr. Virginia Ramos Foster, Tempe, Arizona, 2008

Top l to r: Marilyn Barmash, Sue Richards, N/A, George Bell, Cecilia D. Esquer, Jennifer Cote, Bob Yegge, ABA Legal Assistant Standing Committee, Chicago, Illinois. 1998

Bottom l to r: Elías Y. Esquer, Tom Reade, Cecilia D. Esquer, James P. Walsh, Phoenix, Arizona, November 5, 2002

UNIVERSIDAD DE GUANAJUATO

Dr. ALFREDO DE LOS SANTOS
Vice Chancillor
Maricopa Commnunity Colleges

Guanajuato, Gto., Diciembre 4 de 1996

La que suscribe Licenciada Clementina Vargas Hernández, Secretaria Académica de la Facultad de Derecho de la Universidad de Guanajuato, por este conducto me permito hacer constar que tal y como obra en Archivos de esta Unidad Académica la LICENCIADA CECILIA D. ESQUER, realizó estancia académica durante el semestre de Agosto-Diciembre de 1996, en nuestra Facultad. Durante ese ciclo escolar la Lic. Esquer atendió los cursos de DERECHO CIVIL IV relativo al estudio de CONTRATOS CIVILES; el curso DERECHO PROCESAL CIVIL I, relativo al JUICIO PROCESAL CIVIL EN MEXICO; asi como el curso de DERECHO ADMINISTRATIVO I, referente a FUNCION ADMINISTRATIVA Y ACTOS ADMINISTRATIVOS. Además, hago de su conocimiento que la Lic. Esquer participó en las actividades académicas universitarias que tuvieron lugar durante este semestre, siendo prácticas en Juzgados, Despachos Jurídicos, así como su asistencia a Conferencias y Congresos desarrollados en nuestra Unidad.

Sin otro particular, reciba Usted un cordial saludo.

ATENTAMENTE
"La Verdad os Hará Libres"
LA SECRETARIA ACADEMICA

LIC. CLEMENTINA VARGAS HERNANDEZ

Facultad de Derecho
Lascuráin de Retana No. 5
Tel. (473) 2-00-06 Ext. 3092, 3093 y 3094 Fax 2-50-51
C.P. 36000 Guanajuato, Gro. México.

Letter from: Lic. Clementina Vargas Hernández, Registrar, University of Guanajuato College of Law to: Dr. Alfredo de los Santos, Vice Chancellor, Maricopa Community Colleges confirming my attendance at the University of Guanajuato.

LA FACULTAD DE DERECHO
DE LA
UNIVERSIDAD DE GUANAJUATO
otorga la presente
C O N S T A N C I A
a

CECILIA DENOGEAN ESQUER

Por su asistencia, participación y aprovechamiento en el CONGRESO DE ESTUDIANTES DE DERECHO PENAL, en el que dictaron Conferencias Magistrales los reconocidos catedráticos:

Prof. Dr. FRANCISCO MUÑOZ CONDE, Universidad de Sevilla, España.
Prof. Dr. ALVARO BUNSTER BRISEÑO, UNAM, México.
Prof. Dr. JUAN BUSTOS RAMIREZ, Universidad de Chile.
Prof. Dr. AUGUSTO SANCHEZ SANDOVAL, ENEP-UNAM, México.
Prof. Dr. VICTOR MORENO CATENA, Univ. Carlos III de Madrid.
Prof. Dr. MOISES MORENO HERNANDEZ, PGR, México.

Celebrado los días 12, 13 y 14 de Septiembre de 1996, con una duración total de veinticinco horas. ·
Dado en la ciudad de Guanajuato, Gto., a los catorce días del mes de Septiembre de mil novecientos noventa y seis.

A T E N T A M E N T E
"La Verdad Os Hará Libres"

El Director de la Facultad

Dr. Manuel Vidaurri Aréchiga

La Secretaria Académica
de la Facultad

Lic. Clementina Vargas Hernández

Certificate of Attendance: International Conference on Criminal Law; First Conference of the University of Guanajuato Criminal Law Students [included presentation by Dr. Francisco Muñoz Conde, Professor, University of Sevilla, Spain.

20

ANOTHER POLITICAL ADVENTURE
Arizona Redistricting 2000
Personal Agendas Win, Democrats Lose

Background

THE Arizona and United States Constitutions require the states to redraw legislative and congressional district lines after the decennial U.S. Census. In Arizona, the state legislature was charged with redrawing the district lines. Arizona voters felt this process benefited incumbents or the majority political party.

In the general election of November 7, 2000 voters passed Proposition 106 (Prop 106) that amended the Arizona Constitution.[1] Prop 106 created a five-member Arizona Independent Redistricting Commission (Redistricting Commission) to redraw Congressional and Legislative district boundaries following the 2000 Census. The Redistricting Commission must redraw the boundaries so that districts have a population as equal as possible, which is required by the Arizona and U.S. Constitutions.

The 2000 redistricting process was especially important in Arizona because Arizona had gained two house seats since the 1990 Census. While the Redistricting Commission is supposed to be independent from the legislature, it turned out the legislature had a lot to do with the resulting district lines. Prop 106 mandated a rapid process for the selection of the five commissioners who would then be responsible for redrawing the district boundaries.

Process

Prop 106 placed the initial step under the jurisdiction of the Commission on Appellate Court Appointments (Commission). The Commission was required to nominate twenty-five candidates by January 8, 2001. Ten had

---

1   http://www.azredistricting.org/?page=prop106

to be Democrats, ten had to be Republicans; and five "Other." Ed Delci, an ASU Academic Advisor, MEChA sponsor, and César Chávez activist, thought it was crucial for Hispanics to be named to the Redistricting Commission. Ed sent out an email to his Hispanic distribution list urging each of us to apply to ensure that it could not be said there were no Hispanic applicants. The word got around quickly. Many Hispanics applied.

Even though I was teaching full-time at Phoenix College, I decided to apply. I didn't think there was any chance I would be selected. President Pepicello encouraged me to apply and said she would make sure someone would cover for me if I was selected. About 311 Arizonans applied, including seventeen with Spanish surnames.[2] It appears there were no Hispanic Republicans on the list.

On January 5, 2001, the Commission announced the twenty-five nominees for the new Redistricting Commission.[3] The twenty-five nominees included three Hispanics, all Democrats: R. Aaron Kizer, an attorney, Carlos Vizcarra, and me, Cecilia D. Esquer. I was surprised and very concerned when my name surfaced. I was still teaching full-time at Phoenix College. Despite President Pepicello's support and encouragement, I did not want to leave my students in the middle of the semester. So I waited anxiously for the next step.

The next step in the selection process gives the legislature total power over who is selected for the five-member Redistricting Commission. From the list of twenty-five candidates, Prop 106 provides that the first four members of the Redistricting Commission will be appointed by legislative leaders, and the fifth member will be chosen by the four members appointed. Finally, no more than two members could be from the same political party. The appointments had to be made no later than January 31 of 2001.

The first appointment was to be made by the Speaker of the Arizona House of Representatives (Republican), the second appointment by the Minority Leader of the Arizona House of Representatives (Democrat), the third appointment by the President of the Arizona Senate (Republican), and the fourth appointment by the Minority Leader of the Arizona Senate (Democrat).

---

2 APPLICANTS FOR INDEPENDENT REDISTRICTING COMMISSION AFFILIATION LIST, http://www.supreme.state.az.us/irc/affiliationlist.PDF

3 Annette Corallo, Press Release, Nominees Announced for New Redistricting Commission, Commission on Appellate Court Appointments, January 1, 2001, http://www.supreme.state.az.us/irc/

How did it work for Hispanics?

No minorities were selected. The Republicans had no one to pick from. The two Democratic Party leaders placed their personal agendas before the interests of the Democratic Party. Since I was one of the finalists, I had to launch a campaign. Representative Ken Cheuvront was the House Minority Leader at the time. He announced he was going to have an open process, including interviewing some of the finalists. All Democratic Caucus members would be invited to sit in on the interviews. Many individuals contacted Ken Cheuvront urging him to appoint a Hispanic. Aaron Kizer and I seemed to have the most support.

I was interviewed by Ken Cheuvront on January 12, 2001. A few days before my meeting with Mr. Cheuvront, I had met with Senator Jack Brown, the Senate Democratic Minority Leader, to ask for his support. He told me he would be happy to speak with Cheuvront, but that he felt an obligation to ensure the rural areas of the State were represented, so he had already made his selection. Some legislators, including Senator Jack Brown, sat in for a while at different times. We had a wonderful discussion. Toward the end of the interview Cheuvront asked why I had applied. I responded I did not want anyone to say there were no qualified Hispanic applicants. He was a little surprised at the frankness of my response. He told me he still had a few more people to interview, but would try to make a decision very soon. The process ended with a reception including all the finalists and Caucus members.

The four commissioners selected were: Daniel Elder (Republican), Joshua Hall (Democrat – Senator Brown's selection), James Huntwork (Republican), and Andi Minkoff, (Democrat – Representative Cheuvront's selection). At their first meeting they chose Steve Lynn, (Independent) to serve as the Chair. No Hispanic was selected. This brought a strong reaction from the Hispanic community:

> Hispanic politicians in Arizona last week demanded that the state's new redistricting commission resign, saying the all-white panel cannot adequately represent a state where Hispanics comprise 30 percent of its 5.2 million people.[4]

> Mary Rose Wilcox, a Maricopa County Supervisor, declared: "A sign should be posted on its door that reads,

---

4   John Mercurio, Between the Lines (excerpt), February 19, 2001, http://www.fairvote.org/redistricting/reports/remanual/aznews2.htm#reversal

'Whites only.' We are asking that the Arizona state government start this process over."[5]

I was not involved in the efforts to change Mr. Cheuvront's mind. There were rumors the Democratic Caucus recommended that Cheuvront name me. Andi Minkoff had little support. I heard from several House members that, when Cheuvront selected Andi Minkoff, he lost the support of the Caucus. And, he lost support for any future congressional run.

The two Democrats on the Redistricting Commission were not particularly partisan. Many Democrats from rural areas tend to be more conservative than the Democrats in the urban areas. Their interests often line up with those of the Republicans. So was the case with Joshua Hall. I visited with Andi Minkoff and found her to be an intelligent and engaging person. She was an outstanding fundraiser for Israeli causes, but she had never really been too involved with the Democratic Party. It took her some time to realize the issue of competitiveness was the most important issue to Democrats. In the end, she voted against the proposed plan, but it was too late to influence the result.

The resulting map on the surface seemed to favor minorities: Minorities are dominant in nine of 30 legislative districts. Minorities tend to register as Democrats. Minorities were packed into nine legislative districts. The Democrats wanted them spread out a little more so the resulting legislative districts would be more competitive. In fact, the resulting map was less favorable to Democrats than the existing map. The Republicans on the Commission insisted the grouping was done to comply with the Voting Rights Act that prohibits diluting the minority vote.[6]

According to Democratic State Senator Pete Ríos:

In the real world, having nine minority districts doesn't mean a hill of beans. . . We will control no one's agenda. White Democrats are more likely to be sensitive to the needs of the minority community than most Republican office holders. The Republicans are using the Voting Rights Act to ensure themselves a majority for the next 10 years."[7]

---

5 Ibid.

6 Bruce Rushton, "Send in the Clowns. Don't bother, they're here. After a decade of voter-mandated reform, the Arizona Legislature is as out of touch as ever," Phoenix New Times, January 20, 2005 http://www.phoenixnewtimes.com/content/printVersion/176059

7 Chip Scutari, "Minorities doubt redistricting success," The Arizona Republic, October 16, 2001.

The goal of Prop 106 was to create competitive districts. This was not the result.

Both sides of the aisle agree: The Legislature will never change until the districts do. 'I think the biggest issue about the makeup of the Legislature is always going to be the districts themselves and whether or not those districts are competitive,' says Goodman, the GOP [Republican] consultant [to the Commission].[8]

Republicans ended up with a voter registration edge in 18 of 30 legislative districts. "There is only one competitive congressional district and only four of the 30 legislative districts are considered 'swing' districts where either political party could win. That's fewer swing districts than existed when the Legislature drew up the maps."[9]

This lends credence to Democratic strategist Bob Grossfeld's observation: "One of my favorite reference points is something Mayor Daley used to say:

. . . 'I don't care who does the electing, as long as I do the nominating.' That's what's in play here."[10] ". . . at least one thing is clear: The commission has spent more than $7 million in taxpayer money creating a map that looks an awful lot like what legislators would have come up with for free. And what was supposed to be an open process has become cloistered as the commission meets in executive sessions to plot legal strategy."[11]

The courts have upheld the maps drawn by the commission, stating that the Constitution does not ". . . enumerate the manner in which competitiveness should be considered nor does it require objective testing to show significant detriment."[12] The court cannot substitute its judgment for the commission's judgment, so long as the commission has a rational basis for its decision. In 2009, Republicans continue to have a clear majority in both houses: Senate: 17 Republicans, 12 Democrats; House: 35 Republicans, twenty-five Democrats.

---

8 Rushton, "Send in the Clowns."

9 Scutari, "Minorities doubt redistricting success."

10 Rushton, "Send in the Clowns."

11 Rushton, Ibid.

12 Arizona Minority Coalition for Fair Redistricting v. Arizona Indep. Redistricting Commission, 1 CA-CV 07-0301 (April 10, 2008) (Redistricting II)

Following the completion of the 2010 Census, a new Redistricting Commission will be selected. Will personal agendas once again be placed before the interests of the Democratic Party?

21

WORKING WITH TERRY GODDARD, ARIZONA ATTORNEY GENERAL

ERRY Goddard was elected Arizona Attorney General in November 2002. I was contacted by the transition team, who set up a meeting with Terry and me. I was on leave from Phoenix College at the time, so I hated the thought of dressing up to go downtown. Terry and I were in the same law school class and saw each other through the years when working on various campaigns. I assumed that Terry wanted some advice on Chicano issues. To my surprise, he asked me to be the Chief Counsel for the Public Advocacy Division (PAD), which included the Consumer Protection and Advocacy Section (CPA) and the Environmental Enforcement Section (EES). I asked:

"Are you nuts? I've never done anything like this in my life."

He responded: "No, I need your help."

I was totally baffled and told him I would have to discuss this with Elías, because I was in the process of retiring from Phoenix College.

When I told Elías about the offer, he asked if I was sure I wanted to do this because this job represented a big commitment. I had three separate meetings with Terry Goddard before I agreed to join him. At the third meeting he asked why I was hesitating. I told him I knew I could not stay four years. I could only stay for two years. He said "I'll take what I can get."

I soon found out I was about to experience the greatest challenge in my life, being responsible for a staff of about one hundred employees. I was flattered that Terry thought I could do this. I was not so sure I could, but I was willing to give it my all. One of my first thoughts was how the staff would accept being supervised by a minority woman. Martin Luther King, Jr. said it very well:

> Discrimination is a hellhound that gnaws at Negroes [and
> Chicanos] in every waking moment of their lives to remind

them that the lie of their inferiority is accepted as truth in the society dominating them.[1]

I knew at some point someone would make a comment about my ethnic origin and my qualifications to do this job.

Even though I had worked in the Attorney General's Office in the late 1970s when Bruce Babbitt was Attorney General, I was not very familiar with the administrative structure of the Office. In addition, the Office had grown tremendously since 1979.[2] In 2003, there were more than 1,000 employees statewide, with the majority in the Phoenix and Tucson offices. The Office was organized by divisions and sections. There were seven divisions, each led by a Chief Counsel who was a member of Terry Goddard's Senior Management Team. Each Chief Counsel was responsible for the sections within their division. Amazingly, six of the seven Chief Counsels were women, and two of us were Hispanic. The first challenge facing the Senior Management Team was to deal with the layoffs which had to be made due to the severe legislative budget cuts.

The legislature had cut the Attorney General's budget by ten percent the previous November or December. In effect this amounted to a twenty-percent cut because half of the fiscal year was gone. Terry Goddard had no option but to cut staff. Janet Napolitano, by then Arizona's governor and previous Attorney General, had begun a plan for layoffs, which we picked up and refined. The legislative majority was not too sympathetic about our complaints over the budget cuts. Some legislators were even pleased there would be fewer enforcement actions against the business community. At the Senior Management Team meetings we had to identify the specific employees who were to be laid off. It was an agonizing experience. By April 2003, more than fifty employees were laid off office wide and 120 unfilled positions had been eliminated.[3] This resulted in a big drop in employee morale.

In my Division I had to lay off seventeen employees, which included attorneys, paralegals, and support staff. I had never laid off even one

---

1 Martin Luther King, Jr., speech, Southern Christian Leadership Conference, Atlanta, Georgia, August 16, 1967, http://www.mlkonline.net/quotes.html

2 [In 1979 there were approximately 138 total employees – fewer than 50 Assistant Attorneys General.] State of Arizona Appropriations Report 1979-80 – Statistics provided by the Arizona State Library, Archives & Public Records, Phoenix, AZ.

3 Paul Davenport, Associated Press, "Attorney General to Lay Off up to 60 Workers," The Arizona Republic, January 16, 2003

employee, so this was an incredible challenge for me. I will never forget how I felt when the Section Chief and I would meet with the employee to tell her/him they were being laid off. Most were fortunate to find another job. After the layoffs, it was not easy to walk into someone's office and see the concern in their face. Their first thought was that they were about to lose their job. It helped when I started calling ahead to let the person know the topic for discussion.

Once the layoffs were behind us, we turned our attention to the mission of the Office of the Attorney General. Terry Goddard's mission was to "promote justice to improve the lives of all Arizonans." He asked each Chief Counsel to review and revise their division's goals and priorities. This turned out to be a good experience because everyone became focused on the work ahead. While there was a job description for the Chief Counsel position, the duties were fairly broad and generic, so each Chief Counsel had to set her own priorities. In addition, each Chief Counsel had a role to play in the Attorney General's mission.

I told my team that my role as Chief Counsel was to get the resources needed for the Division to do its work and to secure the appropriate access to ensure the Attorney General was aware of emerging major issues and cases. This was not an easy task due to the budget restrictions and Terry Goddard's extremely busy schedule. He traveled statewide and to regional and national meetings, so it was difficult to get time with him. I had weekly meetings with Bob Meyers, the Chief Deputy Attorney General, which helped to keep the Attorney General informed.

Terry had a lot of issues he thought were up my alley. I served on four committees in the Office and was part of several working groups, including the working groups on Border Issues, Indian Law, Immigrant Assistance, and Attorney General Forums, that included the forums on Predatory Lending, Internet Safety and Identity Theft. I also became the Spanish language media contact for our Division. I worked closely with Terry on the Spanish language DVDs that were developed as a result of the forums. I was impressed with his growing fluency in Spanish. He was actually answering some media questions in Spanish. Terry also devoted a lot of time to Predatory Lending, Internet Safety and Identity Theft issues.[4] He was very successful in increasing public awareness of the dangers involved in Identity Theft and Internet Safety, especially when it came to children. I was not involved with Terry's incredible

4 http://www.azag.gov/

efforts attacking the horrors of methamphetamines.[5]

Border Issues

There is a working group of attorneys general from the border states of the U.S. and Mexico. At the 2004 meeting Terry Goddard agreed to host the 2005 Border Attorneys General Conference. Virginia Gonzales, the Chief Counsel for the Civil Rights Division, and I worked diligently to prepare a briefing notebook for Terry. This turned out to be a great learning experience. In a very short period of time, Terry had managed to move on many issues and had a lot to share with his fellow attorneys general.[6] The border conferences provide an avenue for the attorneys general in the Border States to discuss common issues and explore avenues of working together to resolve them.

For instance, many stolen cars are taken to Mexico. With a joint project, it is now possible to alert border authorities with information about the stolen vehicle. Today more stolen cars are intercepted at the border. When a stolen car does make it into Mexico and is recovered by the Mexican police, Mexican law enforcement agencies now have a cooperative agreement with Arizona that allows them to check the title for the registered owner. There are also better working relationships on more serious problems dealing with narcotics, human smuggling (coyotes) and with tracing and detaining felons who flee to Mexico to avoid prosecution. One of the conditions Mexico demands before it will extradite a suspect is that the prosecution must agree not to seek the death penalty because the death penalty is prohibited in Mexico.

Virginia Gonzales and I worked closely with the Mexican Consulate to make sure his office was aware of the services offered by the Attorney General's Immigrant Assistance Program. I enjoyed the contact with the various Mexican officials we met, including a meeting with Attorney General Goddard and Rubén Díaz Vega, the Attorney General from the State of Sonora, and his senior staff.

Indian Law Working Group

The Indian Law Working Group brought together for the first time some of the Assistant Attorneys General who dealt with Indian law issues and tribal attorneys from various Arizona tribes. There are

---

5 http://www.arizonamethproject.org/
6 "Action Report, The First 100 "Days," Attorney General Terry Goddard, April 21, 2003

many jurisdictional issues that sometimes cause tensions between the offices. This working group provided a positive environment for looking for workable solutions. Terry chaired the meetings, which signaled the high priority he placed on this effort. I was privileged to attend a meeting with Terry when he met with Louis Denetsosie, the Navajo Nation Attorney General in Window Rock, Arizona, the capital of the Navajo Nation. While it was only a get acquainted meeting, the groundwork was laid for future interactions.

Predatory Lending Forums

One of the most frustrating experiences dealt with Terry's efforts to protect consumers from the increasing predatory lending practices. In addition to meeting privately with industry representatives, he established Predatory Lending Forums. This brought industry representatives together to explore solutions to the increasing number of predatory loans. Terry brought in individuals who had lost everything as a result of predatory lending practices. The industry representatives expressed their sympathies with the borrowers, but insisted they did not engage in these practices, but would oppose any efforts by the State to impose any new restrictions on the industry.

In 2004, Democratic Representatives McCune-Davis and Gallardo each sponsored anti-predatory lending bills. Only the industry bill sponsored by Republican Senator Dean Martin received a hearing. No amendments proposed by the Democrats were adopted, so the industry bill passed on strict party lines.

Predatory loans are made by the loan originator and immediately sold to private purchasers and assignees. There is no recourse for the borrower who is the victim of the predatory lending practices of the loan originator because Arizona law does not impose any liability on the private assignees or purchasers for the loan originator's fraudulent practices. When the borrower defaults on the loan, the loan originator is generally long gone, with the proceeds from selling the loan in his pocket.

Many loans were extended to borrowers the lender knew would not be able to keep up with the payments, especially in those loans that had adjustable rate mortgages. The buyer was sucked in by the high-pressure sales approach that focused on the low monthly payments to be made during the first three or five years of the loan. Often the sales person would convince the borrowers to borrow additional money to do other things. The borrowers did not realize their payments would more than double or triple when the rate was adjusted as provided in the contract. As a bottom line, Terry would ask the legislators to require the lender to provide some proof that the buyer would be able to afford the payments as required by the contract. The industry vehemently opposed this simple request. Terry warned the legislators of the long-term impact these practices would have on our economy, but the majority did not listen to him.

Since Terry was elected in 2002, he worked each legislative session with legislators who sponsored bills to curb these predatory lending practices. Each session the bills failed, until the bottom fell out of the market. Then it was too late to remedy anything. Many families lost their homes because they were duped into buying homes the lender knew they could not afford.

I remember one couple testifying at a Predatory Lending Forum before industry representatives. They were retired and thought they were in good shape money-wise until they received an offer to refinance their home mortgage. The persuasive sales person convinced them to borrow money to replace the roof of their home and then convinced them they deserved some other items. The high-pressure sales approach did not give them an opportunity to inquire how the adjustable rate mortgage would work.

When the monthly payment increased tremendously because of the new interest rate, they did not have the funds, nor could they borrow from another lender. The balance on the new mortgage was much more than the value of the house. Their home was foreclosed and they were forced to move in with one of their sons and his family. There were tears in the husband's eyes when he told the forum the shame he felt for being in this position. He and his wife had always been the ones to help their children and never dreamed the roles would be reversed.

If the lender had been required to disclose the real terms of the loan, including the amount that would be due when the rate was adjusted, and to affirm that the borrowers were capable of making the increased payments, they would not have been in this position. After all, the husband had been a manager in his company and considered himself successful and intelligent. Other families lost their homes because they did not speak English nor could they read the contract, which was all in English, so they did not fully understand the terms of the loan.

Despite the testimony from various families and written documentation presented to the forum, the industry took a strong stance against any proposed bills that would increase their responsibility, so the bills did not pass. After all, the loan originator [often the bank] got the money for the loans up front when they sold the loans to investors and to private assignees, who were not liable for the lender's predatory lending practices. In many instances, the homeowner still owed money after the house was sold through foreclosure because there was still a balance on the mortgage.

To this day, Terry Goddard has fought valiantly for legislation to protect consumers and has increased community outreach efforts to inform consumers of their rights and of the many traps in consumer transactions. He also had the website enhanced so consumers could access this information and file consumer complaints online.

Immigration Issues

The Immigrant Assistance Program was created to inform immigrants of their rights and to encourage them to report crimes committed in their communities. On the controversial immigrant issues, Terry Goddard has led efforts to concentrate the limited resources for law enforcement on going after the drug dealers and coyotes because they are largely responsible for the huge increase in violent crimes in the State. He and Paul Charlton, the Republican U.S. Attorney at the time, led efforts to create a task force that included federal, state, county, and city law enforcement agencies.

Joe Arpaio, the Maricopa County Sheriff, was the only one who did not join the task force. Instead Arpaio concentrated on going after the individual undocumented aliens and ran sweeps across Maricopa County arresting workers, mostly Hispanic, many who turned out to be legal residents. This gave him a lot of publicity and made him very popular with the racist elements in the county who are very fearful of the increasing minority populations in the State.

The Public Advocacy Division (PAD)

I had never managed a large staff before. The situation called for someone to lead the Public Advocacy Division (PAD) through these difficult and challenging times. The task of reviewing and revising the

PAD mission and priorities helped me to know most of the staff rather quickly. I also had as one of my priorities to address the issues facing support staff. I am not sure I got any permanent results from those efforts, but the support staff was appreciative of the fact that we were looking at these issues.

One of my main peeves since entering the legal profession is the failure of many attorneys in the private or public sectors to acknowledge the good work performed by support staff. In response to a survey of the PAD support staff, the type of acknowledgement expected was very basic: "A simple 'Thank you' or 'job well done'" would be sufficient. I would remind attorneys that their support staff actually "saved your butts" because they were familiar with the courts' procedures and they made sure that pleadings were properly and timely filed and served. Beginning attorneys generally were very well prepared academically, but most did not know the ins and outs of the court system. The support staff was happy to train them in those areas. Plus, they knew who to call when issues arose.

One of the biggest challenges I faced as a Chief Counsel was insisting that the Chief Deputy[7] respect the "chain of command." I did not agree with him that he could just call up one of our attorneys or paralegals to assign a project to them. When he did this, they assumed they should drop whatever they were doing and turn their attention to the Chief Deputy's project. Initially the attorney or paralegal would fail to tell their Section Chief of this assignment. I felt that some of the Chief Deputy's actions were going beyond oversight of my division and that he was interfering with the running of my Division.

I finally told the Chief Counsel, "If you want to run my Division, go ahead. I was in the process of retiring when Terry called me. I would not mind going home tomorrow." After some discussion, we reached a mutual understanding on how to handle the Chief Deputy's projects and concerns. In 2004, Bob Meyers accepted a position as the Legal Counsel to the Department of Corrections. Jim Walsh was his replacement, someone I had worked with over the years. This helped lessen some stress during my last year with the Office.

Another challenge was dealing with employees who were not in the Phoenix office. There was not a lot of cohesiveness between the offices. I made it a point to visit the Tucson office from time to time. On one trip, I took Rene Rebillot, the new CPA Section Chief, to meet

7 The Chief Deputy is the second in command in the Attorney General's office.

the Tucson staff. We received many positive comments for showing an interest in their work. In reality, the large consumer cases most often came out of the Tucson office because they had quite an eye for recognizing a case's potential.

One of the biggest cases settled during my tenure was the action against the Qwest Corporation involving Qwest's fraudulent billing practices. The case had been filed during Attorney General Janet Napolitano's tenure. Noreen Matts, the Tucson Unit Chief was the lead counsel. A consent judgment was entered on July 7, 2003, with Qwest agreeing to pay the Attorney General's Office $3.75 million for the costs of litigation, and about $1 million in restitution for consumers. The judgment required Qwest to change its business practices and to submit their sales practices to an independent audit for the next five years.[8] I can't tell you how exciting it was to sit in on the settlement conferences.

Tamara Huddleston, the Section Chief for the Environmental Enforcement Section (EES), was instrumental in briefing me on the environmental issues facing the State. I was impressed with the commitment of the EES attorneys. They could go to the private sector and earn a lot more money, but they were committed to enforcing Arizona's environmental laws. I encouraged Tamara to bring attorneys from all divisions together who worked on similar issues.   Terry Goddard took a special interest in environmental cases. He was impressed when Mitch Klein, one of the Unit Chiefs in EES, assembled a working group that brought together attorneys from the various state agencies who were dealing with the same parties responsible for some major damages to the environment in violation of state and federal laws. Attorneys within the Office knew the names of other attorneys working on environmental issues, but some had never met, even though they had been working in the Office for at least five years.

Too often one agency would settle a case before another agency was done with their investigations. This hampered some enforcement actions because the first agency had waived the violator's liability for any actions not included in the settlement. This working group opened up communications and exchange of information and resulted in more successful outcomes of some major environmental cases.

During my tenure, one working group worked on an investigation

---

8   Arizona Attorney General Terry Goddard, 2003 Annual Report, http://www.azag.gov/AnnualReports/2003%20Annual%20Report.pdf

that resulted in a record environmental settlement against George H. Johnson, a land developer, and two other companies. The 2008 $12.1 million settlement was the "largest environmental recovery by state agencies in Arizona history. The suit charged the defendants with numerous violations of state law and destruction of the state's natural and archeological resources."[9]

Budget Restrictions

I had monthly meetings with a person from the Finance Division to review my division's budget and expenditures. This was very helpful because there were important restrictions on the funds recovered in consumer law cases. In the Consumer Protection and Advocacy Section (CPA), there were often big money settlements or judgments in cases, in some instances in the millions of dollars. A large percentage of the funds recovered in consumer enforcement cases went directly to the consumer, while other funds went into the Consumer Protection Revolving fund to help defray the costs of litigation. The legislature imposed a limit on how much could be kept in the Consumer Protection Revolving Fund. Any overage was required to go to the State's General Fund.

Press Secretary

I enjoyed working with Dianna Jennings, Terry Goddard's first Press Secretary. Diana had a great sense of humor. When she left the Office, it took Terry a long time to pick her successor. I heard he had interviewed about fifteen candidates but could not find a good fit. One Friday after 5:00 p.m. Terry came into my office and asked: "What about Andrea?" I looked at him quizzically and he said "for press secretary." When I told him he needed to talk to her, he asked "Do you think she can do the job?" I answered "Yes, but you must understand I am her mother." Andrea was seven years old when I was in law school, so Terry had seen her around for some time.

Andrea called me Monday morning to tell me she had been called in to meet with Jim Walsh and Richard Travis, the Communications Director. She accepted their offer and became Terry Goddard's Press Secretary. Her training and experience proved valuable assets

9   Arizona Attorney General Terry Goddard, 2008 Annual Report, http://www.azag.gov/AnnualReports/2008AnnualReport.pdf

for the Office. She has a degree in journalism, a Master's Degree in Public Administration, and worked about five years for the Clinton Administration in Washington, D.C. She was a "Schedule C" Presidential appointee.

When Andrea returned to Arizona, she worked for four years as a Council Aide for the Mesa City Council. She had great contacts from her experiences. She also knew quite a few of the politicians around the state from growing up in a political family. Her biggest initial problem was to remember not to call me "Mom" at the senior management meetings. I left the office about eight months after she was hired. She turned out to be a good fit for Terry Goddard and stayed for about five years until she decided to go to law school.

Lessons Learned

Working with Terry Goddard turned out to be the ideal way to get to retirement. He has every reason to be proud of his many accomplishments since 2002. The Annual Reports provide a great summary of the many ways the Attorney General's Office effectively serves the public.[10] This experience brought all of my education and training together: Spanish language fluency, law practice, supervisory skills, secretarial experience, teaching, and political experience. I was happy to be a good resource for the Attorney General and for the individuals I worked with and supervised.

Overall I felt I was successful in carrying out the huge responsibilities of a Chief Counsel, but I was relieved that I had limited by commitment to two years. The daily pressures took their toll on my health and my time with my family. I was flattered that Terry Goddard asked me to remain and happy that he understood my situation in the end. I will never forget the confidence Terry placed in me, especially when I had grave doubts about whether I could do the job.

I finally got to the point where I was not tripped up by the "second-class" albatross that hung over me wherever I went. Phoenix College President Myrna Harrison gave me my first real opportunity to be in a leadership position that was not limited to minority issues. Working with Terry Goddard helped me get rid of this albatross and gave me increased confidence in my abilities. Because of his strong support, most who had doubts about my qualifications because I was a minority

---

10   Attorney General Terry Goddard, Annual Reports, http://www.azag.gov/annual.html

woman soon got over those doubts.

Today many minorities walk into a work environment where this albatross is not the prevailing attitude. Activist Anglo women and Chicanas in my generation were a key factor in bringing this change to the workplace culture. However, there is still work to be done, as evidenced from the reaction to President Obama's nomination of Judge Sonia Sotomayor to be the first Hispanic justice on the U. S. Supreme Court, and the hypocritical reasons some Republican U. S. Senators gave when they announced they would not vote in favor of her confirmation.

Many of today's young Hispanics continue to suffer from "the lie of their inferiority," including Judge Sotomayor. "She is a woman who, in public speeches in recent years, has confessed a sense of insecurity, describing herself as 'always looking over my shoulder, wondering if I measure up'."[11]

I share Martin Luther King, Jr.'s dream:

> I say to you today, my friends, that in spite of the difficulties and frustrations of the moment, I still have a dream. It is a dream deeply rooted in the American dream. I have a dream that one day this nation will rise up and live out the true meaning of its creed: . . . . I have a dream that my four little children will one day live in a nation where they will not be judged by the color of their skin but by the content of their character. I have a dream today.[12]

Individuals like Terry Goddard are helping to make that dream a reality.

---

11 http://www.cnn.com/2009/POLITICS/05/26/sotomayor.bio/index.html

12 Martin Luther King Speech – "I Have a Dream," Steps of the Lincoln Memorial, Washington D.C., August 28, 1963, http://www.mlkonline.net/dream.html

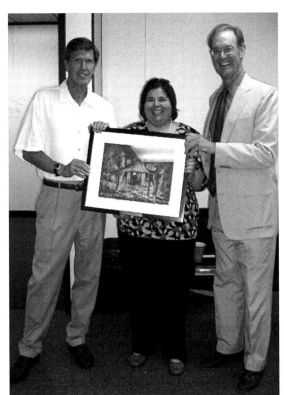

Top: Steve Wilson, Andrea
Esquer, Hon. Terry Goddard
Phoenix, Arizona, July 21, 2008

Bottom: Mexico-Arizona
Border States Attorneys
General, September 2005,
Phoenix, Arizona, La Voz

El procurador de Arizona Terry Goddard y varios de sus colegas, se tomaron la fotografía oficial de la conferencia donde compartierón su preocupación por la inseguridad en ambos lados de la frontera; los acompañó el cónsul Carlos Flores Vizcarra.

WORKING WITH TERRY GODDARD, ARIZONA ATTORNEY GENERAL | 243

Top left: Cecilia D. Esquer, Virginia Herrera Gonzales, Phoenix, Arizona, September 28, 2004

Top right: Cecilia D. Esquer, Hon. Terry Goddard, Phoenix, Arizona, September 28, 2004

Middle front row: Cecilia and Elías Esquer; back row l to r: Sally Ripley, Hon. Terry Goddard, Hon. Patrick Irvine, Arizona Court of Appeals, Phoenix, Arizona, September 28, 2004

Bottom l to r: Steve Wilson, Cecilia D. Esquer, Tom Prose, Connie López, Phoenix, Arizona, December 18, 2006

Top: Hon. Terry
Goddard and Kerry for
President Volunteers,
Tempe, Arizona, 2004

Bottom l to r: Diane
Himelic, David
Moreno, Yolanda
León, Noreen Matts,
Cecilia D. Esquer,
Joanne Roll, Rosa
Armendariz, Tucson
Consumer Protection
and Advocacy Unit,
Arizona Attorney
General, Tucson,
Arizona, 2004.
Photo courtesy of
Noreen Matts

❧ 22 ❧

TEMPE POLITICS
2004 Tempe Mayoral Race

IN 2004, Elías and I got involved in a Tempe Mayoral Race. This was probably the most contentious race in the history of Tempe mayoral elections. The main controversy went back to February 1999, when three City of Tempe workers filed complaints with the Equal Employment Opportunity Commission (EEOC) and the Attorney General's Office claiming racial discrimination. Following the February filings, more than fifteen workers also filed complaints. These agencies conducted investigations, which substantiated many of the complaints. The City denied the allegations.

In 2002, thirteen of the workers filed a lawsuit in Federal District Court. They were represented by attorney Stephen Montoya.[1] The issue became a focal point in the 2004 Tempe mayoral election. Dennis Cahill, an Anglo man and a long-time member of the Tempe City Council, ran against Hugh Hallman, a former one-term member of the Tempe City Council. Hispanic Hallman supporters, some who had known Dennis Cahill since high school days in the 1950s, claimed that Cahill turned "a 'blind eye' to the discrimination of city workers during his 12 years on the council."[2]

In an interview with Cahill, Dennis Welch, a reporter for the East Valley Tribune, reported the following:

> Cahill said he knew racism had existed in the public works department since he moved to Tempe in the 1950s. "But knowing about something your friends tell you about and proving it are two different things," he said.
>
> Since his election to the City Council in 1992, Cahill said he has worked behind the scenes, lobbying the council to implement changes.[3]

---

1 Dennis Welch, ,"Tempe, Arizona: Putting a Price Tag on Bias," East Valley Tribune, July 10, 2005, p. A1

2 Dennis Welch, "Cahill rebuts racism claims," East Valley Tribune, January 31, 2004, web article.

3 Welch, January 31, 2004

Elías and I were Cahill supporters. Elías had known Dennis since the 1950s. We could not understand the comments attributed to Dennis in the Tribune article, so we decided to call a meeting with Dennis and some of his Tempe High School classmates. We wanted to counter the bad publicity Dennis was getting. Elías called Dennis to tell him we wanted to meet with him about the race. He told Dennis we were going to invite a few of his old friends from Tempe High School. Dennis agreed to come.

Elías and I decided to limit the invitees to fifteen individuals. These individuals had to have a connection to Dennis, so most of them would have attended Tempe High with him. When word got out about the meeting, we received numerous calls from people who wanted to attend. We told them it was a private meeting. We met at our house. Janet Regner, a friend and political consultant, called to ask if she could attend as Dennis' friend. We told her she was welcome.

The meeting started out with introductions by John Aguilar, a native Tempean, who retired from the City of Tempe after working for 30 years. Johnny Martínez, who also worked for the City about 41 years,[4] and had attended high school with Dennis, started out. He asked Dennis if he remembered their football days when Johnny was the quarterback and Dennis was his center. Johnny recalled they had won the State Championship their senior year. Then he asked Dennis to come up so they could show the group their formation. Dennis came up, crouched in front of Johnny in his center position. We all broke into laughter. Johnny was pretty short; Dennis was more than 6 feet tall. When Dennis bent over in front of Johnny, we could barely see Johnny. How did this short quarterback lead his team to a State championship? One after the other, individuals who attended high school with Dennis recalled something about their high school days. It was very moving and brought tears to our eyes. These men thought of Dennis as a brother. Irene Gómez Hormell recalled how Dennis had always been generous with his friends. Dennis would bring his pick-up to help people move. He would find a refrigerator for someone whose refrigerator had broken, and would come to help friends with home repairs.

Then John Aguilar brought us to the subject at hand. He recounted some of the discriminatory practices in the City of Tempe. John had been a special assistant to Ken McDonald, the City Manager. John also

4   The City of Tempe named the new Water Treatment Plant in honor of Johnny's 41 years of service to the City. http://lists.tempe.gov/admin/WA.EXE?A2=ind0003&L=tempenews&D=1&P=2215

served in various administrative positions in the City so he had a good idea what was going on. Then he asked Dennis about the comments attributed to him in the Tribune.

Dennis acknowledged he had made those comments to the Tribune. He added that the City administrators were his friends and he had "to protect their reputations." Imagine the shock and dismay that passed through the group. Dennis said that in high school he caught a lot of grief from his Anglo friends for hanging around with Mexicans. Then he repeated what he told Dennis Welch from the Tribune: "You can tell me there is discrimination, but saying it and proving it are two different things." Then he added: "Besides, Mexicans have always been treated this way. Why are they complaining now?" A couple of people in the room got up and headed for Dennis, but they stopped short of hitting him. Several reacted to his comments with rather strong retorts. Johnny Martínez told him: "Dennis, we are trying to help you." Elías reminded Dennis these men were his lifelong friends. "Some even played football with you. Now, when they need you most, you have let them down."

At this point, Janet Regner stepped forward and shook her finger at Dennis. In a trembling voice Janet said: "Dennis, these people are your friends. They are trying to help you. You just don't get it!" Then she walked out. I think this got Dennis' attention. He knew he had offended the group. Dennis became defensive and said he did not think like us because he did not go to college. Very few of those present actually had college degrees. After a couple more exchanges, the meeting was over. I walked Dennis to his car. As we walked out the door, he said "Now you can vote for whomever you want." I responded: "Dennis, you were our candidate. How can you think we would vote for anyone else? We set up this meeting to see how we could help you get elected. Now you have made it very difficult for us to support you."

Some of the City workers involved in the lawsuit were working on Hugh Hallman's campaign and asked if Elías and I would back Hugh. Hallman's campaign ads turned very negative and, in regard to the issues raised by the Hispanic community, really stretched the truth. I told them Hugh Hallman's priorities were different from ours. We could not back him. The ads were below the belt and stretched the truth. Even the local paper ran an editorial on Hugh Hallman's campaign tactics:

A month ago it looked as though Tempe voters would
be treated to the best mayoral contest they've had in years.

Following the dynasties of Harry Mitchell and Neil Giuliano, at the top of the March 9 ballot are two able, experienced men who've served the city well.

But as Friday's front-page headline — "Tempe mayor race gets nasty" — shows, a would-be intelligent contest on issues and styles between Dennis Cahill and Hugh Hallman has degenerated into a mud-wrestling match. And most of the mud has been manufactured by Hallman out of purely phony issues. Too bad, because there are plenty of substantive issues.

Yet Hallman seems determined to build his campaign on SOPHISTRY.[5]

At the same time, I could not lend my name to Dennis Cahill; neither could Elías. We thought Dennis was good on most issues: he worked for improved and expanded social services for the community, support of the unions, senior citizens, important City projects and was an overall nice guy. However, now that we knew how he felt about "Mexicans," we felt we could not overlook this. At some point, we had to show candidates that they could not take our community for granted, or treat us disrespectfully. Nor would we support anyone who thought the way Dennis did. It was a trying time.

During the last two weeks of the campaign, a mailer went out with a group picture of Hugh Hallman with a large group of Latinos claiming these Latino leaders backed Hugh Hallman for Mayor. Sometime after the election, I was at a get-together with a group of friends. At least one of the individuals in the photo said he was very upset when he saw the mailer. The picture had been taken at the end of the annual Diversity Walk sponsored by the City of Tempe. At the time the photo was taken they were not told the photo would be used in Hugh's campaign — neither were they contacted by Hugh's campaign to get their permission to use the photo. When I heard that, I was glad I had not lent my name to Hugh's campaign.

Hugh Hallman beat Dennis Cahill decisively – 10,379 to 8,041.[6] Hugh enjoyed being the Mayor. However, there was some friction between him and a couple of the Council members. Mayor Hallman found it

---

5 Editorial, "Mud Mania in Tempe, Hallman chooses Sophistry over healthy debate on vital issues," East Valley Tribune, February 21, 2004.

6 http://www.tempe.gov/CLERK/election/PastMayorCouncil.pdf

difficult to hide his feelings. He acted as if he was smarter than those around him, including staff and some residents who came before the Council. As time went by in Hugh Hallman's tenure, I did not appreciate the partisanship that had developed in the Council. There had been a long tradition of running the Council in a non-partisan manner. I used to get frustrated when Harry Mitchell was Mayor, because people could not easily identify him as a Democrat. Today I appreciate the pains he took to work in a non-partisan manner. During the 2008 Council election, many voters I spoke with also expressed their concern about the partisan division that had become so evident in the Council.

Ben Arredondo, one of the Council members, and a native Tempean, worked hard to reach across party lines. Although he was a Republican, like Hugh Hallman, he began to challenge Hugh on important issues.

When Ben was elected in 1994, I was pretty skeptical about Ben's commitment to improving working conditions for the Hispanic city workers. Elías attended Tempe High School with Hank Arredondo, one of Ben's older brothers. I felt the Arredondo's were rather conservative and reluctant to get involved in issues affecting Hispanics.

As Ben became more confident as a councilmember, he became more powerful. He developed into a strong advocate for Hispanics and became part of an elite circle of Hispanic elected officials around the State. At the same time, he was able to maintain support from the greater community. Elías and I became strong supporters. But, Ben was not part of a majority on the Council and was often frustrated over being in the minority.

The 2008 election brought about a big change in the makeup of the Council. Of the three seats up for election Hut Hutson, an incumbent, was defeated. Mark Mitchell, an incumbent was re-elected. Two new Council members, Corey Woods and Joel Navarro, were elected. I hope to see a resurgence of the non-partisan tradition and a stronger commitment to fair and equitable treatment of all city employees.

Tribune Editorial 2-21-04

MUD MANIA in TEMPE

Hallman chooses SOPHISTRY over healthy debate on vital issues

Headline, East Valley Tribune, Tempe, Arizona, February 21, 2004

23

WHAT ABOUT RETIREMENT?

Why Did I Retire?

I was very serious when I told Terry Goddard I could only stay two years. As I mentioned before, I had been in the process of retiring from Phoenix College when Terry asked me to join the Office. Perhaps sixty-two is a young age for retirement, but not for me. I looked forward to working on personal projects, and especially to spending more time with my family. Besides, working had become very stressful for me and had affected my health.

From the time I joined the faculty at Phoenix College in 1990 to the day I retired from the Attorney General's Office in 2004, I had gained fifty pounds and suffered from high blood pressure and high cholesterol. I have a tendency to take on more than I can handle. This was the basis for most of my stress. While I apparently did well as an administrator, the responsibilities involved were somewhat overwhelming, so I spent a lot of sleepless nights worrying about things at work. That was the main reason I decided to retire from Phoenix College.

Besides that aspect, my husband Elías was in an early retirement program at Mesa Community College. He was teaching half-time and would soon be fully retired. Since I was working full- time, he returned to being the head cook and primary housekeeper as he had done during my law school years. This time, however, he did not have two young children to care for. In the last few years we had lost quite a few family members and many close friends, so I wanted to spend more time around the house. It helped that I enjoyed spending time with Elías and looked forward to traveling a little more.

I also was burnt out from dealing with the recurrent political issues everywhere I went. Phoenix College was a political hotbed in part because it had become a majority minority college, and some of the faculty did not feel comfortable with the minority students. The lack of diversity in the faculty and high ranking positions were issues I could not escape. I did not enjoy learning that some of the most outstanding faculty had some rather negative attitudes toward minority students and the hiring of minority faculty. However, there was a small cadre of faculty and staff who actively pursued the diversity issue, which meant spending a lot of time outside of class and teaching duties.

At the Attorney General's Office, it was a challenge to try to improve communications between attorneys and support staff and between sections and divisions. The lack of good communications affected the productivity of the office and had a negative impact on employee morale. It is difficult to change long standing practices. It was clear some of the employees who had worked many years in the Office saw each new administration as something that would pass in a few years. They felt they did not have to bother with proposed changes they disliked. Despite this, Terry Goddard's tenure was very successful and productive. I was happy to be in a job where I could not be very active in partisan politics, where dealing with super egos was the standard operating procedure. I vowed not to get too involved in future political campaigns.

Finally, I wanted to pursue my interest in documenting some of the events in the Chicano movement, including our involvement. There is also a story in my father's family circle having to do with the Hayden Flour Mill in Tempe, Arizona. I wanted to find written documentation to verify what I had heard as a young child. In essence, the story is that a distant relative had settled on the property where the Hayden Flour Mill stands, which disputes the many stories that Charles Trumbull Hayden was the first settler on the property. The story describes Mr. Hayden's many efforts to pay an equitable price for the property.

So, how is it going? Challenges, Successes and Surprises

Health and Family

I have been able to devote more time to improving my health, although some days I can't believe how much time it takes to deal with aging issues. I have lost more than 30 pounds since I left the Attorney General's Office. If I lose about 15 more pounds, I may no longer have to take medication for my high blood pressure. I signed up for the Silver Sneakers program at the Tempe YMCA. Priscilla Chomina-Bottz, a friend since undergraduate days, encouraged me to join the aerobics class. It turned out there were a couple of other longtime friends in the class. I have met some great women, many retired educators. A personal trainer guides me through a strength training program, so I have improved muscle tone to accompany the weight loss. I look forward to the sessions at the Y.

I have been able to spend more time with Elías. We often cook meals together and have more time to eat and have great conversations after meals. In Spanish we call that "sobremesas." When I mentioned to Elías how impressed I was with the depth and intellectual nature of his contributions, he observed that he finally has time to read and time to think about what he has read. We enjoy the frequent short trips we have taken and look forward to longer stays.

I have also spent more time with our son Marcos, who for many years felt I was too busy to be a good parent. We have improved our communication and are finding a more trusting and less confrontational relationship. While our daughter Andrea and I have generally enjoyed a good relationship, I am also available to spend time with her and appreciate that she sees me as a source of support and encouragement. Overall, I am pleased with how things are going and know that I made the right decision to retire when I did.

Political Endeavors

Terry Goddard 2006

I have not been too successful in sticking to my commitment to stay out of campaigns and issues. Terry Goddard ran for re-election in 2006 as a Clean Elections candidate.[1] I wanted to make sure the campaign complied with the Clean Elections exacting rules and regulations, so I offered to be responsible for monitoring and entering the seed money donations and the five dollar qualifying contributions. This turned out to be a full-time volunteer job through the Primary Election from January through August 2006. However, I made it clear I would not be available for the General Election campaign. Terry had attracted many young volunteers with a lot of energy and enthusiasm who helped him win re-election in the General Election.

In addition to Terry's campaign, I served as a Democratic Party

---

1 In 1998 Arizona voters passed an initiative establishing the Citizens Clean Elections Act (Act), a campaign reform measure which "provides full public funding to qualified candidates who agree to abide by Citizens Clean Elections Commission (CCEC) guidelines. . . . . To qualify for funding, participating candidates must adhere to strict spending and contribution limits. . . ." "A Media Guide to the Citizens Clean Elections Commission (CCEC), 2006 Cycle," Citizens Clean Elections Commission, 2006.

volunteer attorney. I was assigned two legislative candidates to advise on clean elections issues. I enjoyed the contact with the other volunteer attorneys and was very impressed with each of my candidate's energy and commitment to serve the citizens of Arizona.

Grupo Acción

On June 30, 2005, a jury in Arizona Federal District Court awarded $2.4 million dollars to nine City of Tempe employees after a six-week jury trial over the City's decades of racism and discrimination of workers in the Public Works Department. Elías had known some of the workers because they came from Victory Acres, a barrio in Tempe where Elías's family had settled in 1946. I met some of the workers at community meetings and through mutual friends. Until this trial, I had not been deeply involved in Tempe politics except for supporting candidates for Mayor and City Council. I felt the odds of addressing the racist elements in the City were too great. My time would be better spent getting involved in Chicano issues elsewhere.

As I read the first few stories of the trial that started on May 24, 2005, I decided to attend some of the trial sessions. I was shocked by the testimony presented by witnesses, Hispanic as well as White.

> Depositions in the case as well as testimony at the trial and interviews with some of those involved in the lawsuit who worked for the city since the early 1980s, paint a dark picture of what it was like at the Tempe Public Works Department over much of the past 50 years.

> Archibald [retired Anglo City worker] watched as racial tensions escalated to a potentially lethal level. Street sweepers, garbage truck drivers and other employees would bring knives, revolvers, and sawed-off shotguns to work. . . . .

> Racism had a long tradition inside the department. For decades, work assignments and work crews had been divided along race and ethnicity. Over the years, the Hispanic and other minority crews were handed the worst assignments. They were forced to work nights and weekends. They worked in the summer heat, filling cracks in the streets, while their white colleagues were given jobs out of the sun. . . .

> . . . [R]acial bias and segregated work crews were institutions at the Tempe department. . . . But the racial slurs

were nothing. Dominguez [one of the plaintiffs] kept a journal that he wanted to be used as evidence if he turned up dead. It was the mid-1980s and Dominguez had just blown the whistle on a supervisor who had landscaped his own house, using city equipment and employees. Shortly after that, he began receiving death threats. "People like you turn up floating in the water," one supervisor told him. On any given day, Hispanics were called a number of derogatory names. And hanging on the office wall of a departmental supervisor was an oil painting of a Nazi war criminal.[2]

I spoke informally with some Tempe residents. We decided to attend the July 7, 2005, Tempe City Council meeting to let the Council know we were embarrassed and alarmed by the trial testimony. We also planned to demand that the Council hold top-level managers accountable for ensuring fair and just treatment for each and every employee in the City of Tempe. Unfortunately, the reality today is that although there are new faces in middle- management positions, some are long-time City of Tempe employees who share the views of the managers who were removed when their racist practices were exposed.

I felt some remorse that I had not been more involved in political issues in Tempe. A couple of months after the jury verdict, some of the successful plaintiffs were concerned about the continuing discriminatory treatment of Hispanic employees and asked to meet with me. Twelve of us met on September 6, 2005, to discuss options. It became clear that something needed to be done. However, I was hesitant to lead the effort, so I offered to coach them on strategies for forcing the Mayor and Council to address the issues.

At the end of our second meeting we agreed to call our ad hoc group "Grupo Acción" and convinced Arnold Ruiz to be the group's facilitator. Arnold was a highly respected Tempe resident who retired after 30 years with the Tempe Elementary School District, where he had worked in the District's finance office. In November we had a goal setting meeting where we decided to ask for a meeting with Mayor Hugh Hallman, a request he graciously granted.

On November 30, 2005, we met with Mayor Hallman to discuss our concerns. At the end of our discussion he offered to set up meetings with his senior staff so we could get a better understanding of the

2   Dennis Welch

inner workings of the City. Again, I was not able to maintain a distance from the group and wound up devoting most of my days to gathering information and to working on strategies to present to the group.

Arnold Ruiz was a wonderful facilitator. Unfortunately, he was diagnosed with a very aggressive cancer and passed away before we completed our work. It was important to have the right facilitator. I knew I did not have the patience to do this. Raquel Gutiérrez, a young Tempe leader working on her Ph.D. dissertation, was very active in our group and agreed to become our facilitator. She was the perfect choice. Not only was she a young Tempe native, but she brought fresh ideas and approaches. As we went to the various meetings Mayor Hallman had arranged for us, there seemed to be immediate changes in some procedures underway. The City claimed they were in process before we came around – whatever.

At Andrea's suggestion, we prepared a written report of our findings and recommendations that Andrea edited and formatted. The final product was impressive.[3] We presented the report to Mayor Hallman on May 31, 2006. We asked him to place us on the Agenda so we could present the report to the Council. He was surprised we had prepared a written report. He skimmed through the report. The Mayor seemed upset and took exception to our findings and recommendations. He had expected high praise for the City's efforts to date. Instead, we basically concluded that most of the changes were cosmetic in nature.

We also concluded there was a continuation of many of the practices which led to the lawsuit. Mike Crusa, the Mayor's Chief of Staff, asked if we had a "professional" prepare our report, the implication being that a group of Hispanics could not have prepared such a professional report. Miraculously, I withheld my reaction, deciding to wait until I could meet personally with Mike. Mike was a long-time political acquaintance who had been on Senator Dennis DeConcini's Washington D.C. staff. Although he originally agreed to meet with me after I returned from a month in Guanajuato, in the end Mike refused to meet to discuss this.

Mayor Hallman asked for time to meet and discuss the report with senior management before we presented the report to the Council. Someone leaked the report to the media, so Mayor Hallman did not see why we needed to present it to the Council. It took a lot of political pressure to finally convince Mayor Hallman to place Grupo Acción on the Council agenda.

---

3 Grupo Acción, "A Report to the Tempe City Council," May 31, 2006.

Before our presentation to the Council, we called a meeting to which we invited individuals from the larger community to ask them to attend the Council meeting to show their support. Finally, on November 16, 2006, we made a formal presentation of the report to the Council to ensure that it was included in the Council materials and thus become a permanent public record. At the end of my presentation, I asked for those in the audience who were part of Grupo Acción or supported Grupo Acción to stand. The Council chambers were almost full. Although some were there for another Agenda item, many of them stood in support of our requests. This concluded the work of our hard working ad hoc committee.

Between November 30, 2005, and July 14, 2006, we held seven meetings, where we met with five of the senior management directors and two Council members. Grupo Acción would meet prior to each of these meetings to prepare our presentation. In addition, some of us met individually with Council members. I also made a presentation to the City of Tempe Human Relations Commission. I admire the individuals who took the time to participate in this process, and I am proud of the changes we effected.

However, this set me back almost one year on my writing projects and reminded myself I had to learn to use a very simple word: "NO." I have turned down most requests for assistance and make it a point not to attend meetings that might result in my volunteering for a new project. Some days I feel "out of the loop." Most days I see this as a good thing. There are many younger men and women who are doing a good job taking up the slack.

Corey Woods 2008

Corey Woods asked to meet with me to discuss his plans to run for the Tempe City Council in 2008. He had asked for my support in 2006, but I told him I had already committed to another candidate. For me to support him, he needed to show some record of service to the City of Tempe, since he was a fairly new arrival in Arizona. In two years, Corey undertook more voluntary activities than anyone I have ever known.

He was appointed to at least one City Commission. He joined the local Kiwanis, became a board member for the Boys and Girls Club in Tempe and for the Tempe Community Action Program. I was impressed with his commitment and intelligence and especially his maturity when he was only twenty-eight years old. I agreed to Co-Chair his campaign, with Cecil Patterson as the Chair. I have known Cecil Patterson for many years. He is a fellow attorney and served many years as a Superior Court Judge, then as a Judge on the Court of Appeals. Corey promised not to take up too much of my time. He had a working campaign committee and a loyal group of young volunteers who really came through for him.

Corey was sworn in on July 2008, the first African American Council member in Tempe. Joel Navarro, a young Hispanic City of Phoenix firefighter captain, was also elected for the first time. Joel, Corey, and Mark Mitchell are three of the younger Council members with great promise. Ben Arredondo, a sixteen-year Council member, decided not to run for re-election. Instead, he switched parties and is running as a Democrat for a District 17 legislative seat.[4] Hopefully, Mark, Joel, and Corey will continue Ben Arredondo's outstanding efforts to force the City to treat its employees in a fair and equitable manner.

Tempe History Museum
Oral History Project Advisory Committee

I agreed to serve on this committee because it will be a valuable resource for me when I finally get to continue my research on the Hayden Flour Mill story. I was impressed with the new direction the Museum is taking, one of being inclusive of all the groups that are part of the history of Tempe.

Some years ago I had complained about the fact that the Museum permanent collection had no information on the Native American and Hispanic settlers who were here many years before the White settlers came and took over. I now had a chance to be part of the change and supported museum Director, Dr. Amy Douglass's commitment to make the Museum inclusive. The move toward inclusiveness caused her some difficulty with the long-established Tempe Historical Society, which, through the years, has raised a substantial amount of money for the Museum. They were not too supportive of these changes. I have enjoyed working with the other committee members and with the Museum staff. The committee work does not take a lot of time. The Museum Director and Curator have not lived in Arizona for many years

---

4 Nanez, Diana and Matthew Benson, "Tempe's Ben Arredondo Shakes Things Up in Legislative Bid. http://www.azcentral.com/community/tempe/articles/2009/11/19/20091119tr-arredondodems1121.html

so they rely on committee members to serve as a resource on local history.

How is the Writing Progressing?

I have found it difficult to make time to write on a consistent basis, in part because we are more available to our families and our friends, and because of my inability to stay out of challenging issues. It is taking some time for me to stand firm on my priorities. I did take an on-line class on memoir writing during the spring 2008 semester that was very helpful. I was pleased when Barbara Jordan, the instructor, encouraged me to write my story.

Recently, I stopped to re-evaluate my priorities and almost decided not to write my political memoirs. I read a book on memoir writing that had some writing exercises. One exercise asked me to write about what I would miss the most if it was taken away. I had no problem coming up with an immediate answer: all the family events, like camping trips around Arizona, going to Rocky Point, going to Andrea and Marcos' school events and sports activities, tamale days, and our trips to Spain and Mexico. Not once did I think about my political involvement. I told our son Marcos I was convinced I should not write my story. He understood, but told me I had a duty to write it because it was important for others to understand how things were "back then." So, here it is.

What Was Not Anticipated in Retirement?

I hadn't thought about the fact that in retirement I would have time to reflect on the choices I made through the years and how they affected my family. I realized I have many regrets for the time away from the family, especially for not making time to pay attention to Marcos's dilemmas about me, something that made life very difficult for him. He needed my personal attention in the worst way and would engage in pretty negative behavior to get it. I did not have the patience to deal with him and too often lost my temper and lost the battle. Andrea dealt with our situation in a different way. She made every effort to please me and would become emotional when I would get upset with her. Elías seemed to take everything in stride. He was always supportive and always going that extra mile to make sure they were not interfering with my schedule. Beneath that façade was a very stressed out, over-burdened spouse and father who never complained about our crazy lives. Even though I know there is no way to undo whatever harm I caused, I cannot get rid of the guilt I feel for being so self-centered. I started going to a counselor, who has helped me sort through some of these feelings. I feel I am handling them in a more positive way.

I have found time to establish and build new bridges to my children and have some good feelings about how things are going. Elías has also found his voice and forcefully speaks up when he has concerns about the next project I want to undertake. He continues to be great company and makes me laugh a lot. All in all, things are going in a very positive direction. I can unequivocally say that "I am a happy camper."

The other thing I didn't expect are the emotions I have felt while writing this memoir. I often cry when I think of the abuse I had to suffer simply because I am a woman with brown skin who stands up for herself. On the other hand, I am impressed with the courage with which I faced up to the many challenges that confronted me. Of course it was no small factor that I have such a supportive husband. I also laugh when I remember the angst I caused some of the people I confronted when they were outdone by this Chicana. As I read some of my letters and papers, I wonder why I ever bought into "the lie about [my] inferiority." Those letters and papers were written by a very intelligent Chicana.

Was it Worth it?

Some days I think it was not, yet when I come across a former student who tells me how I was a crucial factor in her success, former clients who let me know how my legal advice helped to resolve their legal dilemma, and from total strangers who read about me, saw me on television, or heard me on the radio tell me that I had a strong influence in their lives, I feel that perhaps I have made some difference. One thing for sure, my life has never been boring, and it is clear that retirement will not be boring. I have so many people to thank for their love, support and confidence. Judge Sonia Sotomayor described herself this way: "I am an ordinary person who has been blessed with extraordinary opportunities and experiences."[5] I cannot think of any better words to describe my life.

---

5 "Who is Sonia Sotomayor?" http://www.cnn.com/2009/POLITICS/05/26/sotomayor.bio/index.html

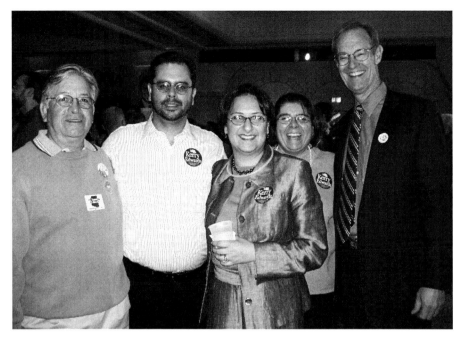

Top: Elías Y. Esquer, Greg Fontes, Gina Ramos, Andrea Esquer, Hon. Terry Goddard, Phoenix, Arizona, Election Night, November 2004

Bottom: Marcos, Elías, Cecilia, Andrea Esquer, Phoenix, Arizona, 2005. Dinner to recognize Elías Esquer and José Torres for their efforts in developing the MCCCD Guanajuato Summer Program.

Top: Marcos
Esquer, Hon. Ed
Pastor, Andrea
Esquer, Phoenix,
Arizona, Election
Night, November 5,
2002

Middle: Elías Y.
Esquer, putting up
Goddard campaign
signs, Florence,
Arizona, 2006

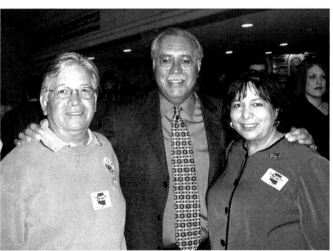

Bottom: Elías Y.
Esquer, Hon. Ed
Pastor, Cecilia D.
Esquer, Phoenix,
Arizona, Election
Night, November
2004

Top: Cecilia and Elías Esquer, Phoenix, Arizona, Somos América, March 2007

Bottom: March – Somos América, Phoenix, Arizona, March 2007

Top l to r: Rachel Villanueva, Rosie López, Esther, Ofelia Cañez, Cecilia D. Esquer, Voter Registration Volunteers, Somos América march, Phoenix, Arizona, March 2007

Bottom: Grupo Acción Meeting, 2005. L to r: Cecilia, Pete DeMott, Raquel Gutiérrez, Randy Bologna, Dan Frank, and John Aguilar

Top: Esquer Park, Tempe, Arizona, October 2008

Middle: Elías and Cecilia Esquer, and Corey Woods, October 2008

Bottom: Swearing In Tempe City Council Joel Navarro, Corey Woods, Mark Mitchell, July 2008

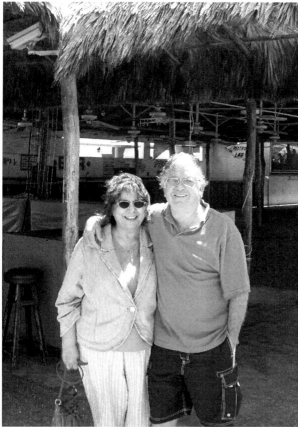

Top l to r: Priscilla Chomina-Bottz, Elías Esquer, Anita Knowlton, Cecilia Esquer, John Knowlton, Frank De Lucia, Ed Delci. Remembering Dr. Paul Luenow, August 2007

Bottom: Cecilia and Elías Esquer, Celebrating 43 Years of Marriage, Puerto Peñasco, Sonora, Mexico, May 2008

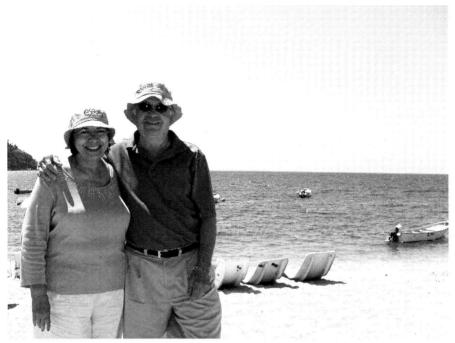

Top: Cecilia and Elías Esquer, Yelapa, Vallarta, Jalisco, 2009

Bottom: Elías and Cecilia Esquer, Celebrating Cecilia's Retirement, Caracol, Belize, March 1, 2005

Top: Cecilia D. Esquer, Dr. Louise Baca, Andrea Esquer, Tamale Day, Tempe, Arizona December 2004

Bottom l to r: Andrea and María Eller, Andrea Esquer, Taylor Homes, Louise and Gloria Baca, Lorraine Homes, Tamale Day, Tempe, Arizona, December 2004

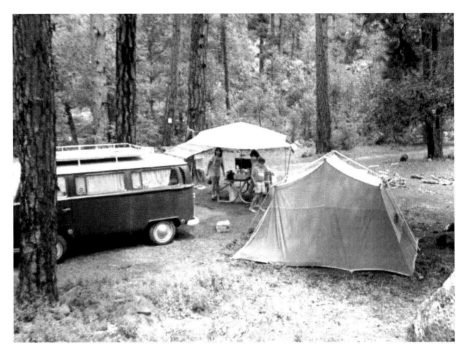

Top: Andrea, Cecilia and Marcos Esquer, White Mountain Apache Nation, Arizona, 1982

Bottom: Elías and Cecilia Esquer, Tempe, Arizona, 2001. Photo by Tom Spitz

BIBLIOGRAPHY

Beach, Bennett H. "One More Narrow Escape." TIME, Inc. TIME, Inc., 23 November 1981.

Castro, Raul. "Ambassador." Phoenix: letter, 22 September 1977.

Arizona Commission on Judicial Conduct. "Summaries of Major Cases, Handbook, Commission on Judicial Conduct." Phoenix: Arizona Supreme Court.

Corallo, Annette. "Applicants for Independent Redistricting Commission Affiliation List." Arizona Supreme Court, 2000.

Corn, David. "Conservative Realism or Disingenuous Callousness?" Blog, Thenation.com/blogs/capitalgames/131091: The Nation, 20 October 2006.

"Editorial, "Mud Mania in Tempe, Hallman chooses Sophistry over healthy debate on vital issues ." Mesa, Arizona: East Valley Tribune, 21 February 2004.

Esquer, Cecilia. "Best lobbyist won." Phoenix: The Arizona Republic, 14 October 1974.

"Guadalupe sit-inners go home." Phoenix: The Arizona Republic, 31 October 1969.

"History of Civil Legal Aid." Washington: National Legal Aid and Defender Association, 2003.

In the Matter of Fred S. Ackel, Justice of the Peace, Tempe Precinct, Maricopa County, State of Arizona. No. 155 Ariz. 34, 745 P.2d92 . Arizona Supreme Court. 1987.

King, Jr., Martin Luther. "Letter from a Birmingham Jail." Atlanta,

1963.

—. "Speech." Southern Christian Leadership Conference. Atlanta, Georgia, 16 August 1967.

Kolbe, John. "Demos Reject Goddard; Tempe Woman Elected." Phoenix: The Phoenix Gazette, 1 October 1974.

Laura E. Garcia, Sandra M. Gutierrez, Felicitas Nunez, Yolanda Broyles-Gonzalez, Editors. "Teatro Chicana: A Collective Memoir and Selected Plays." University of Texas Press, 2008.

"Legal Services Corporation Annual Report." Washington: Legal Services Corporation, 1978. 5.

"Legal Services Corporation Annual Report 1979." Washington: Legal Services Corporation, 1980.

Leuser, David. "Citizens Tell Tempe Councilmen They Are Ashamed to Live There." Phoenix: The Voice of the City, 13 November 1969.

Luptak, Gene. "Guadalupe's anger at Tempe unsoothed by new pipeline." Phoenix: The Arizona Republic, 28 November 1969.

Mercurio, John. "Between the Lines (excerpt)." 19 February 2001.

"Mexican-American Panel Dissolved by Tempe District." Phoenix: The Phoenix Gazette, June 1973. 8.

Noe, Alberto. "Derechos Humanos y Justicia: Una plaza para Victor Noe." Salta: Speech, 30 August 2002.

Obama, Barack. "Dreams from My Father, A Story of Race and Oppression." New York: Three Rivers Press, Member of the Crown Publishing Group, a division of Random House, Inc., 1995, 2004.

Peña, Senator Manuel. Phoenix: Letter to Dean Seidman, ASU College of Business, 23 December 1983.

"Pragmatic Democrats." Phoenix: The Arizona Republic, 4 October 1974.

"Preocupacion por un Dirigente Judio Secuestrado en Argentina." Mexico, D.F.: El Dia, 11 November 1976.

Rushton, Bruce. "Send in the Clowns. Don't bother, they're here. After a decade of voter-mandated reform, the Arizona Legislature is as out of touch as ever." Phoenix: Phoenix New Times, 20 January 2005.

Scutari, Chip. "Minorities doubt redistricting success." Phoenix: Phoenix Newspapers, Inc.:The Arizona Republic, 16 October 2001.

"Tempe woman is named to Dems' national panel." The Arizona Republic.

Waksman Schinca, Daniel. "Argentina: el Antisemitismo Continúa." México, D.F.: El Día, 12 November 1976.

Welch, Dennis. "Cahill rebuts racism claims." Mesa: East Valley Tribune, 31 January 2004.

—. "Putting a Price Tag on Bias." Mesa: East Valley Tribune, 10 July 2005. A1.